CREATION AND LAW

GUSTAF WINGREN

CREATION AND LAW

Translated by
ROSS MACKENZIE

Wipf and Stock Publishers
EUGENE, OREGON

A translation of *Skapelsen och lagen* by Gustaf Wingren,
Copyright, 1958, by AB C. W. Gleerup, Lund, Sweden

AMERICAN EDITION 1961

Wipf and Stock Publishers
199 West 8th Avenue, Suite 3
Eugene, Oregon 97401

Creation and Law
By Wingren, Gustaf
Copyright©1961 by Anna Wingren, Niclas Kedidjan,
and Gustaf Wingren Sallskapet
ISBN: 1-59244-304-4
Publication date 8/12/2003
Previously published by Muhlenburg Press, 1961

FOREWORD TO THE ENGLISH EDITION

THE present work, *Creation and Law*, is the third of a projected series of four related books which began with *Predikan* ("*Preaching*"), published in Swedish in 1949. This has recently been published in English as *The Living Word*. The second work, *Teologiens metodfråga* ("*The Question of Method in Theology*") was published in Swedish in 1954 and has already been published in English under the title, *Theology in Conflict*. While this book frequently touched on Creation and Law, it did not offer any detailed interpretation of these concepts. In the present work, therefore, first published in Swedish in 1958, I propose to analyse these ideas in greater detail.

It might appear that the most obvious point of contact which the present book has with the other two works on preaching and theological method would be at the beginning of the section, "Preaching and the Law," which comes at the end of Part I. Man's actual need is reinterpreted through the preaching of the Gospel, and gets its meaning only from outside the belief in Creation. I have, however, found it more convenient to begin with Creation and then proceed to the Law.

The publication of the present work involves a disadvantage similar to that found in *Theology in Conflict*. Any description of Creation and the Law is bound to touch on the Gospel and the Church, even though it cannot analyse these concepts in fuller detail. It is my hope, therefore, that I shall later be able to take up a detailed examination of these ideas in a work to be published in the not too distant future. It will thus be seen that the present *Creation and Law* will balance and be complemented by the projected *Gospel and Church*.

I should like to emphasise here that only when this latter work has been published will certain essential interpretations of Creation and Law be fully explained. It is necessary to stress that the correct theological treatment of these concepts needs to be worked out in a discussion of Gospel and Church. Conversely, one cannot discuss Gospel and Church *in vacuo* without affecting the proper interpretation of Creation and Law. The two are integrally related. There are certain important aspects of the Gospel and the Church which we shall lose if we do not examine them against the background of Creation and Law. It is my hope that this may prove self-evident and that the formula of Creation and Law on the one hand, followed by Gospel and Church, will prove acceptable and sufficiently well based by the end of the projected work.

Both the present volume and the projected work are concerned primarily with the content and not the method of theology. The second of the three books already mentioned, *Theology in Conflict*, was not so much positive as negative. It dealt with the description of the content of scripture or Christianity which we find in three of the dominant theologians of Europe. In each case their description of this content was dependent on the method which each used. The main question was thus that of theological method. The debate which has followed since the appearance of this work has clearly called in question my own description of the content of scripture, and especially my interpretation of the Law. This compels me now to offer a positive explanation of the content of theology at certain central points. We cannot here speak of the Law by itself. Our discussion has to be in a double context. It has to refer back to the context of Creation and forward to the context of the Church. My attempt to answer the questions which have been raised appears for this reason to have given rise to a doctrinal system. The division of this "dogmatics" into two books is a disadvantage, but only, I hope, a temporary one.

I am again indebted to the Rev. Ross Mackenzie, B.D., for his translation of this work and his preparation of the manuscript for publication.

GUSTAF WINGREN

Lund, Sweden

TRANSLATOR'S PREFACE

IT is a privilege to bring again the work of Gustaf Wingren to the notice and service of English-speaking readers. It is fortunate that the work of this scholar is thus made widely available to those who are unacquainted with the extent and importance of present-day Scandinavian theology.

It is for this reason that in preparing the English edition of this book I have retained most of the footnote references to works by Scandinavian scholars. There is a double purpose in this. First, it will enable English-speaking readers to appreciate better the great amount of theological research being done in Scandinavia; and second, it may encourage younger theologians to learn Swedish, Danish, and Norwegian, in order to profit from this abundance.

At every stage in the preparation of this book I have had the advantage of consulting with Professor Wingren and getting his advice on points of translation. I am grateful also to the Rev. John H. I. Watt, B.D., for reading the translation and making numerous suggestions which have been incorporated into the text; to the Rev. Henrik Svenungsson of Lund for help in preparing the footnotes; to Mrs Barbara Barron of Edinburgh for her competence in typing the manuscript and keeping it accurate; to Mrs Blanche Morris, of Richmond, Virginia, for help in typing the completed manuscript; and to Messrs Oliver and Boyd, without whose care and patient preparation this book would not have had its present worthy form.

ROSS MACKENZIE

Richmond, Virginia

CONTENTS

PAGE

FOREWORD TO THE ENGLISH EDITION ... v

TRANSLATOR'S PREFACE vii

PART I

CREATION

1. CREATION AND THE GOSPEL

The Trinitarian Creed 3

The Creator and Life 18

Christ and Creation 31

2. CREATION AND JUDGMENT

Sin and Wrath 45

The Unrecognised Demand 57

The Last Day and our Death 69

3. MAN IN CREATION

The Creation of the World and our Birth 83

"Dominion" and Freedom 95

Bondage and Constraint 108

PART II

LAW

1. THE CREATOR AND THE LAW

The Old and New Testaments 123

"Government" and Mercy 135

PAGE

2. THE FIRST USE OF THE LAW

Our Neighbour and the Law 149

"Idealism" 162

3. THE SECOND USE OF THE LAW

Man and Guilt 174

Preaching and the Law 187

BIBLIOGRAPHY AND LIST OF ABBREVIATIONS 198

INDEX OF NAMES 201

INDEX OF SUBJECTS 203

INDEX OF BIBLICAL PASSAGES 206

PART I

CREATION

CHAPTER I

CREATION AND THE GOSPEL

The Trinitarian Creed

THE two credal formulae which have predominated throughout the whole of the history of the Christian Church, the Apostles' Creed and the Nicene Creed, are both quite markedly trinitarian in form. Despite their internal variations, we note that faith in God the Creator, in Jesus Christ crucified and risen, and in the Spirit in His work of edifying the Church, was a regulative principle in the formation of both these Creeds. It has, however, been stressed from time to time, particularly within recent years, and notably in Continental theology, that it is difficult to find any good grounds in the New Testament for insisting that the Creed should contain just these three members in exactly this sequence. "The originally most widespread Christian confession is quite certainly the *purely Christological* formula," says Cullmann, and he continues: "This fact is as important for history as for theology."[1]

Without doubt Cullmann is correct so far as he is simply recounting historical facts. The New Testament confession is not trinitarian, but centres rather around the single affirmation that Jesus is Lord (Phil. II.11; cf. Rom. x.9). If this formula had not been the most primitive in the early Church, it would indeed have been remarkable that it was in actual fact with this confession that the Church emerged from its Jewish environment (see Acts II.36; cf. v.30-2). For the Jews did not regard Jesus as Lord, nor recognise that in the life and death of

[1] Oscar Cullmann, *Die ersten christlichen Glaubensbekenntnisse*, Theologische Studien VOL. xv, Zollikon-Zürich 1943, Eng. trans., *The Earliest Christian Confessions*, London 1943, p. 38. See also the same author's *Die Christologie des Neuen Testaments*, Tübingen 1957, pp. 1 f.

3

Jesus the Messiah had come.[2] There was also, however, another article of belief held by the Jews, which the Christian Church by no means denied. And this common underlying confession could not be expressed or made articulate until its content was *denied* in the environment which rejected that belief. The first article of the Creed concerning Creation was not declared as part of the Christian confession until the appearance of the Gnostics, who tried to dissociate the created world from God, in order to assign to the demiurge the power in physical and external existence. It then became a confessional act of the first importance within the Christian Church to proclaim God as Creator of heaven and earth. But what was thereby proclaimed —albeit with full force only at the time of the anti-Gnostic conflict—was not less primitive than the confession of Christ, but rather more primitive, for it was the essential part of the Old Testament which was here being proclaimed. From the first the Old Testament was the sacred book of the early Church. It did not become "holy scripture" by degrees, e.g. in the anti-Gnostic conflicts of the second century.[3] But Creation was one point at which the early Christian Church did not at once become forced into credal conflict with its Jewish environment. Its confession was centred on Jesus as Lord—the confession which we now have in the second article of the Creed—the very point of conflict.

In other words, the confession of a particular belief is always related to the denial of that belief in the particular environment of the Church (cf. Mt. x.32 f., and see also Acts III.13 f.). When Israel was surrounded by a tribe which made images, it was a proof of faith to live without images, and to fear the one invisible God as the Lord of all creation, to whom "every knee shall bow, every tongue shall swear" (Is. XLV.23).[4] The

[2] A typical passage is Jn. IX.22.

[3] When the term "scripture" or "scriptures" is used in the New Testament clearly implying absolute authority, we should note that the authority understood is purely an Old Testament one. The term has no reference to the New Testament scripture. The transition to the situation of the early Church in which both Old and New Testaments are "scripture" is to be seen in a single passage, II Pet. III.16, which appears to be unique. The division of "scripture" into the writings of the Old and New Testaments can also be traced in II Cor. III.14.

[4] The passage comes in one of the sharp attacks made by the author of Deutero-Isaiah on those who make and worship idols. See the context, Is. XLV.15 ff. and cf.

environment which in this kind of situation involves the confession of God as the only God may apparently alter in a different situation, for example, in the New Testament, where even the evil spirits are said also to believe that God is one (Jas. II.19). Now, it is true, it is again stated that "every knee should bow . . . and every tongue confess," but in this instance it is Jesus Christ who is the watershed, in confrontation with whom men either believe or disbelieve, and whose coming dominion over all Creation is hoped for (Phil. II.10 f.).[5] But it is only in appearance that the New Testament fails to give full value to the affirmation that God has created the world, for this particular dogma emerged as soon as the Church encountered the Gentile world and had to deal with those who were not yet obedient to the Gospel. The constantly recurring call for conversion in missionary preaching to the Gentiles points in the same direction (Lk. XXIV.47; Rom. I.18-II.16; Acts XIV.15-17; XVII.24-31).[6] The conviction that the "powers that be" in the world derive their power from God (Jn. XIX.11; Rom. XIII.1-6; 1 Pet. II.13 f.), and that they use it for God's purposes, even when they are evil powers, and indeed even when they permit Jesus to be crucified (Acts IV.27 f.), means that in His government of the external universe God is not dependent on the readiness to believe of the human instrument which He uses, but rather retains His divine freedom to take His enemies and the workers of unrighteousness into His service, as the Old Testament witnesses (see Is. X.5-27, and Gen. XLV.5-8, L.20).[7] There is nothing strange in the fact that this early Christian belief in Creation turns into a direct confession of the divine work of creation as soon as the situation exists in which God's creation and government of the world—and not only Christ's

XLI.1 ff., XL.18 ff., and Bertil Gärtner, *The Areopagus Speech and Natural Revelation*, henceforth cited as *The Areopagus Speech*, Acta semin. neotest. upsal., VOL. XXI, Uppsala 1955, pp. 88 f., 94 f, 220 f., etc.

[5] On the parallel between Is. XLV.23 and Phil. II.10 f. see also Cullmann, *Earliest Christian Confessions*, p. 22.

[6] See also Acts IV.24-30; Rev. IV.11, XIV.7; Mt. XIX.4 ff., and 1 Tim. IV.3 f.

[7] Cf. Gösta Lindeskog, *Studien zum neutestamentlichen Schöpfungsgedanken*, PT. I, henceforth cited as *Studien*, Uppsala universitetets årsskrift, VOL. XI, Uppsala and Wiesbaden 1952, pp. 180-7; and also Stig Hanson, *The Unity of the Church in the New Testament*, Acta semin. neotest. upsal. VOL. XIV, Uppsala and Copenhagen 1946, pp. 24 ff., 58 ff., and the New Testament references in this work.

status as Lord—are denied. This negative situation prevailed at
the time of the appearance of the Gnostics, viz., as early as
the second century.

The young Church which had to face such a situation did
not attempt to formulate any hitherto unexpressed aspect of
its belief. But the emphasis in the expression of that belief
differed from the early Christian emphasis, since the object of
denial now differed. As we have stated, the confession of a
particular belief is always related to the denial of that belief
by those who reject it. The young Church, confronted by the
innovations of the Gnostics, began to formulate its trinitarian
confession, which afterwards was to become the confession of
almost every Christian communion, in the form of the Apostles'
or the Nicene Creed.[8] The young Church was also responsible
for adding together all that was meant by "holy scripture" to
early Christianity, and the oral proclamation or teaching of
the early Christian period, or epistles which had been sent to
various churches, and for setting all this material in a book,
divided into two parts, one for each "covenant," the old and
the new. The assembling of this chaotic mass of writings into
the two divisions of the Old and New Testaments was comparable in its implications to the discovery of the wheel. When
the discovery was made, it seemed impossible that there could
ever have been a time when it did not exist. May I, however,
once more repeat the statement that it is the Old Testament
that is called "scripture" in the New Testament, and is the
only known scripture in the New Testament period. It was only
after the apostolic period, when there was in existence a
particular compilation of early Christian writings, that
"scripture" was divided into an old part and a new.[9] This
double book, consisting of Old and New Testaments, had no
other authority than that possessed by the early Christian
Church—the Church had not "added to" the Old Testament
(for from the beginning it had been the only scripture), nor had

---

[8] Cf. the essay in Bengt Hägglund, *Teologins historia*, Lund 1956, p. x.

[9] Even as late as the 2nd century the word "testament" was not used to denote
the divisions of the Bible, but only the two covenants. Cf. J. Hoh, *Die Lehre des hl.
Irenäus über das Neue Testament*, Neutestamentliche Abhandlungen, ed. M. Meinertz,
VOL. VII, PTS. IV-V, Münster 1919, pp. 1 ff. The basis for this terminology is II
Cor. III.6, 14, I Cor. XI.25 (cf. Jer. XXXI.31).

it "added to" the New Testament (for from the beginning it had been the only word concerning Jesus Christ which had been recognised and directed against the Jews). The Church, which now drew together and interpreted the scriptures against the Gnostics, began to realise the power of the Spirit which it had possessed since Pentecost to lead it into truth. And the content of the credal affirmations of the Church against the Gnostics, possessing the same structure as the Bible itself, was trinitarian in form.

For this reason Creation stands first in the trinitarian Creed, for in the Bible it is first.[10] It did not stand first in the New Testament, but the New Testament was not "the scripture," and never had been, at any rate not by itself. The isolation of the New Testament is a quite modern phenomenon, unknown to the Reformation and Catholic orthodoxy.[11] In our reading of the New Testament we are guilty of an anachronism in forcing a comparatively recent conception of our own production upon early Christianity, by our insistence on making the New Testament writings the repository of every possible belief which the early Church can have held concerning the beginning of things. All this is contained in more than ample detail in the Old Testament—the "holy scripture" of early Christianity. If, however, we begin from the other end, the Old Testament can speak to us only in so far as it is quoted in the New. But if we do this, we produce a Bible different from that known to the early Christians. This "Bible" to all intents now begins with the Gospel according to St Matthew (or chronologically with the earliest Epistles of Paul). It may perhaps be more clearly understood in the light of the Old Testament which precedes it, i.e. in the witness to God's activity in history *before* the new covenant given in Christ.[12] But to claim that this

[10] On this point see the suggestion in Hugo Odeberg, *Skriftens studium, inspiration och auktoritet*, Stockholm 1954, p. 26, that every verse in the New Testament has as its background the chapters in Genesis on Creation and the fall. Cf. *op. cit.*, pp. 113 f.

[11] Luther was a Biblical scholar and lectured variously on Old and New Testament texts. Cf. Karl Bauer, *Die Wittenberger Universitätstheologie und die Anfänge der deutschen Reformation*, Tübingen 1928, pp. 14 ff.

[12] Many of the contributors to *En bok om bibeln*, Lund 1947, are clearly influenced by this attitude. See, e.g. Anders Nygren, "Gamla testamentet i nya förbundet," pp. 111-5.

B

abbreviated "New Testament" Bible is the "Bible" is to separate ourselves radically from catholic and apostolic Christianity, and to shut ourselves off from the word which the Old
Testament has to address directly to us. We should then be
saying that the "scriptures" which speak to us are the New
Testament scriptures, whereas those of the Old Testament are
ancillary, and that the New Testament addresses us more
plainly. To isolate the New Testament in this manner very
soon means that in a strict sense even the New Testament
itself does not speak to us. In our reading of it we adopt an
attitude opposed to that of listening, and we attempt to define
what religion meant to the apostolic writers in the early Church.
But to submit to the word of the New Testament in faith means
something quite different. The New Testament addresses us
only as a witness from men whose intention is to elicit faith
among all their hearers (Jn. xx.31). In offering us their witness
to Christ they at the same time deliver to us and to all their
readers the Old Testament word concerning our creation and
fall, and present us in their appeal with the possibility of
conversion, in the immediate proximity of the Last Day and
therefore of our death.[13] Where the response to this offer is
acceptance, it is quite natural that the response should take the
form of the statement in the trinitarian Creed—first, Creation;
second, the work of Christ; and finally, the expectation of the
final Judgment, forgiveness, and life—all three statements
delivered as the response to the apostolic witness, and all
prefaced with the same verb, "I believe," *Credo*.[14]

It is an unquestionable benefit that we have a science which
deals exclusively with the text of the Old Testament in its
proper context, and alongside this a scientific study of the New
Testament text in *its* proper context. But there ought to be a
method by which to address theological enquiry to the writings
of the Bible as a whole, a method which is not exclusively
contained in one or other of the two exegetical systems, and
does not coincide with them, but which stands simply alongside
the other two. In other words, there ought to be a method of

---

[13] See Henrik Ivarsson, *Predikans uppgift*, Lund 1956, pp. 35 ff.

[14] From the beginning the confession of faith was a song of praise. Cf. Regin
Prenter, *Skabelse og genløsning*, 2nd edn., Copenhagen 1955, pp. 135 f.

enquiry in which the Old and New Testaments are read together under the presupposition that there is a common factor expressed in both the "Testaments," and therefore in the Bible. There have been ages in which the Bible has been read in such a way as to suppose that the narrative of the Fall in Gen. III speaks of a destruction which is remedied and abolished by Christ. This remedy is described in the Gospel narrative in which the removal of the effects of the primal destruction once and for all is the substance of the New Testament hope. It is also described in the form of the promise of the Book of Revelation concerning Christ's coming judgment and victory. Among these interpretations through the ages there have been some preposterous and fantastic suggestions, but where the Bible with its remarkable restraint and lack of exaggeration has been taken as the basis and starting-point of interpretation, some of the exegesis has been sane and worthy of examination. When, however, we do examine these interpretations, we find much to perplex us, for neither Old nor New Testament exegetics alone can provide a basis for examination. The perplexity which we feel here is exactly the same as we experience when we wish to examine the conformity of the trinitarian Creed to scripture, provided, that is, our examination relates to the fundamental question of whether the threefold division is a reasonable one, and also whether this particular sequence of each of the sections (Creation first, and then the Incarnation) is right. The New Testament offers little support for putting Creation first,[15] and the Old Testament little support at all for a trinitarian Creed. Only the Bible as a whole can provide the basis for the formulation of the threefold confession. Our present division of Biblical studies into two separate exegetical systems leaves us poorly equipped to study the Bible as a whole.

It is unnecessary here to go into all these difficulties of Biblical theology. On the other hand there are certain propositions beyond dispute, but easily forgotten in spite of their self-evident nature, which we must emphasise in regard to the confessing congregation. Where a congregation is assembled

[15] Cullmann also criticises the threefold Creed of the early Church on the basis of his hypothesis; see *Earliest Christian Confessions*, pp. 50-3.

for an act of Baptism or the Eucharist and makes declaration
of the trinitarian Creed, we may state the following propositions
concerning them: (1) They are confessing that they are God's
creation and possession, and presuppose that the account of
the fall in the Bible relates to their own condition; (2) They
are confessing that Christ is their Lord, and presuppose that
His Lordship is still proceeding against all evil; (3) They are
confessing that the Spirit is now gathering them to form a
Church, and they await the time when sin and death will be
completely deprived of their power in the coming Judgment
and Resurrection. In so confessing they are holding together
Creation (the first page of the Bible) and victory (the last)—
both are the works of God, and both relate to themselves as
they make the confession. But in so confessing they further hold
together their defeat (that is, Adam's defeat) at the beginning
of the Bible and the purity which they obtain through Christ's
word in the New Testament. The destruction and the healing
both relate to themselves as they make their confession. But
since they are confessing the creation of heaven and earth, life
and existence in its wholeness, and since they are awaiting the
judgment over all things, "the living and the dead," it is not
possible for those who make this confession to limit it to themselves.[16] The works of God which they confess (and their
confession is a hymn of praise) are works which as yet are
extolled only by those who confess them. These works, however,
have been done for the world and precisely by this confession
extend to all other men for whom they are intended, "that at
the name of Jesus every knee should bow . . . and every tongue
confess that Jesus Christ is Lord" (Phil. II.10 f.). The common
proclamation of both Old Testament and New is of God's
dealings with all that is meant by mankind. If man ceases to
be thought of as the hearer of the Word, the one to whom the
Word is addressed, the parts of the Biblical Word become
relics of purely antiquarian interest from two religions of an

---

[16] Cf. Cullmann's emphasis on world mission as the obligation of the Church
in *Christus und die Zeit*, Zollikon-Zürich 1946, p. 138 f., Eng. trans., *Christ and Time*,
London 1951, p. 157 f. It is a question, however, whether Cullmann does not go
beyond the New Testament evidence, and in consequence err in his judgment on
the Bible as a whole. The narrowing line of the Old Testament (pp. 110 ff.) is not
strictly speaking based only on the New Testament.

early period, Israel and early Christianity. The only way in which the Biblical unity is seen to be held together, and not separated from the recipient to whom it is addressed, is in the situation where the Word is opened and preached to a congregation assembled to hear it. It is in this situation—in worship, the cult—that the trinitarian Creed, the hymn of praise for the saving works of God, is heard.[17]

These primary works of God, which are enumerated in the confession of faith, are recited in the order in which God has performed, or continues to perform, them—Creation, the Incarnation, the Death and Resurrection of Christ, the outpouring of the Spirit, and the Last Judgment. It is the same order generally followed in the Biblical narrative. The same simple, epic, and anthropomorphic form of narration characterises the Bible itself. Genesis is first, Revelation last. Within the New Testament the Gospels are first, the Acts and the Epistles come afterwards, and within each Gospel there is the same order as in the second article of the Creed—first the nativity, and last the ascension to heaven together with the promise of the Second Advent.[18] It is only if this order is followed that God and His works remain central. Strangely enough, it is a modern and designedly theocentric theology which tends to put the statements about Creation into a secondary place in relation to the fundamental word concerning the revelation in Christ. The motive for moving the confession to Christ forward in this theology and placing it before the confession to the Creator seems to be based wholly on the assumption that we acquire certainty concerning the work of God in Creation only by hearing and receiving the Gospel concerning His work in the Incarnation. This, however, is an argument which puts man and his knowledge, rather than God and His works, into the centre. There was an earlier anthropocentric period in theology during which a doctrine of man's natural knowledge of God employed the first article of the Creed in

[17] Originally both the Apostles' Creed and Nicene Creed had a liturgical function. They were intended as acts of praise to God for His works. Cf. Prenter, *Skabelse og genløsning*, pp. 138 ff.

[18] The Fourth Gospel speaks of the Ascension and outpouring of the Spirit in a special way. See C. H. Dodd, *The Interpretation of the Fourth Gospel*, hereafter cited as *Fourth Gospel*, Cambridge 1953, pp. 429 f., 442 f.

order to detract from God and His works. Now in opposition
to this there is a contrary doctrine of man's *lack* of any natural
knowledge of God, which is replaced by the revelation in
Christ. When we have received this revelation we then turn to
an understanding of Creation, which is now provided for us
clearly in the second article of the Creed.[19] In this concept of
revelation, however, there is a radical failure to understand
Creation as the continuing work of God which is independent
of the Gospel. The idea of creativity, which is reproduced in
the simple statement, is lost, and the decisive factor is not the
order of God's acts, but the order in *man's* progression from lack
of certain knowledge to ascertained knowledge. Man and his
knowledge determine the Creed, and not God and His works.
The fact that we now acquire our knowledge of God from the
second article of the Creed, whereas an earlier "liberal"
generation derived theirs from the first, is a comparatively
small change.[20] But the anthropocentric character is
unbroken.

In a peculiar way, and one which it is particularly difficult
to criticise, this false systematic construction is connected with
perfectly correct historical assertions concerning the earliest
New Testament credal formulae. These, as Cullmann shows,
were Christological formulae, and did not mention Creation.
It is common in science, and perhaps particularly so in theology,
to find an incorrect general view supported by correct specific
details. In this particular case the questionable Christology,
which goes right back to Karl Barth's earliest writings around
1920, was affected by a curious, anti-liberal mania, which from
the first made the calm accumulation of many specific details
difficult. The historical results had to be made full use of
quickly, and therefore the exegetical foundation had to depend
on relatively few statements, preferably those which were fairly
consonant with one another. The consequence, however, was
that the liberal predilection in Germany for the first article of

[19] Torgny Bohlin in his *Den korsfäste Skaparen*, Uppsala 1952, p. 123, is typical:
"It is only from the standpoint of the Cross that we can speak about the Creator,
who before that was only dimly recognised." Cf. pp. 129, 362, etc.

[20] Cf. Benkt-Erik Benktson, *Den naturliga teologiens problem hos Karl Barth*, Lund
1948, pp. 124 f.

the Creed passed into a propensity for an ideology based on race and blood during the 1930's. This in turn confirmed the conviction of those who advocated putting the article concerning Creation second, after the Gospel concerning Christ. We find in this period theological works, particularly those of Barth, which are at once characterised by a brilliant and scholarly perception which compels the admission that these works constitute the most able of our time, but which at the same time are marked in style by an ebullient passion with deep political involvements.[21] From the theological aspect, the critical point in these writings of Barth is the role which *knowledge* plays with regard to the order of precedence in the doctrines with which he is dealing. Since the Law is revealed and its meaning fully perceived only when the Gospel is revealed, Gospel has priority over Law.[22] Since social righteousness is comprehended within justification, justification has priority over justice.[23] And since only the Church is aware of the basis on which the State rests, the Church has priority over the State.[24] This theological approach makes human knowledge and insight the organising principle for the sequence of the acts of God within the confession of faith. In so doing, however, it displaces the order of God's acts, and in fact it is the sequence in which we acquire knowledge of God which comes to determine the order of the confession.[25]

If the sequence of God's acts has been thus altered at a critical point, then the whole sequence has been disrupted. Thus, in the theology which has been influenced by Barth, the

[21] In regard to politics, for instance, the roots go deep down into Barth's own youth. See Eduard Thurneysen,"Die Anfänge," in *Antwort*, Zollikon-Zürich 1956, pp. 831-64.
[22] Karl Barth, *Evangelium und Gesetz*, Theologische Existenz heute, VOL. XXXII, Munich 1935, p. 9.
[23] Karl Barth, *Rechtfertigung und Recht*, Theologische Studien, VOL. I, Zollikon 1938, p. 39.
[24] Karl Barth, *Christengemeinde und Bürgergemeinde*, Theologische Studien, VOL. XX, Zollokon-Zürich 1946, pp. 8, 21, 23 f.
[25] Cf. Barth's two interpretations of the Apostles' Creed, *Credo*, 3rd edn., Munich 1935, pp. 14-30, Eng. trans. *Credo*, New York 1936, pp. 11-29, and *Dogmatik im Grundriss*, Zollikon-Zürich 1947, pp. 16-57, Eng. trans. *Dogmatics in Outline*, London 1949, pp. 15-64. His great work on Church Dogmatics has the same starting-point. For a criticism of this starting-point, cf. Gunnar Hillerdal, *Gehorsam gegen Gott und Menschen*, Stockholm and Göttingen 1954, pp. 209-87.

relationship between the present time and the eschatological future is not marked by eager expectation in the present time of new works which God is still to accomplish in the future. The Apostles' Creed and the Nicene Creed enumerate the events which have taken place, but when they pass from the present—and in the present God's work is Christ's rule at the right hand of the Father—the verbs become future: He shall return, He shall judge, of His kingdom there shall be no end. The belief in the works which God has already accomplished extends towards the works still to be done. The theology which takes the second article of the Creed as its starting-point is based on the conviction that our certainty concerning the meaning of God's work in Creation is acquired through the incarnate Christ. It therefore clearly tends to let the relationship of the eschatological consummation to the present time be conditioned by the fact that the future—which, according to the New Testament, will bring perfect vision, sight face to face—will bestow still greater certainty than faith in Christ at present possesses.[26] There is no objection to the simple statement that our certainty concerning the existence of God increases in proportion as God continues to act. But statements about this increasing certainty could also be included in a progressive account of God's works, and this dogmatic structure would do greater justice to the Bible in its entirety and to the trinitarian Creed. It will be from this aspect that we shall deal with Creation, the Law, the Gospel, and the Church, in the exposition that follows.

It is of fundamental importance that the basis of this exposition is not purely New Testament in character. In 1943 Cullmann stated that the Christological form of the earliest New Testament credal formulae is in its very lack of three members essential for present-day theology. In 1946 he offered in his *Christ and Time* a broad, comprehensive view of the whole of redemptive history from Creation to the Incarnation and the resurrection of the dead. The whole of this long sequence of events, however, is for Cullmann a single "Christ line" (the second article of the Creed has extended into and absorbed the

[26] Karl Barth, *Die kirchliche Dogmatik*, VOL. III, PT. III, Zollikon-Zürich 1950, pp. 419-24. Cf. Bohlin, *Den korsfäste Skaparen*, pp. 404 ff.

other two). The events with which it deals, and from which his broad perspective is formed, are fundamentally New Testament in character, although in certain minor respects he has borrowed from the Old Testament.[27] What we fail to find in Cullmann, however, is the object for whom all these mighty acts of God are intended—man, man in Creation, man who receives his life from God, and who is sought and redeemed in these acts by God who is Creator and Redeemer. To use Luther's language, we could say that Cullmann does not "use personal pronouns" or describe the application of God's works. He loses the "*pro me*" and "*pro nobis*" for whom the acts of God are intended. This means that any description of a Biblical time line which does not reckon with the object of God's acts thereby lacks half its theological content. If the idea of man as the object to whom God addresses His acts is lost, thus creating a need for an anthropology, apparently the only way in which this need can be met in modern theology is by connecting to the dogmatic system an already existing philosophical doctrine of man, as Bultmann does through his connexion with Heidegger.[28] If this is done, it almost always becomes unnecessary for some reason to base theology on the whole of the Bible, including the Old Testament.[29] The result of this is either a long "Christ line" emptied of anthropology, as in Cullmann, or an existential interpretation filled with anthropology, as in Bultmann. In both cases it is the New Testament alone which is being expounded. The Bible, however, begins with the Old Testament, and the Old Testament begins with Genesis. This is the word which God speaks to us concerning Creation and man in Creation, who later defies the Creator. God, however, continues to deal with man until the very end, and this end is still awaited and still spoken of as being in the future on the last page of the Bible and in the last part of the trinitarian Creed. To begin with Creation and man in Creation is to start at the

[27] Cullmann. *Earliest Christian Confessions*, p. 38 f., *Christ and Time*, p. 108 f. and his index of scripture references on pp. 245-50.

[28] Rudolf Bultmann, "Neues Testament und Mythologie" in *Kerygma und Mythos*, VOL. I, Hamburg 1948, pp. 35 ff. We could also quote Nygren as another example, but will pass over his work for the present.

[29] Both Bultmann and Nygren give little place in their theology to the Old Testament, and work rather with philosophical presuppositions.

point from which the subsequent succession of God's mighty
acts develops, and which these acts "recapitulate."[30]

The contrast between Cullmann, who works with New
Testament material which is unrelated to the object of God's
dealings, and Bultmann, who tends to destroy the content of the
New Testament in favour of the object for whom it is intended, will
often concern us in what follows. The main point which I shall
make is that it is only on the basis of the Old and New Testaments together, and by commencing with the work of Creation,
i.e. the order which the trinitarian Creed represents, that it is
possible to escape the false alternative of an early Christian
faith expressed in a purely theoretical form, or an anthropology
derived from philosophy. The Old Testament describes a
humanity which has been created by God and has turned
from God, and which, represented by the peculiar people
who had been chosen for the salvation of the whole of the
human race, could do no more than await the outpouring
of the Spirit. This humanity which awaits the Spirit, created
by God, and subject to the discipline of the Law, is the same
humanity into which the Spirit comes in the present time
through the Gospel and the Church. The Old Testament
fulfils the legitimate theological need of an anthropology, and
deals with men on as high a level as the New Testament. All
that the New Testament bestows and promises—the forgiveness
of sins, the resurrection of the dead, and life eternal, which in
part is already a present experience, and in part is still a future
hope—all these blessings are not given in a vacuum, but are
always given to *man*, whose creation and defeat are described
in Genesis. In the "new covenant" the works of God right up
to the Last Judgment are always works of restoration and
recapitulation. For this reason the perspective of the New
Testament opens out into world mission and the Last Judgment.
Hence, too, the New Testament addresses itself to "all nations,"
πάντα τὰ ἔθνη. These are the very nations involved in the
world mission of the Church, who will be judged in the Last

[30] Cf. Gustaf Wingren, *Människan och inkarnationen enligt Irenaeus*, Lund 1947,
pp. 12 ff., Eng. trans *Man and the Incarnation: A Study in the Biblical Theology of
Irenaeus*, henceforth cited as *Man and the Incarnation*, Edinburgh 1959, pp. xiii-xv.
On the difficulty of translation see especially p. xv, footnote 5; see also the references under *recapitulatio*, p. 230.

Judgment (cf. Mt. xxv.32 with Mt. xxiv.14 and xxviii.19, and with Lk. xxiv.47 and Rom. xvi.26), who were created by God (Acts xvii.26), and who have fallen into sin and walked in their own ways (Acts xiv.16).[31] The New Testament needs not only its own interpretation of the Old Testament, but also the Old Testament itself. In isolation from the Old Testament it is in danger of evolving a philosophical anthropology.[32]

If, however, as suggested above, we want to take the Bible in its wholeness as our basis, and in particular as our basis for an exposition of Creation and the Law, we must at the same time note that with our present division of exegetical studies into two parts, Old and New Testaments, such an undertaking is not possible in purely exegetical terms. To read the Bible as a unity, consisting of a single long narrative, is to read the Bible as it was read before the Enlightenment. No modern interpreter reads the Bible in this way, though every congregation does so in public worship, especially if it makes confession of the trinitarian Creed. In this case, however, such a congregation has to depend for its picture of the Bible or the Creed *as a whole* on the outmoded interpretation provided by many earlier exegetes. In regard to the *parts* of the Bible or the Creed, on the other hand, it gets most help from more recent commentators. As far as a picture of the Bible as a whole is concerned, we have still a great deal to learn from the very earliest Biblical commentators who wrote at the time when the scriptures of the Old and New Testaments were first gathered together, and when, significantly enough, the trinitarian Creed began simultaneously to develop.[33] The foremost among these Biblical interpreters was Irenaeus.

[31] Cf. Gärtner, *The Areopagus Speech*, pp. 229-33. Gärtner's important work shows the connexion on the one hand between Acts xvii and Rom. i-ii, and on the other between these different New Testament texts and the Old Testament. In systematic theology, especially that part of it which has been influenced by Barth, texts such as Rom. i.19 ff., ii.14 f., Acts xiv.17 and xvii.24 ff. have often caused great difficulty. See, e.g., N. H. Søe, *Kristelig etik*, 4th edn. Copenhagen 1957, pp. 21 f., 54 ff. We shall return later to this work.

[32] By connecting itself with one particular philosophy in this way theology does not become more open to philosophy in general, but less. Cf. Gustaf Wingren, *Teologiens metodfråga*, Lund 1954, pp. 205-14, Eng. trans. *Theology in Conflict*, Philadelphia 1958, pp. 155-68.

[33] It may well be asked why modern exegetes refer to the Old Testament as the "Old Testament" and the New as the "New Testament." If we are unable to

The Creator and Life

It may be appropriate to begin this section with some aspects of an argument which appears in Irenaeus, whom on this particular point we might well suppose to represent the Old Testament interpretation of life, including man's physical life. But in fact Irenaeus (and in his case we are dealing with a particular criticism of the Gnostic denial of God's work of Creation) represents a belief which is common in the Old Testament and is retained in the New (Acts XVII.25, XIV.17; Mt. VI.25-32, V.45). This was a belief in God's preservation of the *body*. Irenaeus defended this belief against his opponents who separated the body from the soul, and who were prepared to admit that the soul could have eternal life, but denied that the body could. This denial of the body and separation of body from soul was expressed in their unwillingness to accept the doctrine of the resurrection of the dead. It was on this particular issue that the conflict between Irenaeus and the Gnostics took place. But it was characteristic that the problem of the participation of the body in the life which is received in the Resurrection was not restricted by Irenaeus to its future participation in that life, but is extended to include the whole life of the body. All life is created, and is thus bestowed by the Creator. But what does it mean to say that the body "lives"?

"It is not possible to live apart from life, and the means of life is found in fellowship with God."[34] To live means to receive life from outside oneself. As soon as we are cut off from this external source, life is extinguished. The resurrection life is the receiving of life from an external source, from which even now

explain the unity of the Bible, the Old Testament is merely a piece of Semitic literature and the New Testament a piece of Hellenistic writing. The terms "Old" and "New" are as meaningless as the term "Testament." If, however, we retain the terminology, we do so on the grounds of a very ancient method of Bibilical interpretation which we clearly cannot abandon, even though we reject it in its details. Cf. L. S. Thornton, *Revelation and the Modern World*, London 1950, pp. 163 ff., etc. For Thornton the contribution made by Irenaeus is fundamental.

[34] Irenaeus, *Adversus haereses*, henceforth cited as *A.h.*, IV. xxxiv. 6 (Harvey's edition; Stieren's edition IV. xx. 5). In subsequent references *A.h.* will always refer to *Sancti Irenaei episcopi Lugdunensis libros quinque adversus haereses*, ed. W. W. Harvey, Cambridge 1857. The reference in *Sancti Irenaei episcopi Lugdunensis quae supersunt omnia*, ed. A. Stieren, Leipzig 1848-53, will follow the Harvey reference in brackets, since the Bibliothek der Kirchenväter follows Stieren.

in faith man draws his sustenance. But the same thing holds good even now of the bodily life, and not just that of believers, but of all bodily life. Breathing, searching for food, protection from danger, and warmth, all these are the conditions of our human, created life, and are afforded by the contact which human life has with other created things. This contact keeps life in being and sustains human weakness against death. The Gnostics in their very denial that their bodies had received life from God used their lips and tongues to make the denial, thereby manifestly contradicting their whole assertion that the body is incapable of receiving life. "The flesh, therefore, is not destitute of participation in the wonderful wisdom and power of God. But if the power of Him who is the bestower of life is made perfect in weakness[35]—that is, in the flesh—let them inform us, when they maintain the incapacity of flesh to receive the life granted by God, whether they do say these things as being living men at present, and partakers of life, or acknowledge that, having no part in life whatever, they are at the present moment dead men. And if they really are dead men, how is it that they move about, and speak, and perform those other functions which are not the actions of the dead, but of the living? But if they are now alive, and if their whole body partakes of life, how can they venture the assertion that the flesh is not qualified to be a partaker of life . . . ? For that the flesh can really partake of life, is shown from the fact of its being alive; for it lives on, as long as it is God's purpose that it should do so . . ."[36]

To read a passage like this which comes from the second century is like reading a modern description of the Old Testament concept of life, e.g. that in Pedersen's *Israel*. In this, it is true, the body is thought of as frail, but not as being of less worth than the less visible and "more refined" soul. When the body is alive, it is wholly permeated by the life which God has breathed into it.[37] It is nowhere suggested in the Old Testament that there is a contrast between body and soul, as if these were

[35] The allusion is to II Cor. XII.9.

[36] *A.h.* v. iii. 3 (Stier. ibid.), trans. in *The Ante-Nicene Fathers*, VOL. I, New York 1896.

[37] Johannes Pedersen, *Israel*, VOLS. I-II, Copenhagen 1920, pp. 124 f., Eng. trans. *Israel*, VOLS. I-II, London and Copenhagen 1926, pp. 171 f. See Gen. II.7.

two constituent parts possessed by men, but ultimately two
opposed parts.[38] Whenever the Bible speaks of a contrast
between body and soul (or body and Spirit), it is man or the
creature that is being contrasted with God, who is the giver of
life: "The Egyptians are men, and not God; and their horses
are flesh, and not spirit" (Is. xxxi.3).[39] Man, who receives his
life from God, cannot set himself up against God in defiance
without dying. By his defiance he shuts himself off from the
source of life from which he receives his own life. Death in this
instance comes slowly, as disease spreads slowly from a poison
or wound, but it does come. Even in the time of Israel, therefore, and before the New Testament period, the concept of
salvation includes the destruction of death (Is. xxv.8).[40] The
failure of later theology, particularly after the beginning of the
eighteenth century, to say much about the body was related
to the prevailing avoidance by theologians of the problem of
death.[41] It is only when death is conceived of as something
unnatural and tyrannical, and when life in all its forms,
including the outward and bodily life of man, is related to God
and His continuing work of Creation in the present time, that
it is possible for us to understand the immediacy and self-
evidence of the Biblical faith in God, and discover how realistic
it is.

Its immediacy consists in the fact that our relationship to
God is given in and with life itself. It can never, properly
speaking, be created or established from man's side, as though
there had been a time after a man's birth when this relationship
was not yet established. Man cannot live, without living from
God. But his relationship to the Creator may take different

[38] Einar Billing, *De etiska tankarna i urkristendomen*, hereafter cited as *De etiska
tankarna*, 2nd edn., Stockholm 1936, pp. 74, 122. Billing shows how at this point
Israel is to be distinguished from Greek thought. On the one hand Greek thought
always understands the spiritual in man as something which ought to rule over his
lower part, while no crisis in a man's life can ever, properly speaking, affect this
spiritual self. In Israel, on the other hand, man is thought of in a completely
different way as constituting a unity, and anything which affects him affects him
as a whole, and in particular afflicts him in his innermost being. But it is only in
his encounter with God the Creator that this judgment on his "heart" ceases.

[39] Pedersen, *Israel*, VOLS. I-II, p. 176 ff. Cf. Ps. LVI.5.

[40] *Op. cit.*, pp. 333 ff.; cf. pp. 330 f.

[41] Cf. Tor Aukrust, *Forkynnelse og historie*, Oslo 1956, pp. 259 ff.; Adolf Köberle,
Der Herr über alles, Hamburg 1957, pp. 106 ff.

forms. There can be a relationship of wrath and judgment, or one of forgiveness and mercy. Whatever form it may take, man's relationship to God begins by being that of a creature who has been born, who lives, who never ceases to be created from first to last. As such he receives all that he has from the Creator, independently of what his attitude to the Creator may be, just as a son may receive from his natural father, even when he curses him. This relationship is given with life itself, and cannot be created or come into being as a result of some human decision. Within this unbroken relationship to God, which cannot cease, man receives wrath or love, and is put to death or is made alive.[42]

The self-evidence of the Biblical faith in God is such that we cannot put the question of His existence. When God is conceived of as being given along with life, much of this self-evidence disappears. It is not that this kind of belief in God is free from any problems—on the contrary, it is full of them; but these difficulties and problems are such as men have anyway by the very fact of their being alive. "Why should a certain thing happen?" "What is the correct choice?" "How shall I be able to bear it?" Men ask themselves questions like these because of the very fact that they are alive. They can ask them, even though they have no belief in God at all, but what they are really questioning is their relationship to God. For this relationship is *given* with life itself, and even when men have ceased to use the term "God" they do not cease to be related to Him, because *He is*, even though they deny Him.[43] On the other hand, it is probable that the one particular question which men put concerning the existence of God has nothing to do with their relationship to Him, since in using the word "God" they do not mean by "God" the One from whom they receive the gift of life. If we are beginning from the Biblical

[42] On Deut. xxxii.39; 1 Sam ii.6 f., cf. Aubrey R. Johnson, *The Vitality of the Individual in the Thought of Ancient Israel*, Cardiff 1949, pp. 105 f.

[43] This is important for preaching. Preaching which reveals this true relationship to God gives the listener something, even though he may be an atheist. Conversely, both the preacher and his listener may have a common store of religious terms without any contact being made with their true relationship to God when these terms are used. This true relationship to God may in fact be revealed through an everyday occurrence or expression.

faith in God with its immediacy and self-evident character,
we may state in the first place that the question of the existence
of God has nothing to do with the God *of the Bible* (although,
of course, our question about His existence may really conceal
a question about His *mercy*, in which case it *is* directly related to
the God of the Bible). Again, if we are beginning from the
Biblical faith in God, we may also state that a positive answer
to the question of the "existence" of God is generally of little
interest and indeed rather misleading. The real questions of
this relationship—which Job, for example, asked—were questions which are raised in the course of human life and which
can at times simply be confused by the bald answer, "God is,"
while on the other hand the so-called atheists may often live
in a real relationship to God with greater intensity and sim-
plicity.[44] The statement that God exists means in Biblical terms
that God helps, governs, or creates man, and here the activity
on God's side is always related to receptivity on man's. If there
is no such relationship, then what exists is not *God*.[45] For this
reason too it is of little importance from a theological point of
view if we reverse the statement and say that thus God does
not exist.

Either, then, we proceed from God, in which case we are
unable to discuss His existence; or else we are discussing something other than God, in which case it makes little difference
(if we are taking Biblical faith in God as our point of orienta-
tion) whether our discussion ends by affirming or denying His
existence.[46] It does not follow from this that a belief in God has
no problems. It has, on the contrary, to deal with a God who
by definition gives man all that he receives and who is not
excluded from anything that happens to man. At the same
time God demands credence, willingness to receive, and a love

[44] Cf. the "non-religious interpretation" in Dietrich Bonhoeffer, *Widerstand und
Ergebung*, Munich 1955, pp. 183 ff., 246, etc.

[45] Cf. Ps. x.4 with its parallelism and also Pss. xiv.1, liii.2. To deny the
existence of God in one way means to adopt an attitude of superiority and power
over something that is then regarded as powerless. Cf. Gärtner, *The Areopagus
Speech*, p. 100, n. 1 and the passage referred to.

[46] These negative statements concerning the existence of God refer only to what
is actually expressed in words. It may be, of course, that the words themselves
conceal a completely different problem. It is these hidden problems which may be
the important ones.

which gives freely. This demand is implicit in Creation independently of His Word in scripture, and becomes articulate as soon as the Word or any part of it is preached. This kind of faith is filled with problems because it has to deal with every one of life's circumstances, and these are always hard to bear with continued willingness to give and receive. If this willingness disappears, it is easier from one point of view to bear life's circumstances.[47] The fact that this kind of belief is filled with many problems never means that the primary question is whether a spiritual reality exists. Even when we speak of a spiritual reality, we have still made no statement concerning its content. We are assuming rather that as soon as we have discovered something that is likely, viz., the existence of God, we may then go on to discuss His nature and what we think He can do. But in this very sequence we have already denied God's work in Creation, and our denial continues even when we ask whether a spiritual reality exists. If it is God who creates, then we have said something concerning the content of the spiritual reality as soon as we have asked questions about it, for the very existence of the questioner is something that is already determined in regard to its content. What the questioner is doing is to direct his question at the One who determined and continues to determine what this content shall be. A belief in Creation cannot, therefore, speak of God without using anthropomorphic terms. The very avoidance of anthropomorphic language in a general discussion of "spiritual reality" is virtually a denial of the content of the belief in Creation.[48] As soon as we begin with the work of Creation as the first of God's works, it follows clearly that we must adhere to a simple anthropomorphic account of the subsequent works of God, to which both the Bible and the Creed testify. In the extension of the act of Creation there lies the life of a man (Jesus Christ),

---

[47] This relationship between faith and what happens in human life constituted the main problem in Billing's theology. See *Vår kallelse*, Uppsala 1909, pp. 37 f.; *Herdabref*, Stockholm 1920, p. 50; *Försoningen*, 2nd edn. Stockholm 1921, pp. 124, etc. From another point of view, of course, it is harder to bear life's circumstances if the willingness to give and take has disappeared.

[48] On the necessity of some kind of anthropomorphic language see K. E. Løgstrup, *Den etiske fordring*, Copenhagen 1956, p. 234, n. 1. Cf. H. Østergaard-Nielsen, *Scriptura sacra et viva vox*, Forschungen zur Geschichte und Lehre des Protestantismus, VOL. X, PT. X, Munich 1957, pp. 29-32, 109-19, 194, etc.

C

whose circumstances form the substance of the Gospel (the second article), and the Church, the very gathering of which initiates the events of the last period (the third article).[49]

Because faith in God possesses this character and because it is incapable of excluding any aspect of man's life from his relationship to God, it contains everything to do with man's life without being contained in any part of it. This is important from the point of view of the question of method in theology. Our best starting-point in regard to method is that which proceeds on the one side from a given empirical fact, e.g. the fact that certain scriptures have been and are being expounded to men. On the other side it makes as few assumptions as possible concerning the significance of this fact. Its interpretation of these scriptures is quite free and open.

This kind of phenomenological starting-point allows room for the relatively exact historical discipline of theology, but at the same time leaves the door open for a systematic judgment. The actual demands under which man lives are reinterpreted by the proclamation which is directed to him, and which extends to a belief in Creation from which these demands take their meaning. The actual proclamation which we may observe in its phenomenological aspect is significant only in so far as it is addressed to created man and extends to a doctrine of the Church and the Resurrection, which is the restoration and the recapitulation of Creation.[50] Such a theology is free in regard to philosophy, but for this very reason is capable of dealing with philosophical problems and different philosophies, and is not bound to one particular philosophy. Furthermore, such a theology is exclusively concerned (when it puts the question of method) with working rules, and is not interested in discovering a total view. A theologian who assumes that, while he under-stands the Christian faith, he lacks this total view, as long as the philosophical basis of his theology remains unsettled, has a false picture of the Christian faith and a false view of philosophy. Philosophy, and in particular science, has no such total view to offer. The object of such a theologian is an attitude to life, and

---

[49] On the "pictorial" or narrative preaching of the Reformation see Ivarsson, *Predikans uppgift*, pp. 43-55.

[50] See the section, "Preaching and the Law," in Part II, chapter III.

philosophy is unable to provide him with this without becoming a religion. In science it is only a step from one subject of study to another, and it is scientifically impossible to link the various subjects of study together by a particular view of life.[51] On the other hand there is a total view in the Christian faith precisely because the Christian faith is concerned with a belief in Creation and all that follows from this.[52] When this theological content, namely, a belief in Creation, has been lost, we must look for a total view elsewhere. In this case the consequence is always that the Christian faith becomes incorporated into an alien subject of study, which is assumed to be greater and more comprehensive.

Often this method in theology is combined with a special content in theology. We take the New Testament as the basis of our theological discussion rather than the Old Testament, in which we begin with Creation and the defeat of Adam—created man—and we start with the second article of the Creed rather than the first. To begin with the New Testament and not the Old Testament and the doctrine of Creation involves having to introduce some kind of philosophical framework before the New Testament, into which we then insert the Christian faith or the early Christian *kerygma*. To adopt a particular method in theological discussion will often involve the alteration of the theological content, either by omission or by over-emphasis. In this particular case what disappears is the belief in Creation, if this has not already disappeared for other reasons at an earlier stage. We shall then feel no contradiction if in determining our method of procedure we separate the belief in Creation, assuming it was already there in the first place, from any other part of the content. Against this we must stress, first, that the Christian faith is faith in Creation; second, that we alter most of the other aspects of the content of faith if we begin by denying Creation; and finally, that our theological method ought to be developed in such a way that

[51] Cf. Friedrich Gogarten, *Verhängnis und Hoffnung der Neuzeit*, hereafter cited as *Verhängnis*, Stuttgart 1953, pp. 138 f. Gogarten's conclusions, however, may be disputed.

[52] This total view cannot be proved scientifically, but can only be confessed and preached. Cf. Wingren, *Theology in Conflict*, p. 154. This book nowhere states that theology expounds Biblical texts. It interprets them, but does not expound them.

26 CREATION

Creation remains the starting-point of our discussion. But Creation means at the one time both the creation of the world, the creation of heaven and earth, and my personal creation, that is, my birth.[53] This was Luther's great understanding of both the first and the second articles of the Creed: ". . . He has created *me* . . . given me body and soul . . . He is *my* Lord." He interprets the third article in a similar way. There is no doubt at all that there are good New Testament grounds for Luther's interpretation of the second and third articles concerning Christ and the Spirit, but we must emphasise that the Old Testament itself also thinks of the work of Creation as continuing in the present time, and, as it were, personalised, in such a way that birth is seen to be the same act of formation as the work of Creation itself, though more intimately related to myself, and coming to an end in my own life, with all that this life implies (Is. XLIII.7; Ps. CXXXIX.13; Job XXXI.15; cf. Jer. 1.5).[54] For this reason faith in the Creator in the Old Testament, as well as in the quotation from Irenaeus which we have cited in this section by way of introduction, is universal in its reference. There is no part of man's life which is isolated from his relationship to God. "Thou dost beset me behind and before, and layest thy hand upon me." (Ps. CXXXIX.5).[55]

The question whether this belief in Creation is also characterised by closeness to reality and not just by immediacy and self-evidence cannot be answered, at any rate if proof in the normal sense is demanded. We have no proof of the accuracy of statements of faith in relation to the reality of which they speak. The idea of such a proof, moreover, presupposes the kind of spiritual reality which the belief in Creation cannot confirm. Just as belief in Creation means that we cannot

[53] See the section, "The Creation of the World and our Birth," in Part I, chapter III.
[54] Cf. Walter Eichrodt, *Theologie des Alten Testaments*, VOL. II, Leipzig 1935, pp. 78 f., and also Hans Schmidt, *Die Psalmen*, Handbuch zum Alten Testament, VOL. I, PT. XV, Tübingen 1934, pp. 244 f. See also Job XII.10, XXXIV.14 f.; Ps. CIV.27-30.
[55] The problem is not where to find God, but where to escape from Him (Ps. CXXXIX.7 ff.). There is no place to hide from God. This is the starting-point of the preaching of the Gospel. What we find in the Gospel is God's new, saving work in Christ. See Acts XVII.27 f., and Gärtner, *The Areopagus Speech*, pp. 230 ff., and cf. Rom. x.6 ff.

isolate a "religious" part, our soul, from the rest of us, or separate body from soul on the false assumption that only the soul can have any relationship to God, so the basic fact that we live constitutes the primary relationship to God. Proof of the accuracy of statements of faith in the foregoing sense is excluded. All that we can prove is the ability of various types of faith to come to terms with the circumstances of life which Einar Billing refers to as "scope, capacity, or elasticity."[56] This ability which we have referred to as "closeness to reality" is quite obviously varied in its form. In some types of faith most of life's circumstances fall outside the relationship to God and indeed at times can be understood only as a disturbance of existing peace, ἀταραξία, which only the Wise One can get rid of.

The belief based on the second article of the Creed which is represented in several forms of modern theology is generally characterised by its failure to become involved in human relationships and circumstances. There is a sense in which it feels little point in involving itself in the human situation. In this connexion we can see quite clearly the contrast between the present time and the Reformation, which was involved in and concerned with all human relationships.[57] This lack of contact in modern theology with human relationships is undoubtedly connected with the neglect of the belief in Creation and therefore also with the neglect of the Old Testament and the first article of the Creed. Where the belief in Creation which we find in Genesis is taken seriously, we must begin our discussion of the relationship to God in human life in all its aspects. Our point of departure is thus not a book which speaks about Creation, viz., the Old Testament, but is in fact Creation itself, i.e., the fact that man lives.[58] Since the waning of liberal

[56] See Billing, *De etiska tankarna*, p. 12.

[57] Barth with his doctrine of *analogia relationis* is an exception here. His doctrine, based on the statements in the Creation narrative concerning "man and woman," (Gen. 1.27), brings the whole of social ethics into the centre of his Dogmatics. See Barth, *Die kirchliche Dogmatik*, VOL. III, PT. II, Zollikon-Zürich 1948, pp. 344; VOL. III, PT. IV, Zollikon-Zürich 1951, pp. 127 ff., and many of his essays on social ethics written in the 1940's and 1950's.

[58] To a certain extent this is where Grundtvig begins, and in his contact with life he is an exception in the process of spiritualising which marks the 19th century (taking "life" in the sense of "human life" as given above). For this reason Danish

theology, this point of departure has been denied or understood
as anthropocentric. It appears, however, that this denial and
interpretation are connected with certain debatable assumptions concerning the risks involved in taking the belief in
Creation as a starting-point in our theological discussion.

In the first place, it is assumed that if we start here, viz. with
the doctrine of Creation, we are attributing to natural man a
more or less sovereign knowledge of God which is independent
of the revelation in Christ, and which already exists in man
himself.[59] It may be that in the eighteenth and nineteenth
centuries the belief in Creation was interpreted in this way. If
so, this interpretation should be challenged, for it rests on a
concept which goes quite counter to the belief in Creation,
viz. that at the beginning of Creation man was independent
of God. Thus the priority of the second article, on this argument, is that it would make man dependent. As we have seen,
however, Creation in fact means that the creature depends for
his existence on the Creator. To live means to receive life, and
in one sense to be created. By making man's start in Creation
the basis of a false independence on man's part, modern
theology is in turn admitting a false interpretation of the first
article of the Creed.

In the second place the dangers of a false anthropocentric
independence of God, which are a direct consequence of concentrating on the second article and isolating the New Testament from the Old, are barely recognised. To be surrounded
by conditions and relations which have no connexion with the
relationship to God, and to conceive of this relationship as
being non-existent among those who are born, live, eat, beget
children, and work, but who have not heard nor received
the historically given word concerning Christ, is in itself a

society and the life of the Danish people form part of his total view, and for this
reason too he follows the early Church in interpreting salvation as restoration
"*recapitulatio.*" Løgstrup, *Den etiske fordring*, p. 127, n.1., discusses Grundtvig, but
he makes use of the terminology of Gogarten: "The ordering of our civil or political
life is not a religious but a secular achievement." The term "secular" hardly does
justice to Grundtvig with his affinity to the early Church any more than it does to
Luther (cf. Løgstrup, *op. cit.*, pp. 115 f.). On Gogarten's use of language see
Gogarten, *Verhängnis*, pp. 129-43.
   [59] It is on these grounds that Søe criticises natural theology, *Kristelig etik*, pp.
15 ff.

tremendous declaration of independence of God and of fellowship with Him, and this declaration cannot be modified or balanced by statements affirming Christ's lordship.[60] Creation does not mean that a knowledge of God is given, but that life is bestowed. According to the Bible, independence of God is not a consequence of Creation nor a gift of God in Creation, but is an effect of the Fall (Gen. III). God's intention in Creation (Gen. 1.26) is not fully realised in Creation, but in His works between Creation and the end of the world of which the Bible and the trinitarian Creed speak.

We can hardly use the second article of the Creed in order to dethrone man from his position as a sovereign being over and against God. On the contrary, if we do not begin with the fact that life itself constitutes an established relationship to God the Creator, then all statements about God's sovereignty in Christ will be meaningless.[61] In this case His sovereignty will be a sovereignty over man in which man's submission will be dictated and not voluntarily given. In actual fact God's sovereignty in Christ is a sovereignty of victory over the Destroyer of man and Creation. The proclamation of this victory is therefore also the offering of freedom to men (Heb. 11.14 f.). God's continuing works give man salvation, which means that they give men life, and this in turn means that they extend the work of Creation, which was threatened by its bondage to sin and death, but is now saved through forgiveness and resurrection. Since these works of God give life, and recreate and develop life, man also achieves certainty, new knowledge of God, and even an insight into God's work from the beginning, which he did not previously possess; but his growth in knowledge is simply one aspect of the greater fact, that God renews man.[62] There is no reason for making man's lack of knowledge of God a regulative factor, or for defending oneself by trying to argue against the fact that the first article is actually first, i.e. the word which describes God's first mighty

[60] Cf. N. H. Søe, *Religionsfilosofi*, Copenhagen 1955, e.g. pp. 96, 106-10, where "special revelation" is contrasted with human seeking in such a way that man's independence of God is accentuated rather than lessened.

[61] Cf. K. E. Løgstrup, *Den erkendelsesteoretiske konflikt*, Copenhagen 1942, pp. 114 f., 154.

[62] Cf. Irenaeus, *A.h.*, v. ii. 1-3 (Stier. ibid.).

act upon which all His subsequent works until the end of the
world are based. The very fact of life proves that God has begun
to give. The "*opus proprium*" of God, which is to give and which
is seen most clearly in the Gospel, is already operative in
Creation and is expressed in the primary fact of life.[63] It is for
this reason that the present section, "The Creator and Life,"
is being treated under the chapter which deals with "Creation
and the Gospel." A radical demand, however, follows from the
Creation and bestowal of life. Life has not been established in
Creation once and for all, to be maintained and preserved
subsequently under certain orders defined by God. This is a
false consequence of the belief in Creation; or rather, if the
concept of Creation itself is false, this doctrine of order will
follow. In this misinterpretation of Creation which has generally
arisen through confining God's work of Creation to a particular
point in the past, there is no real understanding of God as
continuing to create in the present, or of life itself as God's
continuing Creation. There is rather a conception of certain
static results of the work of Creation which has isolated certain
abilities or qualities in human nature, or social institutions, or
at times a combination of both, in some time long since past.
These, however, are always substitutes for God Himself, and automatically exclude any new creation, i.e. the critical and
refashioning work of the Word.[64]

The distinguished Scandinavian theologian K. E. Løgstrup,
from whose notable work, *Den etiske fordring*, I shall frequently
quote, has vigorously returned to a quite definite interpretation
of the radical demand which is given along with God's work
of Creation. His interpretation does not involve a theology of
order, but develops into a doctrine of an ever-new and increasing relationship of concern for our neighbour, in which we

---

[63] Cf. the transition from the first article to the second in the Larger Catechism
of Luther (Weimar edition, *Kritische Gesammtausgabe*, ed. J. C. F. Knaake, 1883–,
henceforth cited as **W. A.**, 30-1, pp. 183.30-186.28).

[64] It cannot be denied that Brunner's theology of order presents certain difficulties at this point. In spite of this much of Brunner's criticism remains correct.
See, e.g., E. Brunner, *Das Gebot und die Ordnungen*, 2nd edn., Tübingen 1933, p. 109.
Eng. trans., *The Divine Imperative*, London 1937, pp. 140 ff. It does not necessarily
follow from this, however, as Brunner suggests, that we must adopt a conservative
position, nor is the question of the "preservation" of life the main one. Ethical
demands can be defined only by use of the term "neighbour."

see that we are inseparably involved in our neighbour's well-being. We find his clearest interpretation of the demand which is inherent in the life which is given at Creation in the work already quoted.[65] Every encounter between human beings involves an unexpressed demand to be responsible for one another's life as long as we are able to do so. To receive life means to be implicated in this reciprocity of demand. Where we regard the life which has been given to a man as his own to do with as he pleases, we deny both the work of Creation and the need of our neighbour. Thus guilt comes into being.[66]

Christ and Creation

It is frequently stated in the Old Testament that God creates by His word. In the New Testament several passages state that God has created everything in Christ, through whom He continually creates anew (Col. 1.16 ff.; Heb. 1.2) These two lines of thought are connected in the affirmation that the Word became flesh in Christ (Jn. 1.1-14). The Word who was active in creation, invisibly, finally "dwelt among us and we beheld His glory" (Jn. 1.14). A second and too much neglected factor linking the two lines of thought is the Spirit. Creation by the Spirit and Creation by the Word are the same thing. Jesus was anointed by the Spirit and is therefore Christ and Creator. "By the word of the Lord the heavens were made, and all their host by the breath of His mouth" (Ps. xxxiii.6).[67] The whole of the New Testament bears witness to the Spirit who was poured forth by Christ and is actively engaged in His continuing work of Creation in the present time.

But all points of contact such as those are nevertheless unsatisfactory. They belong to a past time, linking concepts which cannot be applicable to our life simply because they

[65] It is true that Løgstrup fails to make room for the critical and reforming work of the preached word, but from other points of view his contribution is valuable.
[66] See Løgstrup, Den etiske fordring, pp. 126-9, 161 f., 189 f. The preaching of the death of Christ should be connected with this demand.
[67] Cf. Is. xxxiv.16 on the wild beasts and Lorenz Dürr, Die Wertung des göttlichen Wortes im Alten Testament, hereafter cited as Die Wertung, Mitteilungen der vorderasiatisch-aegyptischen Gesselschaft, VOL. XLII, PT. I, Leipzig 1938, pp. 22, 38 ff. 153 f. Cf. Lk. iv.18 with Ps. civ.30 and Rom. viii.11.

belong together. The Creation of the world in Christ is in any
case a difficult concept. Instead of reading Biblical and dogmatic ideas into this concept to a greater extent, I propose in
this present section to outline a problem which is directly
connected with the theme which was developed in the preceding
section on the Creator and life. Our discussion is still under the
general heading which relates Creation to the Gospel. We shall
afterwards examine its relation to Judgment.

Any unfamiliarity which we feel in the concept of Creation
in Christ is often due to the fact that we have put the Creation
of *the world* into the centre. The Creation of the world is
important in its place. Man has, it is true, been put into the
world to govern and to subdue the earth and all that is in it
(Gen. 1.28 ff.),[68] but it hardly helps our understanding of
Creation in Christ to put the Creation of the world into the
centre from the first. In the New Testament picture of the
eschaton, Christ has a cosmic position, and His power extends
to the world in a way which also is as hard to understand as
Creation in Christ itself. But Christ now exercises His rule over
men in the Church through His Word and sacraments.[69] If we
think particularly here of Christ's rule over men in faith, i.e.
His kingdom in the hearts of men, it is possible for us to form a
correct understanding of His kingdom only if man as man, as
one who has been born on earth, is created in Christ. Belief in
Creation does not mean primarily that the world has been
created but that "God has created me and all creatures." My
life depends on the fact that God creates. Our relation to the
Creator is given through life itself and remains even if men do
not use the term "God." The question of God's existence
becomes meaningless. The central point in the encounter
between Christ and man who has been created by God, i.e.
in the Gospel, is the rule which Christ exercises in the conscience. He is able to attain to this rule in man's assent to the

---

[68] See the section, " 'Dominion' and Freedom," below, Part I, chapter III.
[69] This is characteristic of Christ's rule in the Church in distinction from His
future *"regnum"* in Creation as a whole. Connected with this is the fact that according to Genesis even now men have a special place in Creation—they are
appointed to "have dominion" over it. Cf. Oscar Cullmann, *Königsherrschaft
Christi und Kirche im Neuen Testament*, hereafter cited as *Königsherrschaft Christi*,
Theologische Studien, VOL. x, 2nd edn., Zürich 1946, pp. 38 f.

whole corpus of scripture and dogma, but He can also attain
to it even when, because of insuperable intellectual difficulties
concerning dogma, men regard Him as no more than an "ideal
man." Christ comes to men in as many different ways as He
did in the Gospels. Just as it is inadmissible in the introduction
to theology to put the question of the existence of God, so we
may not put the question of Christ's divinity in the introduction
to Christology.[70] Let us temporarily shelve the question, and
in its place ask whether man *is destined for Christ* from his own
inescapable existence and position as created man. The concept
of Creation in Christ will then cease to be unfamiliar and
difficult, and become rather the presupposition of and a
positive element in almost every kind of affirmative relation to
Christ consistent with widely different dogmatic positions. It is
quite reasonable to approach the problem of Creation in Christ
from this angle.

Even though we shall have many opportunities of returning
to the question further on, we must first answer the accusation
which may be raised, that we have destroyed the dogmatic
content of the second article by what we have just stated. There
is a close connexion between the manner in which the content
of dogma in many forms of present-day theology and preaching
is offered for man's acceptance before "faith" may be assumed
to exist, and the fact that eschatology has practically disappeared. Modern theology by and large does not reckon
seriously with the fact that Christ is preached *now* in order that
His visible rule may succeed His Word. Where no division is
made between sowing in the present and reaping in the future, it
will always become necessary to anticipate the future Judgment
by bringing it into the present time as a matter of self-interest.

[70] The question of "the divinity of Christ" has usually been put in such a way
that one has first defined what divinity means independently of Christ, and then
gone on to see whether this kind of divinity is present in Christ. In fact, however,
everything turns on how *God* has defined it in what He has done. Christ destroys
a great many conceptions of what divinity means at the same time as He creates
a new conception of the divine by what He does (cf. Gustaf Aulén, *Den allmänneliga
kristna tron*, 5th edn., Stockholm 1957, pp. 64 f., 202, Eng. trans. *The Faith of the
Christian Church*, Philadelphia 1948, pp. 50 f., 181). God the Creator is to be defined
in terms of His work of Creation, and God the Saviour in terms of His work of
salvation. These two works belong together, and in the Consummation will merge
into a unity.

The Church with its Creed then becomes judge and proceeds
to adopt the same attitude towards those who hesitate on its
threshold as the Jews took towards the Gentiles when they
awaited their submission, astonished that it took so long to
come. It was to the Jews who thought in such terms that Jesus
said, "The men of Nineveh will arise at the judgment with
this generation and condemn it; for they repented . . . The
queen of the South will arise at the judgment with this generation and condemn it; for she came from the ends of the earth
to hear . . ." (Mt. XII.41 f.). The strangers outside Israel here
referred to have not received all God's works or revelation, but
in relation to what they have received all has taken place that
was to take place—they have been afforded the opportunity
of hearing the Word of God and of conversion, i.e. the critical
judgment which is contained in the Word.[71] We do not know
where in relation to Christ's Gospel all this took place. The
Church with its Word and Creed is a servant of this event and
attempts to bring it about, but she is not to judge where it has
happened or failed to happen.[72] It is certain, however, *how* it
happens—Christ claims obedience in the commands which He
lays on men's consciences.[73] This demand may vary with
individuals. Those who want to accelerate this process and
assent indiscriminately without any inward compulsion to a
number of dogmatic propositions are in spiritual danger. If
in such a situation he forces this assent upon himself, a man
will easily lose his capacity to hear a clear command later on,
and will certainly demand the same "faith" from others which
he has forced from himself. Such spiritual compulsion indicates
that liberal theology has not really been defeated, and therefore
must be forcibly restrained [74] against any such tendency. We
must insist that the description of Christ in the second article
serves to give us an understanding of Christ's image and

---

[71] Cf. Prenter, *Skabelse og genløsning*, pp. 604 f.

[72] Cf. Nils Johansson, *Bibelns värld och vår*, Lund 1949, pp. 71-6.

[73] What Christ commands may be an act or it may be faith itself. Cf. Reidar
Hauge, *Gudsåpenbaring og troslydighet*, Oslo 1952, p. 190.

[74] Cf. the description of the present-day situation in the "Denkschrift" of the
Tübingen Faculty, *Für und wider die Theologie Bultmanns*, Sammlungen gemeinver-
ständliche Vorträge Nos. 198-9, Tübingen 1952, pp. 8 ff. What is said there of
Germany is true *mutatis mutandis* of many European nations.

likeness, but this likenessis a mystery. Men can grow into it only slowly, and perfectly only at death. We must also insist that the question of where Christ has found obedience among men is a matter to be decided in the Judgment and not in the present time.

To say that man, as a creature who has been born on earth, is created in Christ, is to use a term which is quite unmythological. It means simply that what man is offered in the incarnate Son is "life." The Creator who lets man live and who thereby creates him, creates him in His image (Gen. 1.26 f.), and this image in which every man has been created is Jesus Christ, who is "the image of the invisible God, the first-born of all Creation " (Col. 1.15).[75] The "new man" whom the believer in Christ "puts on" (Rom. XIII.14; Gal. III.27) is Christ Himself. This is what God the Creator intended man to be in Creation. To become like Christ, therefore, is also to conform to God's will in Creation and to receive "life" (cf. Col. III.10; Eph. IV.24).[76] These many New Testament passages about the "image" and "likeness" are marked by their reference both to Christ and to the believer. They have undoubtedly derived their form from the important Old Testament passage on Creation in Gen. 1.26, and are fully comprehensible only in the light of this passage. The early Christian exegesis of Gen. I. 26 is distinguished from the Jewish by its strong emphasis on the *new Creation in Christ*, on being raised with Him, growth, and the abundant life which He offers, etc.[77] This contrast between that which has been given in Creation from the beginning and that which is bestowed in Christ does not destroy the profound connexion that exists between Creation and Christ. Adam's defeat in his temptation (Gen. III) and Christ's victory in His (Mt. IV) involve both connexion and transcendence (see Rom. v.12-9). The life which Christ gives to the world through His victory (Rom. v.15, 17) is the life which Adam lost (Gen. II.

[75] See N. A. Dahl, "Christ, Creation, and the Church," in *The Background of the New Testament and its Eschatology*, hereafter cited as *Background*, Cambridge 1956, p. 434.

[76] *Op. cit.*, p. 436.

[77] *Op. cit.*, pp. 429 f. Cf. I Cor. xv.45-9; II Cor. IV.4 ff. See also David Cairns, *The Image of God in Man*, London 1953, pp. 32-52. The analysis, however, does not go deep enough.

17; III.17-9).[78] When Adam was tempted, his destruction was a possibility, but after Christ's victory Adam's downfall can no longer affect man: "Death no longer has dominion over him" (Rom. VI.9 f.). Destruction and death can certainly still afflict those who in faith belong to Christ (1 Cor. x.), but in the eternal life which Christ bestows upon them they are also removed from the possibility of the Fall and thus enjoy the life which Adam was still able to lose in Creation. In this "transcendence," therefore, there is a unity which stretches from the beginning in Genesis to the end in the book of the Revelation, from the first article of the Creed to the last parts of the third article. Throughout life is life, death is death, and sin is sin, even although the combat fluctuates from side to side until the destruction of evil in the last Judgment.

Because man is created in a "likeness" which is afterwards raised to life in Jesus's resurrection from the dead, life becomes a reality for him; but he is brought into Christ's life which flows over the limits of Creation and stands open in hope to still greater possibility of development which "no eye has seen." Yet that which has been received, as well as that which is still to come, remains simply "life." It never transgresses what God has already ordained and intended in Creation.[79] It is, therefore, always true and natural life if it is regarded from man's side. To lack this life is death. It is something that is unnatural. It is to participate in the enmity between rebellious man and the Creator which runs counter to the purpose of Creation.[80]

[78] Even in Gethsemane, where our Lord had to choose between "my will" and "thine" (Mt. XXVI.39, 42), there was still the possibility of defeat. It is part of the greatness of the Epistle to the Hebrews that Christ's resemblance to Adam in His temptation is not veiled over but openly declared, thereby emphasising His humanity and conflict (Heb. V.7 ff.). As we go further from the New Testament the idea of the divinity of Christ tends to displace these aspects of His humanity. In the Christocentric theology of the present time it is thought of as being "liberal" to speak of Christ "learning" obedience through what He suffered, even though Hebrews says this! We can also discern a certain disinclination to accept the Gethsemane narrative with its strong emphasis on the humanity of Jesus.

[79] "For our glorification" God has decreed and prepared "what no eye has seen nor ear heard" *before the ages* (1 Cor. II.7 ff.). According to the New Testament the decree of God to give life in abundance in the Consummation already existed in the beginning, before the creation of man. God created the heavens and the earth with this object in view.

[80] Cf. Rev. XX.2, 10 with Gen. III.1-15. The restoration of Creation means that the forces which are opposed to man lose all their power to lead him astray.

When men are given life through the incarnate Son in the Church, they receive it by making use of and having contact with created things. These, unlike man, still belong to God. They have not fallen, but on the contrary are more ready than he is to serve their Creator—for example, water, bread, and wine. This external aspect and relation of the sacraments of Baptism and the Eucharist is not accidental, but more important still is the element in each of them which we may perhaps describe as their *epic* character. Baptism is an event, something that takes place. In Baptism there is a submersion and a rising again in purity, just as Joseph was lowered into the well and came up again; as Ebed Jahveh fell in death and rose; and as Jesus died and now for all eternity has risen again. What happens in Baptism always points forward to new acts, a daily putting to death of the old self and a daily resurrection of the new, until the last age itself is present. What happens in Baptism is the direct opposite of what happened to Adam in Gen. III. Adam longed for exaltation and deification—"You will be like God" (Gen. III.5)—but he died. Baptism completely reverses the primal injury and restores us to health.[81] The Eucharistic act has the same character. The words of institution which are the centre of the act are again *epic* and descriptive of something that actually happens: "He took . . . He broke . . . He gave . . ." And all these acts took place on the night on which He was betrayed. "This cup" which we share in the communion (1 Cor. XI.25) is the same "cup" from which Jesus in Gethsemane asked to be delivered, but which in the end He drank willingly (Mt. XXVI.39, 42) and the same "cup" of which He promised that His disciples would drink when He refused their request for exaltation (Mk. X.37-40).[82] The act of communion points also therefore to the events of the last time and the great communion in heaven. The true meaning of the sacrament will be fully realised only then.

---

[81] The practice of the early Church of baptising only at Easter connects the events of Easter and Baptism in a way that corresponds to their significance. In the well-known hymn of Fortunatus, "Sing, my tongue, the glorious battle," we can hear the Easter joy of the early Church. The hymn is based on the idea of recapitulation.

[82] Cf. Jn. XVIII.11 and Prenter, *Skabelse og genløsning*, pp. 498, 532, on the Eucharist as the sacrament of preparation for death. See also Gustaf Aulén, *För eder utgiven*, Stockholm 1956, pp. 183 ff.

But even when Baptism and the Eucharist are thus connected
and man's final transformation into Christ's likeness is referred
to Christ's future return (as it is for example in Phil. iii.10 ff.,
20 ff.; cf. Rom. vi.3-8); yet the whole of this protracted event
is the working out and accomplishment of God's primal
decision for Creation and of "Creation in Christ" (cf. Rom.
viii.29). When preaching "sets forth" Christ and His life
among men, it is the original "image" that is set forth to the
listener. There are innumerable ways in which this setting
forth of Christ may accomplish its object of restoring in the
heart of the listener the true "image" which will not be fully
realised in the present age. Perfection and revelation belong
to the period which "no eye has seen."[83] Not only is the Church,
which is charged with the responsibility of "setting forth"
Christ (cf. Gal. iii.1), a mystery to those who are outside her,
but those who are outside the Church (all of them created in
Christ even before the Church begins to address them) are a
mystery to her. If our own generation fails to understand
death as other than natural, it likewise finds difficulty in
understanding Baptism and the Eucharist with their final
point of reference in a life beyond death, and their employment
of a particular death as the means used by God to bring men
a still richer life which destroys death.[84] But the narrow extent
of men's earthly life before death, which they cling to as the
one known reality, is also a sphere in which the "image" is to
be manifested. Even though modern man, created as he is in
Christ and conscious of his own destiny to become the image
which is set forth to him, can do no more than employ the
term "ideal man" in order to describe what he believes to be
his true pattern, we may also see this impoverished understanding eschatologically as being affirmed in hope as a form
of God's Creation and Christ's rule in the heart. The Church,

[83] See also Luther's important exposition in W. A., 24, pp. 49.23-50.34, 37,
pp. 452.20-453.22.
[84] F. W. Dillistone, *Christianity and Symbolism*, London 1955, pp. 285 ff., maintains that the sacraments have lost their value as symbols on account of urban-
isation, e.g. the loss of contact with something as elementary as water. It is a
question, however, whether the conscious flight from death means any more. As
long as men must die there is an immediate point of contact even in our big cities
with Baptism and its symbolism of submersion, but if death is concealed, as it
often is in the cities, the contact is lost. Cf. Aukrust, *Forkynnelse og historie*, pp. 260 f.

which makes use of only a narrow part of its wealth of dogma, becomes judge of a great deal that is not actually wrong but, seen in the light of the trinitarian Creed as a whole, is merely a beginning which continues in an extended series of events. Independently of how death may be interpreted, it has an integral part in this series of events, of which the judgment of the living and the dead is the conclusion. It is often maintained against all such concepts of Christ as creating and forming man in the image and likeness which are his destiny that, if this line of thought is carried through, man will occupy the place of priority rather than Christ, because it is he and he alone who has to reach his destiny.[85]

It is this objection which most clearly exposes the errors of a particular theological attitude. In the life of those to whom Christ has not yet been preached there is only one subject, one active force, i.e. man himself and not God the Creator. But if life can be lived only when God wills, and if this life which I live is a manifestation of the fact that God creates, then it is His own work of Creation which God is achieving against the Man-slayer in the events described in the second article (Heb. II.14 ff.; 1 Jn. III.8). When modern theology brings forward the second article against man instead of against the Destroyer of man, this merely shows that it interprets man in Creation as a completely independent partner of God. His being alive does not mean that he receives or that he is created. When it is assumed that the second article alone can put a limit to man's independence of God, this shows that the first article has failed to do so and is held rather to establish this independence.[86] This must mean that we are then interpreting the

[85] When N. H. Søe, *Kristelig etik*, pp. 42 ff., accepts the criticism of the idea of conscience made by empiricism, and on pp. 52 ff. analyses the meaning of conscience from the standpoint of Christianity, it is quite clear that he is separating human life from the work of God and regarding it as an expression of man's independence of God. This is connected with Søe's Barthian doctrine of the Trinity. Cf. his *Religionsfilosofi*, pp. 105 f.

[86] On this point Luther's statements in his Shorter Catechism on the first and second articles are typical. Both physically and spiritually man is the recipient and God the giver. In his explanation of the first article Luther describes man' external or temporal sphere in such a way as to preclude any idea of man's independence of the Creator. The idea of man as a "partner" or "ally" belongs to a different theology (see Barth, *Die kirchliche Dogmatik*, VOL. III, PT. II, pp. 267 ff).

D

first article in terms of idealist theology, and misinterpreting it
in such a way that to criticise it we have to begin from the
interpretation of the second article. The whole of faith in Christ
will then become anti-human, while the belief in Creation will
continue to be denied. When a limb in the body is sick, we
cannot cure it by strengthening another limb and leaning the
whole weight of the body on that. If we do, the first limb will
remain uncured and there will be a danger that the other
limb will also be afflicted.

The fault we have referred to in the second article of the
Creed has been the over-emphasis on *the giving of knowledge* in
Christ.[87] The first article has been misinterpreted to make
man's possession of a knowledge of God his natural endowment.
In consequence the second article was made to stress that man's
knowledge of God is given and is not a natural possession. If
instead the first article had been allowed to testify simply to
the life which God bestows on man unceasingly as long as he
lives; if Creation as the first of God's mighty acts had been
given its proper place; and if man had been regarded in his
primary relationship to God as the one who receives from the
Creator in the very fact that he lives, moves, and has his being
(Acts XVII.25, 28), then the central point in the second article
would not have become *knowledge*, but (as we see in Heb. II.
10-18) the *Incarnation*. In this passage Creation is put first as
the given condition of human existence before the Captain of
our salvation came to share in our humanity.[88] Then comes the
Incarnation: "Since therefore the children share in flesh and
blood, He Himself likewise partook of the same nature, that
through death He might destroy him who has the power of
death, that is, the devil" (Heb. II.14). After this the Temptation,
as in the gospels (Mk. I.13; Mt. IV.1-11; Lk. IV.1-13), is
characteristically seen as the immediate result of the Incarnation (Heb. II.18).[89] In this latter passage there is a clear
parallel to the account of the Fall in Gen. III. Here is described
the temptation of Adam which brought death in its train, but

[87] This is characteristic of Søe, both in his *Kristelig etik*, pp. 15 ff., etc., and his
Religionsfilosofi, e.g. pp. 96 ff.
[88] Cf. Dahl, *Background*, pp. 433 f.
[89] At the same time the Epistle to the Hebrews also teaches that the world was
created in Christ (Heb. 1.2). The two go together.

which was reversed in the Temptation of Christ. This means that sin (and sin rules in *man*, in Adam) is a revolt which God's work of salvation defeats. It also means that His work of salvation restores man. It takes place on the basis of Creation.[90] The article of the Creed which refers to Creation must precede the second article which deals with redemption, even when the Creation referred to is Creation in Christ. The order in which the two are given does not represent the sequence in our acquisition of knowledge concerning God, but the sequence in God's dealings with us.

What we have just said means that from one point of view man is more depraved than the rest of Creation. Man is destined to stand above Creation. He is appointed to govern it, but in yielding to temptation he finds that the will of the Creator is now contrary to his, while the same will continues to govern the rest of Creation. The sun and the rain are the willing servants of God. Man may also therefore be invited to attempt to emulate these natural phenomena which in their workings quite clearly better image Christ than man is able to do.[91] It is man's deprivation and recapitulation that form the theme of the Biblical drama. The rest of nature is purer than corrupted man and was cursed not on its own account but on man's (Gen. III.17 f.; Rom. VIII.20). Nature therefore groans and waits for its liberation which will come when man has been fully restored (Rom. VIII.21 f.) "For among the creatures," says Luther, "Creation or nature remains as it was created. Unlike man, they have not fallen through sin."[92] Even in the world of men the purity of nature from time to time thrusts itself through and compels man to do good in spite of his evil. "If ye then being evil know how to give good gifts unto your children . . ." (Mt. VII.11).[93]

The more we take this goodness in an elementary sense, and

[90] We may again refer to the Catechisms of Luther, e.g. the explanation of the second article of faith in the Larger Catechism, especially the first half.

[91] In regard to Mt. v.44 f., cf. the interesting essay on "Natural Law" in C. H. Dodd, *New Testament Studies*, Manchester 1953, pp. 136 ff.

[92] See Heinrich Bornkamm, *Luther und das Alte Testament*, Tübingen 1948, p. 51.

[93] Cf. C. H. Dodd, *Gospel and Law*, New York 1951, p. 80, and F. K. Schumann, *Wort und Wirklichkeit*, Schriften des Theologische Konvents, VOL. I, Berlin 1951, p. 19.

the more closely we relate it to the primary content of the
concept of Creation, viz. the fact that men are *given* life, the
more easily we can understand the reference in such passages
as Rom. 11.14 ff., to the Gentiles "who have not the law" but
"do by nature what the law requires." We also see more
clearly how the phrase "earthly government" in the sixteenth
century came to have reference to the obtaining of food,
protection to life and limb, etc.[94] Only when pietism has turned
its back upon Creation; only when the goodness for which we
pray as "daily bread" has degenerated into something that is
a mere matter of course, too profane to pray for and too cheap
to give thanks for—only then do we begin to ask questions
about this natural ethic. We therefore analyse it for the purpose
of letting the second article alone provide us with knowledge
even about the Law, order, and justice. But we are then allowing
the knowledge specifically given by the second article to negate
a universal knowledge given through Creation. The reverse
may rather be true. Since the first Creation was Creation in
Christ even before Christ's Gospel and the proclamation of the
Gospel, God is actually working in this Creation, speaking to
man, and ordering and compelling him to goodness and to
outgiving love.

There is no contradiction between this natural order and the
idea that Christ has a new command to give man.[95] Christ's
command is at one time as old as Creation and as new as
salvation. If, however, Christ's law is opposed by an evil power
which resists Him, but which loses its power through His
coming and His work on earth, it then becomes at the same
time both flexible and unyielding. To care for one's children
and to sacrifice oneself for one's enemies may appear to be two
different things from the point of view of a barren ethical
system. From the point of view of murder, however, they merge
into one another in the commandment, "Thou shalt not kill,"
which Jesus interpreted: "Everyone who is angry with his
brother shall be liable to judgment" (Mt. v.21 ff.).[96] In

[94] Cf. Schumann, *Wort und Wirklichkeit*, pp. 18 f.; Dodd, *New Testament Studies*,
pp. 136-42; id., *Gospel and Law*, pp. 81 f.

[95] See Dahl, *Background*, pp. 439 f. Cf. the Pauline passages listed in Erling
Eidem, *Det kristna livet enligt Paulus*, Stockholm 1927, pp. 313-41.

[96] Cf. Helmut Thielicke, *Theologische Ethik*, vol. 1, Tübingen 1951, pp. 687-706.

obeying this sharpened demand of Jesus the disciple is not breaking away from the natural law. On the contrary he is still subject to its demands. He is still in contact with the Creator who has sustained His Creation by all these command-ments in expectation of the One who has now come, and who accentuates the old laws given for the preservation of life. In Christ the life abundant has now appeared. This "sharpening" is the reverse side of grace and forgiveness, and also a sign that opposition has been defeated and Creation restored.[97]

At this point, viz. the harmony of the natural law with the commands which Christ gives in His Word, we can now under-stand that aspect of the belief in Creation which at the begin-ning of the present section we saw to be the most difficult of all concepts, viz. the Creation of the world in Christ. External creation, which is always pouring out its gifts upon men, speaks the same word to man as Christ, in whom God gives not only His gifts but also Himself. There is a force prompting man in his external relationships in the same direction as the command of love. On the other hand man's corrupted nature since the defeat of Adam works against this force and obstructs the promptings which he feels. It tends to make him acquisitive rather than free in his giving.[98] In the "Theologie der Schöp-fungsordnungen" which was formulated on the Continent in the 1930's, the assumption was generally quite different. It was that man had inwardly through faith a relatively un-damaged form of love, but that with the appearance of the "orders" he was compelled to descend to a lower form of love. "Order" is here interpreted as being at the one time both divine and incapacitated, a "broken" form of love.[99] All this was connected with the institutionalising of the concept of order as a relatively permanent and self-preserving form of community, and therefore the result of a completed work of Creation.[100] To use the terms of the Reformers, we may say that theology described order without using the categories of "use" and "abuse." It was characteristic of Luther that he

[97] Cf. *A.h.*, IV. xxiv. 1-3 (Stier. IV. xiii. 1-4).
[98] Cf. Løgstrup, *Den etiske fordring*, pp. 124 f., 161, 275, and Prenter, *Skabelse og genløsning*, pp. 107 f., 115 f.
[99] Cf. Brunner, *The Divine Imperative*, pp. 329, 337 f.
[100] Cf. Prenter, *Skabelse og genløsning*, p. 211, especially the footnote.

conceived of created things in part as being wholly good and in
part as being subject either to man's use (*usus*) or abuse (*abusus*).
In so doing he located sin in man and not in creation.[101] In
commerce, for instance, we cannot think of money in ab-
straction from its use. Nevertheless it is of particular importance
to understand clearly that, in so far as we speak of sin in
matters of business, it is always men's "hands" that are impure.
It is men, that is, who are impure and not the coinage itself.
We could as well say that the Bible is impure, for there is no
paper which has not been touched by impure hands; or that
the wine and the bread of the Eucharist are impure, and so
on. *But the things of creation are always purer than man is.* Sin does
not lie in the things that are created, but in man's use of them.[102]
The institutions which the theology of order regarded as orders
of Creation have undoubtedly a "broken" form of love, but
this is due to the fact that an institution cannot be thought of
apart from those who are involved in it, and if there is any
"break" it is from man himself.[103]

The problem is solely man, his injury and his cure. Man's
incapacity to rule over external nature is due to the fact that
he is fallen from his place in Creation in relation to God, and
therefore also in relation to his neighbour.

[101] W. A., 40-2, p. 203.6-11 (Commentary on Ps. 11).
[102] Cf. Søe, *Kristelig etik*, p. 193. Søe speaks here of "dirty money" and a "background" which requires forgiveness (see pp. 174, 192 f., 318, 363).
[103] See Mk. VII.14-23; Rom. XIV.14; Tit. 1.15. 1 Tim. IV.4 f. may also be
included here.

CHAPTER II

CREATION AND JUDGMENT

Sin and Wrath

IN the Biblical narrative the account of Creation (Gen. I.
II) immediately precedes the account of the Fall (Gen.
III). At the beginning of the present century this fact
caused some difficulty and embarrassment to those who would
have preferred the Bible to offer a somewhat brighter picture
of man's condition. In our present situation, however, it is the
account of the Fall that strongly determines the theological
interpretation of man. The Genesis account of Creation
accordingly causes difficulty since (in the case of the Apostles'
and Nicene Creeds) it provides the basis for an article of faith
which deals with Creation before the Incarnation. This was a
Creation "in" the Son who later became incarnate. It related
to all men, and was accomplished before the Gospel and apart
from any human understanding of its meaning.[1] These changes
and shifts of accent in regard to the relation between Creation
and sin are significant. They point to a real difficulty and not
simply to a fluctuation of theological fashions. The difficulty
consists in the fact that the goodness which belongs to Creation
and the perversity which belongs to sin are interpreted rather
as attributes which, when ascribed to the same subject, namely
man, are mutually contradictory. If we say of man the sinner
that even after the Fall he still remains created, and as such
therefore good, we tend to underemphasise his sinful nature.
We appear to be suggesting that there is still something in
him which is incorrupt, something which is good and not sinful.
When on the other hand we say of man the creature that he

---

[1] It is evident from his *Earliest Christian Confessions*, p. 47, that Cullmann would
prefer that the second article were first. Cf. p. 48 f.

is perverted by the Fall, we appear to be denying the goodness of Creation, if we do not expressly say that he is only partially a sinner.[2] The difficulty may perhaps be attributable partly to the common interpretation of Creation with which we came in conflict on two occasions earlier in the present work. When the word "Creation" is used, one is inclined to think of a *result* of the act of Creation, something which comes into being as a result of the creative act, and which now exists by itself. We find this way of thinking in an institutional form in the theology of order, which thinks in terms of result. We find it again in institutional form in the attempt to think of the Church as a reality involved in the world which is unrelated to God's activity, and in the strenuous avoidance of any idea of the Word as creative of the Church.[3] But this way of thinking which deals in terms of results may also appear without any trace of institutionalism at all in anthropology, and there appropriate to itself a concept of Creation. Here man comes to be understood as the completed result of God's creative activity and as having been equipped with reason and other talents to enable him to do various things. The attempt is then made in this "created result," i.e. in man, to distinguish between the parts which have been affected and those which are unaffected by the destruction which is wrought by sin.

If we are determined to look for results in this way, we shall cut the nerve of the belief in Creation, viz. the assurance that God is actively creating *now*, and that life itself is the other side of God's continuing creative activity. It is quite clear that the Biblical texts which deal with Creation do not deal primarily with man's endowments but with God's power and goodness.[4] To consider first a single result and move backwards from the result to its cause may be the typical method of the later proofs

[2] On these difficulties and the attempts to overcome them in the post-Reformation conflicts, cf. Lauri Haikola, *Gesetz und Evangelium bei Matthias Flacius Illyricus*, Studia theologica lundensiensia, VOL. I, Lund 1952, pp. 97 ff.

[3] In particular the Church is generally interpreted in the same way as Creation and vice versa. The Church is modelled after Creation, Creation after the Church. Present-day theology overemphasises the idea of the Church and generally regards the Church as being prior in this process, but the process can also be reversed.

[4] Cf. Barth, *Dogmatics in Outline*, p. 50, "(The Creed) does not say, I believe in the created world, nor even, I believe in the work of creation. But it says, I believe in God the Creator."

of God, but it is not characteristic of the Bible, which in speaking of Creation points to God who creates.[5] God was not active only when the world of men came into being, so that what we have now to deal with are the end-products of His original Creation. But when we move and breathe we are in a living relationship to the Creator whose work is still continuing.[6]

God's continuing work is also good. His goodness is perfect and complete. One of the aspects of God's continuing work is the dealings which other people have with us, or the effects which they have upon us. There is the obvious instance of our own birth, and the protection and help which we later receive from parents—their supplying of the basic necessities of life through the work of others, the neglect by others of their own pleasures on our behalf, and the assistance and readiness of doctors and nurses to give their time when life is in danger, etc. There is nothing lacking in this goodness which flows through human life, but throughout it is the Creator's own goodness flowing out into the continuing life which God has created, preserving it from harm. We cannot isolate this goodness and change it into a quality possessed by an individual before God. When God's gifts and goodness come down upon man, the individual (parent, doctor, nurse, etc.) may well have complaints to make about the necessity of having to give. These necessities of life are not given to us only when the goodness of an individual emerges, and do not cease when the evil will of the individual rebels against the Creator.[7] Everything in man is evil, since evil consists in man's usurpation of this position and his selfish keeping of it for himself. But no such evil in the individual is able to disrupt the flow through human life of the actions and dealings of God which serve to sustain and preserve life. These actions are God's. Man is not the complete result of God's perfected work of Creation, partly good and partly evil. Rather, man is used by the Creator as the object of His continuing work of Creation. God's works are good, even if man corrupts and distorts them.

[5] Cf. Gärtner, *The Areopagus Speech*, pp. 138, 192, 197, etc.

[6] See the section, "The Creator and Life," in Part I, chapter I, and the Biblical references given there.

[7] Cf. Løgstrup, *Den etiske fordring*, pp. 161 f.

It is necessary first to emphasise the continuing goodness of this work of Creation which comes through men before we attempt to define the relationship between Creation and Judgment, and in particular to define what constitutes sin and wrath. At the present we have often of necessity to isolate the negative side as earlier we isolated the positive, viz. the relation between Creation and the Gospel. It must be made clear that this will not imply any denial of goodness or prevent God from using all men as the agents of His works, i.e. as doers of good (cf. Mt. VII.11; Rom. II.14 f.).[8] There is nothing to prevent this doing of good from increasing and reaching its height, even when the one who is doing good is egotistically benefiting himself. A doctor, for instance, may increase his income and surpass his colleagues, precisely because he endeavours to heal the sick and take care of them. Fishermen and farmers, whose thoughts are wholly taken up with the catch, the harvest, and other chances of making money, nevertheless still do things which continue among men God's life-giving activity. We must not detract from the egoism—nor from the goodness. For the goodness is God's in His work of Creation, encountering and subduing in the world of men the attitude of hostility to the Creator, and making use of it to endue life with power to resist death. This goodness of God remains the same when it becomes flesh in Christ, when it is poured forth through the Spirit, and when it speaks in the commandment of love of one's enemies and prayer for one's persecutors. It is one and the same, even though the works which it then accomplishes in the New Covenant shatter what is in opposition to it—the "old man"— to a far greater extent than before.[9] This conflict will not

[8] The one point which I wish to emphasise in all that I have to say about Creation and the Law is God's sovereignty over man's sinfulness. My criticism of the theology which has neglected the first article and put the second in its place is not primarily that this rearrangement has concealed man's responsibility, but that it has concealed God's sovereignty. See Brunner, *Der Mensch im Widerspruch*, 3rd edn., Berlin 1941, Eng. trans. *Man in Revolt*, London 1939, pp. 215-36, cf. Wingren, *Man and the Incarnation*, pp. xi ff.

[9] Where there is difficulty in reconciling the demands made by God in the "earthly government" and through the natural laws with the demands in which Christ is the example and the Gospel is presupposed, this is to a great extent due to the fact that the idea of "opposition" to God in the world has disappeared. Where, however, we retain the idea of conflict, natural law and the imitation of

cease entirely until the Resurrection of the dead (Gal. v.17).[10]

The Bible does not tell us how this opposition arose. The account of the "serpent" in Gen. iii.1-15 is not primarily concerned to explain, but simply to point to the inexplicable. The text must be read in conjunction with the statements in Rev. xii.9, xx.2, and xx.10, where the "serpent" reappears in John's vision of the future which deals with the defeat of all opposition and God's cleansing of Creation from this evil.[11] What the Bible does speak about is the meaning of this opposition after it has arisen, not only in Gen. iii but in many other passages, and perhaps nowhere in so concise and detailed a way as in Rom. i.18-32. If we take the word "death" in an extended sense and include within it the whole dislocation of God's life-giving activity, i.e. His continuing Creation, and the complete destruction of human relationships, in other words, if we include in death envy, slander, etc., which are a form of murder (cf. Rom. i.29-32), we may then say that man through sin has come under the dominion of death (Gen. 1.17, iii.19; Rom. v.12).[12] Included in the dominion of death is eternal death—the rejection from the presence of God (Rev. xx.10 ff. and the chapters on Judgment generally). But what we ought in particular to notice here is the extent to which this dominion of death dislocates *Creation*.

The main aspect of sin is, of course, disobedience, which is also unbelief and lack of trust in the God who creates and commands. Adam's temptation resides primarily in the serpent's attempt to destroy this trust: "Did God say, 'You shall not eat'?" (Gen. iii.1, 5). This breach of trust meant that man used against his Creator the power which he possessed. But since this power disrupts fellowship with the Creator, it is in fact powerless and corruptible. From this act of hostility comes

Christ will then go together, and yet at the same time remain two different works of God. Cf. Ivarsson, *Predikans uppgift*, pp. 98-163, who deals with these points in Luther in a notable way.

[10] Cf., e.g., 1 Cor. xi.31 f.

[11] Cf. also W. Eichrodt, *Theologie des Alten Testaments*, vol. iii, Leipzig 1939, pp. 96 ff.

[12] The destruction of death is therefore a part of God's salvation in both the Old and New Testaments. See Is. xxv.8; 1 Cor. xv.26; Rev. xxi.4.

man's destruction and continual flight from God. He feels
compelled to hide himself from God (Gen. III.8). But his
relation to God cannot be affected without also damaging his
relation to his neighbour. It is surely no coincidence that the
Genesis account of the Fall (Gen. III) is immediately followed
by that of the murder of Abel (Gen. IV).[13] In Rom. I Paul
shows how mankind's denial of the Creator leads to a terrible
corruption of relationships between human beings (Rom. I.
28-32). Here the breach of trust in God is the primary factor.
First there is unbelief in regard to God, and then disregard for
one's neighbour.[14] This act of acquisitiveness which constitutes
the basic attitude of unbelief towards the giving and creative
God automatically implies an attitude of lovelessness at the
point where man as a link in Creation ought to be giving himself in love, viz. in his relation to his neighbour. We are not
here dealing with two sins, but simply with two aspects of a
single sin. To live in a false relationship of independence of
God who gives is likewise to be in a false relationship of independence of one's neighbour who receives. God's creativity
and giving of life means that man has received from God and
has been used by God as an instrument of new and continued
giving. But now at both these points there is an obstacle,
opposition, and denial.[15] Sin also expressed itself at a third
point in man's relation to the rest of Creation, of which,
according to God's original will for man, he was to be ruler
and lord (Gen. I.28 f.). Man has turned the creature into an
idol.

This aspect of sin occupies a dominant position in the Old
Testament and is stated in Rom. I to be characteristic in its
essence of paganism, upon which the wrath of God is revealed.
It is organically connected with the breaking of trust in the
Creator. In the narrative of Jesus's Temptation, which corresponds to the temptation of Adam, Jesus's refusal to bow
down to any but God is a decisive aspect of His obedience and

[13] See Gerhard von Rad, *Das erste Buch Mose*, Das Alte Testament Deutsch,
VOL. I, Göttingen 1949, p. 88.

[14] Cf. Günther Bornkamm, *Gesetz und Schöpfung im Neuen Testament*, Sammlungen
gemeinverständliche Vorträge No. 175, Tübingen 1934, pp. 17 f.

[15] Cf. the connexion between the receiving of life and the fundamental demands
made upon man in Løgstrup, *Den etiske fordring*. p. 134.

trust, and therefore also of His victory (Mt. IV.9-11). When
Luther states that man must worship either God or idols, and
that the possibility of his being "irreligious" does not exist, he
is on a clear Biblical line of thought.[16] It is a necessity for man
to "have a God," i.e. to have something from which one
expects good, and to which one turns to find refuge from evil.
The necessity of having to "deify" something means that man
has to seek life from some source or other. As a created being
he is still dependent on the provision of life from outside himself,
and cannot escape this necessity. By seeking his God in Creation,
which itself needs what man needs, he does not achieve the
life which he seeks but only death, and his unbelief grows
stronger. By clinging to the things of Creation without being
capable of abandoning them for fear of losing them, the door
through which man ought to pass in order to give to his neighbour becomes barred even more tightly, and his unkindness to
his fellow beings grows stronger. By thus bowing down to what
is created, as though he were subordinate to it, and by making
himself a slave to it, man loses the possibility of standing over
Creation and "ruling" it and "subduing" it to himself (Gen. 1.
28). This means that he becomes hardened in his turning from
God's destiny for him in Christ. All these three aspects of sin
are related to one another and constitute a single unity, the
mark of which is death. This unity appears clearly in the New
Testament usage of the term "idolatry" in reference to covetousness. Here all three aspects are present.[17] The unity appears
in the same way when man's perversion itself is eliminated in
faith. In trusting in God, man escapes from his fear of losing
life and can in consequence adopt an attitude of benevolence
towards his neighbour. When man in faith thus dares to take
the position of servant, he is "the most free lord of all Creation,

[16] Cf. Vilmos Vajta, *Die Theologie des Gottesdienstes bei Luther,* hereafter cited as
Theologie, Stockholm 1952, pp. 8 ff. We should also remember that during the
period of martyrdom in the early Church the choice to be made was between
obedience to God and obedience to something else. Cf. Erich Fromm, *Psycho-
analysis and Religion,* New Haven 1952, pp. 117 ff.

[17] When the New Testament speaks of a false god, it does not usually use the
name of a god in some other religion, but calls it Mammon, i.e. men's possessions
(e.g. Mt. VI.24). On covetousness as idolatry see Eph. V.5; Col. III.5 (note "the
wrath of God" in Col. III.6). Cf. Phil. III.19; Rom. XVI.18.

and no servant."[18] Faith means a recovery of man's original
and natural position, for which both he and Creation alike
were destined and equipped.[19]

We now come again to deal with the constantly recurring
question of *knowledge*, that is, of how we attain knowledge of or
information concerning our perversity. As before we find that
we are dealing with the proposition that it is only through the
revelation in the incarnate Christ that man gains an insight
into his sin.[20] The alternative to this is not that man has insight
into his sin through his own life. In general, God's continued
activity means that He reveals new aspects of His existence;
and this general proposition, which we have already had
occasion to repeat, is applicable also to judgment and wrath,
and therefore to man's insight into the depths of his own perversity. The full revelation of the meaning of sin is given only
in Christ and through the word of scripture.[21] Only when the
injury is cured is it revealed how deep it is and how much it
costs to bring healing to the afflicted part. Only when Christ
submits anew to the temptation of Adam, i.e. of man, in the
wilderness, in Gethsemane, and on the Cross, is the tremendous
power of temptation and sin exposed.[22] But this revelation of
sin and of man's perversity does not mean that sin and corruption in human life are unknown apart from the preaching
of the Gospel. If I am incapable of diagnosing my illness and
of finding a cure for it, it does not follow that I am well. We
are here again confronted by the peculiar predominance of
the second article of faith in contemporary theology and the
consequent rejection of the first article. Because sin is in fact
an intrusion in the life which is given in Creation; because man
to a greater degree than Creation itself has fallen from his true

[18] No writer has so consummately described this freedom as Luther in his *De
libertate christiana.*

[19] The absurdity of man's worship of the creature is to be seen especially in the
fact that the object of man's worship is something which he has at his disposal
and over which he ought therefore to have control. Deutero-Isaiah frequently
refers with sarcasm to the makers of idols. See, e.g. Is. XL.19 ff., XLI.5 ff., XLIV.
9-24, XLVI.6 f.

[20] Cf. Søe, *Kristelig etik*, pp. 58, 220.

[21] Cf. Brunner, *Man in Revolt*, p. 116 f.

[22] On the two Temptation narratives, cf. Dietrich Bonhoeffer, *Versuchung*, 3rd
edn., Munich 1956, pp. 14-25.

nature; and because the work of Creation is not ended but continuous, and man is thus ordained and compelled to serve his neighbour even in the midst of his rebellion, he constantly comes up against the works of God and the need of his neighbour. In this he is reminded that there is something wrong with him.[23] If this were not the case, it would be man and not God who is the lord of Creation.

The same rule holds good here as elsewhere. If we put knowledge into the centre and place the second article before the first, we obscure the sovereignty of God. Paul's argument in Rom. 1.18-32 does not use Creation as a completed act as the basis for the assertion that "there is a God." It cannot, therefore, be made to support the speculative interpretation of the first article, for which the possession by natural man of a knowledge of God which is independent of the revelation in Christ is the principal point.[24] The starting-point in Rom. 1.18 is not Creation as a completed act, but God's dealings with all men.[25] The conclusion of the argument, therefore, is not that God exists, but that man is guilty, and has no defence before God. This guilt would exist, even on the basis of God's works in Creation.[26] A full insight into the depths of human guilt is given only in the preaching of the Gospel. But the accusation is directed against man by the very fact of his living and moving in the world, and coming into contact with his neighbour. Man is still aware of the accusation against him, even though he may long since have excluded the term "God" from his vocabulary,[27] for his own life is *given*, and depends upon the goodness of other men.[28]

This accusation is directed against man and is apprehended by him. Not only so, but the "wrath" of God is even now

[23] Cf. Prenter, *Skabelse og genløsning*, pp. 107 ff., and Ivarsson, *Predikans uppgift*, pp. 74 f., n. 22. Ivarsson develops Prenter's line of thought with certain modifications.

[24] Cf. Anders Nygren, *Pauli brev till romarna*, Tolkning av Nya testamentet, VOL. VI, Stockholm 1944, pp. 111-7, Eng. trans. *Commentary on Romans*, Philadelphia 1949, pp. 105-9.

[25] Cf. Gärtner, *The Areopagus Speech*, pp. 82, 138.

[26] Cf. Günther Bornkamm, *Das Ende des Gesetzes*, Beiträge zur evangelische Theologie, VOL. XVI, Munich 1952, pp. 23-6.

[27] Cf. Prenter, *Skabelse og genløsning*, p. 108.

[28] Cf. Løgstrup, *Den etiske fordring*, pp. 160 ff.

afflicting him. There is a certain similarity between wrath and
judgment on the one hand, and life and the Kingdom on the
other. God gives life now, the Kingdom is at hand now, but
at the same time faith still awaits life without death and the
Kingdom without the enemy. So wrath will come upon men in
"the day of wrath" (Rom. II.5; cf. Rom. II.2 f. on judgment),
but this does not mean that corrupt men are now to be free
from the wrath of God. The main stress in Rom. I.18-32 is that
wrath is now being revealed from heaven. Moreover, this
revelation of wrath corresponds to the completely different
revelation (through the Gospel and apart from the Law) which
is described in Rom. I.16 f. and III.21 f. We find a manifestation of wrath in the present time in God's "giving up" of men
to their sins (Rom. I.24, 28), and therefore in the growth of all
evil and increase of what is unnatural.[29] Man is aware of his
perversion as a burden and punishment to be borne, or as an
unpleasant confrontation with his "destiny" or whatever he
chooses to call it. As in any ordinary disease it is impossible for
the afflicted person not to have some suspicion of what may be
wrong with him, so in their perversion men are aware, even
though they may have ceased to use the term "God," that they
are in fact confronting the wrath of God in action. Just as the
gifts of the Giver pass through human agents and are coloured
by human goodness, so also His Judgment passes through His
human agents and is coloured by their wrath.

The most striking passage of this kind in the New Testament
is the statement in Rom. XIII.4 on the "power" or "authority"
which wields the sword and inflicts punishment as "the servant
of God to execute His wrath on the wrong-doer."[30] It is a
common New Testament concept that the judgment which is
passed upon men now, and to which we willingly submit, in
other words, civil judgment, is a foretaste of the future Judgment. Indeed, Paul can say of judgment in the present that
"when we are judged by the Lord, we are chastened, so that
we may not be condemned along with the world." (I Cor. XI.

[29] Cf. Rom. VII.8 ff.
[30] See here C. A. Pierce, *Conscience in the New Testament*, Studies in Biblical
Theology, London 1955, especially the chapter on "Conscience and Wrath." On
pp. 66-74 Pierce examines Rom. XIII.1-6 and on p. 85 f. Rom. I-II. He also discusses
the Areopagus speech in Acts XVII several times.

32). According to Rom. xiii.4, God uses human punishment as the instrument of His wrath. This punishment is inflicted by those who are unaware of Christ, and in particular unaware of whom they are serving in doing so.[31] This is the central point in Luther's doctrine of the "earthly government"—not that men have any knowledge of God and His law apart from the revelation in Christ, but that in dealing with the world, God uses human beings in order to give good gifts to men or chastise them with His wrath. God is not bound or impeded in all His dealings either by the knowledge or lack of knowledge of Himself in His human instruments.[32] To hold that God's use of His instrument is conditional on the possession of knowledge about or insight into His revelation, is to obscure His sovereignty.

Even though wrath and judgment come upon sinful man in the course of human life, and even though it is in his relations to his fellow men, whether Christians or not, that wrath is most frequently to be seen and his egoism stands self-accused, it is always *God's* wrath. The guilt of sinful man is revealed and judged in these person-to-person relationships, but it is guilt *coram deo*—man's guilt comes between Him and God, and is the guilt of the Last Judgment.[33] Creation and giving, the *opus proprium* of God, are throughout *God's* Creation and giving, even though they are realised in that human goodness which is given separately to every human being, so that all men can remember occasions when they have received goodness and feel shamed by it. In the same way God's *opus alienum*, even though it is painfully connected with person-to-person relationships and guilty memories of injuries done or inflicted, is *God's*

[31] This ignorance of the existence of the true God characterises the powers that be, whether or not the explanation in terms of angelology is correct. Here it is irrelevant. In any case the authorities are pagan. For a criticism of the explanation in terms of angelology, cf. Hillerdal, *Gehorsam gegen Gott und Menschen*, pp. 211-27. See also G. B. Caird, *Principalities and Powers*, Oxford 1956, pp. 24 ff., and also I Thess. ii.16 (on the destruction of Jerusalem).

[32] Since the wrath of God points beyond itself to its own cessation, it serves the mercy of God. See Pierce, *Conscience in the New Testament*, pp. 68 f., in regard to Acts xvii.26, 28.

[33] In the passages which deal with the Judgment it is always God or Christ who judges, but the criterion of judgment is a man's dealings with his neighbour. Cf. Mt. xxv.31-46 and the many passages which deal with "judgment according to works," e.g. Rom. ii.6; ii Cor. v.10, etc.

E

wrath throughout, even to the last day. But this wrath was revealed fully in human history only when the Son of God broke its power in Gethsemane and on the Cross, and in so doing drank the cup which He prayed He might avoid.[34]

If the wrath is God's and establishes guilt *coram deo*, this means that ultimately the one who suffers this wrath is man, the one who does evil. When the authority appointed by God takes action against evil deeds, this "civil" wrath is directed primarily against deeds and not persons. Its concern is as far as possible to get rid of certain behaviour by punishing it (cf. Rom. xiii.3 f.; 1 Pet. ii.14).[35] When we come later in the present work to deal with the "civil use of the law," one of the main points I shall make will be that God wills such a structure for society. The Law is not addressed only to the conscience in order to judge it *coram deo*, "inwardly." But when we say that this purely earthly punishment executes the "wrath" of God and communicates His Judgment, we are not isolating the demand for outward civil righteousness from man's self-criticism *coram deo*. The wrath which is manifested in human society may at any time compel man to call into question the whole of his existence and arouse him to hear the inward voice which shows that his whole life is lost and wasted. The Law is at work in its "spiritual use" when men acquire this conviction of the waste which they have made of their lives, even though in expressing their need men may not use the term "God" or "condemnation."[36] For man has only one life, and his conviction that the life which he has is wasted brings him back to the source of his life, to the Creator, even though he does not know His name. He is brought back only to find that the source of life is blocked. In a situation such as this in which he is forced to make idols of the things of Creation, thereby losing more and more of his freedom, man experiences the wrath of God as an objective reality. In so doing he has a foretaste of

[34] The word "wrath" is also used in the New Testament in the stereotyped phrase, "the wrath of God," e.g. Jn. iii.36; Rom. 1.18; Eph. v.6; Col. iii.6

[35] Both in Rom. xiii.3 and 1 Pet. ii.14 "approval" or "praise" are both mentioned in connexion with men's acts as well as punishment. The former refers to good conduct, the latter to evil.

[36] The civil and spiritual uses of the law are dealt with below in Part II, chapters II and III, "The first Use of the Law," and "The Second Use of the Law."

the wrath of the Last Judgment, even though he may still escape it.

The Unrecognised Demand

When man disbelieves in God, disregards his neighbour, and makes an idol out of Creation "without excuse," this means that he has definitely rejected demands which, however indistinctly he may have been aware of them, should have been sufficiently powerful to lead him to act differently. We are not concerned here with whether by answering these demands a man would have succeeded in obeying the commandments which Jesus gave, e.g. in the Sermon on the Mount. We may leave aside here the whole problem of whether "natural" ethics are identical with "Christian" ethics. Indeed, to raise this question means that we have failed to think of God as the One who acts in the universe and whose dealings with humanity will culminate in His Judgment of the whole world on the last day. If we had regarded God in this way, we could not have raised this particular problem of "natural" versus "Christian" ethics. The problem recurs in a new form in the relation of the "old" and the "new" covenants, etc.; but then, characteristically, it appears as a problem concerning a differentiation within the sphere of God's activity and not as a distinction between Christian and non-Christian. Whenever the Bible begins to speak of the Last Judgment, it becomes clear that the Biblical writers are concerned with God's dealings in general with all men. In the Last Judgment every man will be held accountable for the insight which God has given him into the demand which is laid upon him, and he will be judged by whether this insight, be it great or small, has forced him to the "improvement" which God has intended for him. It may well be that those who have had least insight will arise in the Judgment and condemn those who have had greatest insight.[37] This separation which is to be made in the Judgment is the

---

[37] Cf. Mt. viii.10 ff. (the centurion and the many from east and west contrasted with the sons of the kingdom), Mt. x.15 (Sodom and Gomorrah contrasted with the towns to which the apostles are sent), Mt. xi.22 ff. (Tyre, Sidon and Sodom contrasted with Chorazin, Bethsaida and Capernaum), Mt. xii.41 f. (the men of Nineveh and the queen of the South contrasted with "this generation"). Cf. also Rom. ii.14 f. on the Gentiles who have not the law and Lk. x.25-37 on the Good Samaritan contrasted with the Priests and Levites.

one significant reality for the writers of the Bible. It will destroy
all lines of distinction between "natural" and "Christian" made
previously.[38] Since the Bible looks to this final separation, it
has no clear answer to such anthropocentric questions as, What
constitutes a departure from "the natural ethic"? and, What
is characteristic of "the Christian ethic" as such?, etc. These
are un-Biblical questions and do violence to the typical Biblical
point of view.[39]

We cannot say by way of answer (as we often do) that faith
in God sees Him as being active even where no faith exists, but
that theology must be concerned with a limited Christian ethic
which is based only on the Christian faith. Theology, that is,
can never be forced by any scientific norm to deal with questions which are unrelated to the historic subject-matter with
which it is dealing and which alters it. Here again we see an
instance of the subjection of the first article to the second. The
specific Christian ethic which differs from all natural ethics is
based on the revelation in the incarnate Christ. When we stress
its *difference* from all natural ethics, we are saying that the God
who reveals Himself in Christ is also the Lord of the world who
has governed and continues to govern the world. This is a
concept which has always been central in all Biblical exegesis
to the present day. But we find that this idea becomes suspect
and tends to weaken the distinctive character of the specifically
Christian ethic. In consequence, this aspect of the historically-
given Christian revelation is often repressed in spite of the fact
that it appears quite clearly in the Bible.[40] Theology must in

[38] The specific characteristic of the Last Judgment is its *separation*. The emphasis
on this final separation is often connected in the New Testament with a direct
refusal to make a separation between men now before the Judgment. See Mt.
XIII.24-30, 37-43, 47-50, XXIV.40 f., xxv.32. Similarly the frequent repetition of
the phrase, "the last shall be first," implies a rejection of the idea that this separation is a *fait accompli*.

[39] When Anders Nygren, *Filosofisk och kristen etik*, 2nd. edn., Stockholm 1932
(see, e.g., pp. 267 f., 306, 323), discusses a strictly Christian ethic derived from the
Christian experience of faith alone, he clearly disregards the Law as the instrument
by which God compels men to obey His will.

[40] Søe, for instance, does so. See his *Kristelig etik*, e.g. pp. 19 f., cf. pp. 34 f.,
55f., 203 f. Wherever the idea of a "natural law" appears, whether in Schol-
asticism, the Reformation, or Orthodoxy, Søe regards it as non-Christian. Consequently he sees the Synod of Barmen in 1934 as a late purification of the Christian
Church from non-Christian doctrine.

fact find how to leave room for what is here called "the un-recognised demand," in such a way as to allow the idea of God's universal demand for faith and love to be a link to the new commandment in Jesus Christ.

This demand is a work of God. To speak of its constraint upon man is not to speak of a quality in man. We do not say, for instance, that the Gospel is a quality in man. The fact that the Gospel has a work to accomplish in man does not mean that it is a quality in man. Such an assertion would be completely wrong. But we often find that those who reject any such statement about the Gospel as a human quality assume as a matter of course that to speak about God compelling all men by means of the Law is to ascribe to man an ethical quality. This assumption is false, and constitutes the main obstacle in formulating a correct theological discussion of the problem of Creation and the Law. In speaking here of the "unrecognised demand," we are dealing with a work of God. In speaking of man's apprehension of this demand, we are not dealing with any quality by which man conforms to the demand which is laid upon him. Man does not conform to it even when he renders external obedience to it. We are not, therefore, speaking of any quality which deprives the Gospel, or the new covenant in Christ, of any of its functions. But if we lose the idea of God's universally relevant demand from our theology, then the Gospel which is preached in the non-Christian world as the *kerygma* of the missionary Church, and the new commandment which is presented in the New Testament as the "sharpening" of the old command, will lose some of their typical functions, e.g. forgiveness and "sharpening."[41]

[41] Forgiveness and the summons to conversion in the missionary preaching of the Church to the Gentiles presuppose that there is a work of God in Creation which has already been discerned and experienced before the preaching of the Gospel. It is in fact in the *missionary preaching* of the New Testament that reference is made to the Creator (see Lindeskog, *Studien*, pp. 180 ff., and Gärtner, *The Areopagus Speech*, pp. 169, 229-41). In regard to the new commandment as a "sharpening" of the old, we should note that what is sharpened is not simply the Decalogue nor even something that is purely Israelitic. In Mt. v.47 this sharpening applies equally to Gentile law and custom. The type or pattern of the sharpening is nature itself, e.g. the sun and the rain which obey the Creator better than man does (see Mt. v.44 f. where the new commandment ("But I say to you") is contrasted with what was said "to the men of old").

Because the demand is not a quality in man, we gain no greater understanding of the Gospel by reducing the universal relevance of the demand, or cutting it down to a bare minimum. The tendency to give as meagre a content as possible to the demand makes it clear that if we do so we are understanding it as a human quality, either epistemological or ethical. We are therefore allowing it to exercise only a moderate demand upon man in order to avoid rendering the Gospel unnecessary.[42] In Rom. 1 Paul shows that God's revelation in Creation is the primary basis for His demand for *faith* and not simply for refraining from heinous offences, or for adopting an attitude of regard for one's neighbour. The unrecognised demand, which is addressed to men by the very fact of their living in the world, is a demand for faith and trust in God, and also a demand to put away "idols" (i.e. the worship of the creature rather than the Creator, Rom. 1.19 ff., 23, 25) and to love their fellow men (Rom. 1.30 ff.). The Gospel gains in clarity only when the universal and unrecognised demand is presented in the whole of this context.

When we refer to this demand in Creation for faith and love as an "unrecognised" demand, the term may perhaps call for some explanation. We can best explain our meaning by trying to see where the demand is "recognised."[43] It is recognised where the Gospel is clearly proclaimed, i.e. where Christ's death and resurrection are preached. It is obvious to those who hear the Gospel that this proclamation of Christ's life and work *is news*. In the case of the demand, the requirement which is laid upon those who hear it is not wholly and completely new. It never was, even when the Gospel was first heard in an uncivilised and barbarous environment.[44] In other words, when

---

[42] Søe, who makes the question of knowledge central, characteristically interprets every statement about natural law as an expression of some power or capacity in man. Cf. his *Kristelig etik*, pp. 15 and 54 (where the whole of the discussion deals with this power), and *Religionsfilosofi*, p. 107: "God cannot be reached by man. He can be known in so far as He gives Himself to be known and thereby gives man the power to know Him." See Benktson, *Den naturliga teologiens problem hos Karl Barth*, pp. 129 f., n. 108.

[43] Cf. Wingren, *Theology in Conflict*, p. 140 f.

[44] Justin Martyr, for instance, writing about A.D. 150 can say that men of every nation hear God's Law and in hearing it stand under its curse. The new thing that Christ brings is deliverance from the curse of the Law. See *Dialogue with Trypho*, XCIII-V.

the proclamation of Christ involves the submission by those who hear it of their lives to its judgment, this judgment is not based on the assertion in preaching of a law with "retroactive power." Here as elsewhere any such element of retroactivity in the Law is dubious in the extreme. But when the Gospel is proclaimed together with the Law in preaching, the hearer resumes an obedience to a demand which he has continually defied. It is true that it now grows more profound for him, but it is still an "old commandment." In this reference backwards, man's lack of excuse is due to his guilt. As we saw earlier, Christ in His restoration of man is more than man. The new life which He brings is raised and heightened, as well as restored; for Christ is free for all time to come from the possibility of the Fall, as Adam never was even in the pure and primal Creation.[45] The demand for faith and love becomes recognised in preaching and is grounded in Jesus Christ, the Restorer and Saviour of human life. It is further grounded in the Creator Himself who has hitherto been apprehended as active in Creation in *compelling* man to obedience, but is now revealed in His Incarnation. This demand becomes clear and precise when the Gospel is preached, but is not received by man as something new and hitherto unexperienced. The relevance of this demand was felt by man even in his perversity and in spite of his rebellion. But this was due to the fact that his perversity is unnatural, and as such continually in conflict with God's constant and continuing work of Creation. When theology denies this universal demand, this denial is connected with the rejection of God's work of Creation in favour of the second article.

The demand is thus made "recognisable" in preaching. We are not yet, however, discussing man as the one who is addressed in preaching, nor are we any longer considering him as the object of God's giving in Creation (which in itself contains the *opus proprium* of the Gospel). We are thinking of man rather as being under judgment in Creation, doomed by sin, and the object of wrath. For such a man the demand is unrecognised, and is expressed in the requirements made by his fellow men and in the external needs which press upon him. It is the duty of every individual to give of any goodness which he has to

[45] See the section above, "Christ and Creation," Part I, chapter I.

those around him. When he continues to avoid his responsibility towards his brothers, their needs come into conflict with his attitude.[46] This is also expressed in the perpetual failure to which his "idols" are liable, viz. their inability to help man or fulfil his hopes of getting some good from them.[47] This failure, to which man's false gods are liable, and the demand laid upon man to give, of which he is conscious in the needs of those around him, together imply an unrecognised demand for *faith*. It is strange that this demand, without ceasing to be unrecognised, can in fact be a demand for faith and trust. This is because the unrecognised demand witnesses in the requirements which it makes to the wrath of God, and is seen to be unrealised as soon as it is made.[48] But the unreasonable nature of the demand can never silence it. On the contrary, living in the world means constantly having to listen to the demand anew, and having no means of evading it. Its unreasonableness, however, does not make it easier for man to reject it, when he hears it. On the contrary, he recognises the demand which is being made of him, since he is aware of his own unnatural condition. His recognition may be concealed (but not destroyed) by the misrepresentations which he makes of the faith which he is aware is laid upon him—he must "be strong," he must be "independent of men's opinion," etc., he must conceive of a faith which he lacks, but which is still demanded of him by a wrathful God, for whom he has no other name than "life." However concealed God may be to him, man is in a real relationship to Him, and when he fails or falls short, it is God's judgment that he experiences.

How then can we relate this unrecognised and unformulated

---

[46] Luther, following many others, regards the golden rule in Mt. vii.12, which makes human need our guide to action, as the basic rule of the natural law. Cf. Herbert Olsson, *Grundproblemet i Luthers socialetik*, hereafter cited as *Luthers socialetik*, vol. i, Lund 1934, pp. 19 f.

[47] Man is aware of the inability of his idols to help him, and yet he continues to worship them (Is. xl-xlvi). This inability to help may be seen not only in this failure but also in the fact that man assisted in making them. They ought, therefore, to be subject to him and not he to them (this is the point stressed by Deutero-Isaiah). The same thing is true of position, money, etc. We are responsible for these things, and yet we fail to control and subordinate them, because we worship them. That this is unnatural and perverse is evident even apart from the Gospel.

[48] Cf. G. Bornkamm, *Das Ende des Gesetzes*, pp. 25 f.

demand for faith and love to Christ and to His words which we read in scripture? It is relatively easy to see the connexion between the demands for care for one's neighbour which arise from the very fact of living together in the world, and the commandment concerning love, given by Jesus, e.g. in His heightened demands in the Sermon on the Mount.[49] In Lutheranism the *usus civilis* of the law has often been reduced to a demand for care for one's neighbour, and the commandment of love demanded by the earthly government has been linked to the commandment of love found in the New Testament. The problem becomes more complicated when God's revelation is made the basis of a demand for faith, and this required trust and confidence imagined to be those given and established by Christ in the Gospel. It is only when we comprehend the unrecognised demand for faith that we properly see the connexion between God's works in Creation and in the Incarnation, and discern the recapitulating and restoring aspect of Christ's work. It will be appropriate at this point to try first to define this connexion with "the sphere of faith."

There are two important truths here, and both occur in the Gospels. In the first place, faith in Christ is not an attitude which, having been absent before the appearance of Christ, can be adopted by a believer after His appearance. Faith exists only in conflict with unbelief (cf. Mk. ix.24).[50] As the Spirit strives against the flesh (Gal. v.17), so faith operates by defeating unbelief, i.e. by defeating false trust and confidence (for man must always believe in something). Temptation has not disappeared with the awakening of faith. The man of faith is still tempted to a false trust. He must prove himself to see whether he has faith (ii Cor. xiii.5). False trust is usually directed at something which is good in itself—property, good works, etc. These are not evil in themselves, but, as the object

[49] Cf. Løgstrup, *Den etiske fordring*, pp. 125 f., where the demand of a purely human ethic for the preservation of the life of our fellow men is identified with the ethical demand in the preaching of Jesus. Løgstrup, however, seems to offer too easy a solution.

[50] Cf. Ragnar Bring, "Kristen tro och vetenskaplig forskning," in *Svensk teologisk kvartalskrift*, hereafter cited as *S.T.K.*, 1949, p. 235 f. The New Testament gives a number of instances in which the apostles displayed unbelief. On the whole question of the continual summons to faith as contrasted with unbelief, see Ivarsson, *Predikans uppgift*, pp. 35-69.

of man's trust, are of no worth whatever, since they are not God, and cannot create life. In the second place, Christ answers the cry made to Him by the sick and the needy. This is the case throughout the Gospels. He does not correct the petition made to Him by the needy, but answers it as it is. The many passages in the New Testament about Christ as Healer have lost most of their meaning for present-day theology. This is not simply due to the fact that they mostly concern healing *miracles*. One of the important reasons for our inability to interpret these passages correctly is that we lack the concept of salvation as the restoration of Creation. It therefore seems strange to us that the texts which deal with the healing of the sick so often refer to men's appeal to Christ for help as *faith* (Cf. Mk. v.36, x.46-52, xi.22 ff.; Mt. viii.5-13, ix.28 f., xv.21-8; Lk. v.17-20, viii. 22-5).[51] The fact that faith lies thus embedded in a seemingly unspiritual and purely human prayer for help in need, and that Christ can accept this prayer and regard it as faith without first correcting it, is connected with the first of the two points which we emphasised above, and therefore with the fact that faith exists in distorted form in every man. It may be faith which cleaves to an idol, and is therefore faith distorted into unbelief—but it is still faith. When faith becomes "true" faith, this is simply because man's vague cry for help has become a cry to Christ[52] who transforms it.

The faith which is required from man in the unrecognised and "wrathful" demand for faith is none other than the true faith which ought to be truly present whenever men turn from idols. When this turning from the worship of the creature is radical, faith reaches out to Christ and the true God. Here, as in the case of Abraham, men are rejecting all "works" and waiting only upon God Himself. It is just this waiting that is impossible for man under "wrath." He may temporarily turn

---

[51] Many of these passages (e.g. the story of the centurion, the woman of Canaan, etc.) were Luther's favourite illustrations of a faith that triumphs, but he sees them as examples of triumph over the oppression of the Law and a reaching out for forgiveness (cf. Ivarsson, *Predikans uppgift*, pp. 48 ff.). We have to turn to the early Church for an explanation which gives significance to the actual healing of a physical sickness. The actual sickness in these passages is not incidental but is of importance.

[52] Cf. Vajta, *Theologie*, pp. 12 ff.

away from his idol, and appear to have abandoned his worship of the transient and creaturely, thereby becoming once more, if only in appearance, something of the lord which he was destined to be in Creation. Sooner or later, however, the idol which he looks to for support will fail him. When it does, it will be seen that what man has been trusting in all along is precisely the transient and creaturely. From this and not from God he has drawn his life and being. With the collapse of his idol he now falls into despair and loses his lordship again—or rather, shows that in fact he never possessed it. Having fallen, he regains his equilibrium only by acquiring some new idol to believe in. Such is the nature of the life lived by man under wrath and death. He is continually struggling to abolish fear and build "a world without fear," trusting in new healing media (for instance, in the power of science), and allowing his fear to take concrete form in petty fears of minor and avoidable dangers. At the same time he conceals from himself his deepest fear, the fear of death itself, against which he is powerless.[53] He uses his power to "govern" Creation in order to avert the external aspects of the tyranny of death. These can be averted, since they are simply the outward "masks" of death, and not death itself. In so averting them, man comes to put his hope and trust in the means which he has used to prevent the onslaught of death. In this confidence he begins to worship the creature, although he knows in his inmost being that nothing can ultimately help him, and that the tyrant will come against him in a different mask and destroy him.[54] His ruling over Creation does not save him from making idols. On the contrary, it forces him to do so, for he is unable to produce in himself the faith which can withstand death without idols. Yet this faith is demanded of him, and he knows that this power alone will mean victory. He knows that he is running away and hiding like Adam (Gen. III.8).

For man death is a fact, because he lacks life from the Creator. When man has chosen to live to himself, he loses his life, for to

[53] Cf. V. E. von Gebsattel, *Prolegomena einer medizinischen Anthropologie*, Berlin 1954, pp. 384, 408, etc.
[54] On Heb. II.15, cf. Otto Michel, *Der Brief an die Hebräer*, Meyers Kommentar VOL. XIII, 9th edn., Göttingen 1955, pp. 85 f.

live means to be created, and to resist the Creator is to die.
When this defiance and rejection of God occurs in God's world,
where God continues to create, it means that man is unable
to escape from God. He comes into conflict with Him wherever
he turns. Judgment, wrath, and the unrecognised demand, are
simply expressions of the fact that *God continues to be God* and to
rule His Creation. Life still flows from Him, not from any of
man's idols. For man, nevertheless, it is a mystery where life
comes from. When he asks about life's origin and meaning,
without finding any answer, he comes up against a baffling
wall of silence—God's silence. This silence of God means death
and judgment for man. Now God's silence is not a meaningless
void, but is the omnipotence which refuses to speak.[55] Only a
theology which has determined in advance the question of
human knowledge, and has thereby intellectualised the content
of revelation, can interpret this kind of silence as the absence
of any revelation at all and tie revelation solely to the Incarnation, when God the invisible becomes visible. When the
silence is connected with an unceasing constraint upon man,
and a creative power which continues to create (to create life,
for instance, or even danger, both of them unexpected), it is
an exacting and bewildering silence. It is, to use Paul's phrase,
a revelation of "wrath" (Rom. 1.18).[56] It is hard to see how we
can ever describe this aspect of God's work if we stick to the
order "Gospel and Law," and then proceed on this basis to
argue that every demand and claim made by God is to be
derived from the Gospel, and can never be made upon us
where the Gospel does not at the same time come to us.[57] One
thing is certain. If we thus put the preaching of the Gospel

[55] The Old Testament belief that human life is brought into being by the creative
word of God is balanced by the thought that the silence of God is also significant:
"Wilt thou keep silent, and afflict us sorely?" (Is. LXIV.12); "Be not deaf to me,
lest, if thou be silent to me, I become like those who go down to the Pit" (Ps.
XXVIII.1); "Make haste to answer me, O Lord! My spirit fails!" (Ps. CXLIII.7);
and also Ps. LXXXIII.1. Cf. Dürr, *Die Wertung*, pp. 38 ff. Dürr gives many examples
of God's Creation through his Word as a *creatio continua*.

[56] Cf. Pierce, *Conscience in the New Testament*, p. 85.

[57] Søe in his *Kristelig etik*, pp. 22, 58 ff., 205 f., etc., argues this point with some
force. Naturally Rom. I-II and Acts XVII as well as Rom. XIII create some difficulty
for him. It is, however, important to notice that the difficulties in Søe's theory are
not simply problems presented by isolated passages (for we can always remove
such passages from the centre of the Bible, or else state that in comparison with

before the Law, and put the second article before the first, we inevitably obscure the sovereignty of God. What we have here called "the unrecognised demand" is simply an expression of the fact that God is all-powerful, even when man defies Him. The sinner who defies God is surrounded by evidences of His continuing Creation which meet him everywhere, and hold him in bondage to its demands.

At the present time the dominant school of theology in Europe is one which takes the Gospel and the second article of the Creed as its starting-point. It proceeds on this basis to derive the whole of its content from scripture, but refuses to accept that God has any dealings with human life apart from the Gospel. There may, therefore, be some justification in using against this school of theology the argument based on what Harald Eklund calls "experience." In this theology, which is derived from scripture and the Gospel, faith is of necessity opposed to experience, or, at any rate, independent of it. Human experience cannot be taken as the starting-point. This would dislocate the order "Gospel and Law."

Against this, however, we have to think, as we have seen above, of human life itself as constituting, from one point of view, the basis of the relationship to God. This basis is not a book which speaks about Creation, but is Creation itself, i.e. the fact that man lives. Strangely enough, only such a basis can do justice to scripture, because it fully accords with scripture's own understanding of God as Lord of Creation. Any attempt to eliminate God's dealings with the world through the Law will come into conflict with scripture itself, which assumes this very fact. On the other hand, however—and here we must criticise what Eklund says of "experience"—we cannot proceed from experience to the content of the New Testament, let alone

others they are obscure, see *Kristelig etik*, p. 56, on Rom. 11.14 f.). The difficulty in Søe's argument is that he tends to detract from the sovereignty of God, to intellectualise the Gospel by removing the Law as its antithesis, and to treat the Spirit as an epistemological principle which gives man the "power" which according to liberal theology he already possesses (*Kristelig etik*, pp. 15, 54). This mere transfer of power, however, does not change the liberal structure of the theology. It is still man's ability to know, i.e. the question of knowledge, which is central, though now in a negative form. The works of God are described as it were backwards, from last to first, i.e. from Gospel backwards to the Law. This anti-liberal reaction still leaves man in the centre.

to the Gospel.[58] The movement from man's experience of God, which is a real experience and not an imaginary one, to the Gospel, is never direct. The line is a zigzag, and moves through judgment and wrath to forgiveness and grace via the preaching of the Word of the Gospel. The trouble with the so-called "theology of faith" is not that it bases faith on the Word. If we are going to be true to the New Testament, we must do this.[59] The trouble is rather that it fails to allow the Word or the Gospel to extend to God's work in the Law. It thereby deprives the Gospel of its proper character. For modern theology man's experience does not lead to anything at all because it lacks any knowledge of God. Experience does lead to God, but to His demand and judgment, and not to the Gospel.[60]

Part of this demand and judgment is the distress involved in human life—the needs and wants borne by man's fellow beings, which remind us that the basic necessities of life are not easily acquired (Gen. III.17 ff.). Human need, the necessity of having to live in hardship and by the sweat of one's brow, make life on earth a constant cry for help. Man under wrath hears this cry from those around him, and cannot turn it aside if he has any relief to offer. Here is a new threat to his idols. The object of his trust in his worship of the creature is not generally evil, but is in fact really good, though it is incapable of creating, and cannot therefore hear prayer or occupy God's place. In its appointed place under man rather than above him as the

[58] Cf. Harald Eklund, *Tro, erfarenhet, verklighet*, Stockholm 1956, especially pp. 136-48, on the belief in the Resurrection in the New Testament. We cannot separate the passages which refer to the Resurrection of Christ from the idea of *mission* which they incorporate. In this mission witness is borne to a Gospel which for the future, as often as it is preached, constitutes the form in which Christ is seen to be risen among men. According to the New Testament the world in which the Gospel is preached may have no experience of the Gospel, but it does have experience of God. The purpose of preaching is to recall the hearer to the work of God in Creation.

[59] Jn. xx.29 is certainly addressed to those who have lived after the apostolic period, and have not themselves seen Christ, but depend for faith on the Word. See Dodd, *Fourth Gospel*, pp. 185 f., 443, and Hermann Strathmann, *Das Evangelium nach Johannes*, Das Neue Testament Deutsch, vol. IV, 7th edn., Göttingen 1954, p. 260. Whatever else we may say of Bultmann's theology, in this respect at least he is true to the meaning of the New Testament.

[60] Cf. on Luther Hans Rückert, "Luthers åskådning om Guds fördoldhet," in *S.T.K.*, 1952, pp. 231 f., and Ivarsson, *Predikans uppgift*, p. 39.

object of his worship and subservience, the creature is good. It is given to man to sustain him, and to be controlled by him. "Thou shalt not kill," as Luther says in his simple and apposite exposition of this commandment in his Shorter Catechism, is "to help and support him in all danger and need." If this help and support are not given to our brother, we take the first steps towards killing him. The sin which "is couching at the door" in the story of Cain's murder of his brother, and which will be judged and expelled on the last day, has found expression not in what has been committed so much as in what has been omitted—when the hungry have not been fed or the thirsty given drink (Mt. xxv.42). In the world in which death rules, men's hunger and thirst communicate to us the unrecognised demand.[61]

The Last Day and Our Death

In the present section we shall be contrasting two authors whom we have already named, Rudolf Bultmann and Oscar Cullmann. In making this contrast we shall isolate one aspect of their Biblical theology and limit ourselves to the problem of death and judgment, as stated in the heading of the present section. We shall, however, have occasion in what follows to consider certain other related problems, e.g. in the next section the relation between Creation and birth.

Cullmann has offered us an expansive view of redemptive history as a whole, beginning with Creation and concluding with the Resurrection of the dead. Cullmann relates the beginning of this redemptive line (Creation) and the end (the Resurrection of the dead) to the middle event (Christ's work in His Incarnation). The whole of this long line is a single "Christ line." As Creation is "in Christ," so the events of the last age will also be under His control.[62] On the other hand, Cullmann characteristically omits to relate the events on this long line to the *hearer*, and to allow them to gain their significance in being

[61] The anonymity or incognito of Christ is a feature in the account of the Judgment (Mt. xxv.40, 45). We should not jump to the assumption that "the least of these my brethren" are members of the Christian congregation, and so separate them from others who are in need.

[62] Cullmann, *Christ and Time*, pp. 113 f.

preached and *believed.* He finds no *"pro me"* or *"pro nobis"* in
scripture. He correctly assembles the sequence of events in the
Bible, but fails to relate it to the man who hears these events
proclaimed.[63] One of the problems, therefore, in reading
Cullmann's interpretation of Creation is of my personal
relation to Creation, either in the present or in the past. When
the time line is so greatly emphasised, as it is in Cullmann,
individuals have to be inserted into the Christ line after certain
things have taken place, and before others take place. They
have had no part in Creation, and at present have no part in
the last age. They come, therefore, into the sequence of events
after the death of Christ and before the Parousia, i.e. in the
period of the Church, the period in which the Gospel is to go
into the world.[64]

   With Bultmann it is quite different. For him everything in
the Bible is addressed to the man who listens. There is nothing
which it records which is not *"pro me,"* or related to my immediate condition. When the Bible speaks of the Last Judgment
and eternal life, this means that *I* am being judged now, *I* have
eternal life now. When it speaks of Christ's Death and Resurrection, it is not speaking of an episode in history which is
remote from my immediate condition at some point in the
middle of human history. His Death is real now, and His
Resurrection is real now, and I am implicated in both because
they are addressed to me, and because if they are not preached,
they have no meaning.[65] To describe the content of the Biblical
revelation without relating it to the man whom it addresses is
to misinterpret it altogether. If Cullmann never relates the
Biblical revelation to the man who hears it, Bultmann goes to
the opposite extreme, and is exclusively concerned with man
and his existence, and never, strictly speaking, with anything
else. This would seem to be the major decisive difference
between Cullmann and Bultmann, and it may be helpful to
contrast their respective interpretations of this very point. I
propose, however, to limit the discussion deliberately to the one

---

[63] What Cullmann says in *Christ and Time*, pp. 231 ff., directly contradicts any
interpretation which confines eschatology to the death of the individual.
[64] Cullmann, *Christ and Time*, p. 157.
[65] Bultmann, *Kerygma und Mythos*, VOL. I, p. 51.

aspect described in the heading of the present section, viz. our death and the last day.

In the long time line the last day is a day still to come in the future. It is a day which is different from *my* last day. If the linear interpretation of time is as important for the Bible as Cullmann maintains it is, it would seem to be of importance not to individualise the last day too narrowly, or to tie it too closely to the existence of the hearer, but rather to let it lie in a temporal future to which the whole Church looks as a time which is *distinct* from its own. But according to Bultmann's existential interpretation, I already experience the last day in the Now in which my own death bears upon me. It becomes meaningless to speak of another "last day" which is different from the one which I am now experiencing. In faith man attains to salvation, and there is nothing incomplete in this salvation—eschatology is "realised." In order that it may be realised anew continually for all men, the *kerygma* is preached and the word of scripture addressed to those who hear it.[66] In dealing with the two views represented by Bultmann and Cullmann, I am assuming that each has something essential to say on the question under discussion. The solution is not to choose one and reject the other.

First, however, I propose to examine the question on different lines from Cullmann. In attempting to define the specific character of the eschatological future, Cullmann stresses matter and the body. For him, Christ's dominion in the events of the age to come will reach out to include even matter. For this reason, he maintains, the cosmic perspective in the passages which deal with the future period is not the same as it is in the present. In these passages particular stress is laid upon Christ's future power over the "earth."[67] On the other hand, however, Cullmann does not lay nearly so great a stress on the concept of Judgment in the last period, i.e. the Last Judgment of all, after which nothing is left unjudged. Consequently, when he is discussing the relation between the present and the future in

---

[66] This means for Bultmann that we must cease to speak about the last day and speak rather about death (see Bultmann, *Kerygma und Mythos*, VOL. I, p. 145).

[67] Cullmann, *Christ and Time*, pp. 141 ff., with particular reference to Rom. VIII.11, etc.

F

regard to the individual, the important question is, What extra gift does the future add to the salvation which has already been granted? What more does hope add to what faith already possesses?[68] But there is another question which we have to ask in regard to the future, and which cannot be separated from faith in the New Testament—What happens to *me* in the Judgment? Have I already received all my judgment, or is there still another "last" Judgment which I have not yet undergone? If we ask this question, we cannot regard the death of the individual merely as a transition to a salvation which has something additional or extra, but rather as already bearing judgment within itself, and leading man into the final Judgment. Bultmann takes the idea of death as judgment seriously, but in a completely different way from Cullmann.[69] For him death is the end. It does not point beyond itself to some future Judgment, but is itself "the Last Judgment."[70] Eschatology is in all respects present and not future—eternal life is proffered to man *now*. The last day with its judgment also reaches out to man now, and comes to him in death.

This difference of emphasis, the stress on individual judgment in Bultmann and its relative absence in Cullmann, is not fundamental, for Cullmann discusses the concept of judgment in a different connexion. What is fundamental is the vast difference of view in regard to present and future—Cullmann transfers to a temporal future what Bultmann finds realised in the present. This difference is connected with a further one. Bultmann holds that there has already taken place *in me* personally a significant event which Cullmann is unwilling to admit can take place either in me or in my death. If we should

[68] Cullmann, *op. cit.*, pp. 231-42.
[69] This is because Bultmann works according to the formula "Law and Gospel." Cullmann, on the other hand, confines what he has to say about the Law to a footnote in his *Christ and Time*, p. 138, n. 3. There is no explanation in Cullmann any more than there is in Barth of the significance of the Law in redemptive history. Cullmann's long "line" is fundamentally the same thing as Barth's Christocentric "point", only extended. In regard to Bultmann, see *Kerygma und Mythos*, VOL. I, p. 145.
[70] Bultmann, ibid. Cullmann's view of the death of the individual, on the other hand, is less coloured by the idea of Judgment. His problem is whether the whole of salvation is present in the death of the individual, or whether something more will come with the Parousia (*Christ and Time*, pp. 231 f.).

try to define what is true and what is false in each of these authors, we might put it thus: faith brings the future Judgment into the present, i.e. it brings my own personal judgment and anticipates the last day, but this "last" day could not be anticipated if it did not already lie in the future and outside the limits of our human existence. It is this very connexion between judgment and the dominion of death, the revelation of "wrath" in its most intimate and personal form, viz. dying, that makes it possible to submit to, and yet to survive, the judgment of God, and in the midst of a world of wrath and judgment to receive eternal life from God with its freedom from "idols." Those who accept death gladly are free from the worship of the creature, and also from fear. They have already begun to "rule" over the whole world.[71] The mighty power of faith operates in turning the onslaught of its enemy, death, against its other enemies, sin, false belief, and idolatry, thereby destroying them. When these have all been destroyed, God's pure Creation becomes free again. But this power possessed by faith is itself a borrowed one. Whenever a man is freed from the threat of death, it is the power of Christ's Resurrection alone which comes flooding into his life, forcing its way through the barriers, recreating him, and refashioning in him the image of God in which he was created. It is into this death, i.e. the death of Christ, and therefore this victory, that we are baptised.

We shall find a parallel to this view of death in man's "assent" to judgment in the Reformed doctrine of justification, particularly as it was formulated by Luther in his early period. When man acknowledges the judgment of God, he is acknowledging himself to be a sinner, and accepting the judgment which God passes upon him. By thus affirming the judgment of God, which relates to his entire being, and not just to a part of him, he ceases from his sinful preoccupation with self. But is such a man not still under judgment, even in his affirmation of God's judgment, in such a way that even his affirmation

[71] It is this intimate and personal revelation of "wrath," given particularly to the individual and therefore in a sense "isolating" him, which means that the Judgment can affect him without at the same time affecting all men. On this "isolation" by death as the discovery by the individual of his reality in existentialism, cf. Johan B. Hygen, "Tanker om døden i eksistensfilosofi og kristendom," in *Kirke og kultur*, Oslo 1949, pp. 279 ff.

itself is evil, and therefore to be avoided and denied? To this question there is only one answer—man's assent to God's judgment is not an act of his own which he offers to God, but is God's work in man, by which man comes into full fellowship with God.[72] His true fellowship with God is deepened only when he takes God's judgment upon himself, and is lessened when he sees less in himself to be judged. For God gives life by putting to death, and forgives by judging. Law and Gospel are thus closely related. When the Law performs its function of judgment, it is serving the Gospel. This work of God under the appearance of its opposite, a work which in its very heart is always the opposite of what it seems, is nowhere so obvious as in the death of Christ. Here, even to the apostles, the ultimate fact appeared to be the condemnation of Jesus. In fact, however, life continued unseen, and finally issued in the Resurrection on the third day, and thus determined the salvation of all men. To be in Christ, the tormented and condemned, is to be condemned by the Law, but also to know that one is in fellowship with God and at peace with Him. The unacceptable is accepted, to use Paul Tillich's phrase in his interpretation of the doctrine of justification.[73] Such a phrase is unintelligible unless we are dealing with a living and recreating God whose activity is still continuing against the destructive work of His enemy.

In the sixteenth century, when it was still customary to think in the categories of confession and penance, human existence was wholly understood in terms of guilt and forgiveness, etc. In our modern and more pietistic age we tend to connect "forgiveness," etc., not with acts which give men power to stand under the Judgment, but with those rather which lessen it, and therefore tend to detract from it.[74] It will be difficult for us today to receive the Reformed doctrine of the Law, judgment, and guilt, unless we modify slightly the language of the Reformers, and stress more strongly than was done in the sixteenth century the contrast made in the early Church

---

[72] See Ruben Josefson, *Ödmjukhet och tro*, Stockholm 1939, pp. 57-68.

[73] Paul Tillich, *The Courage to Be*, New Haven 1956, p. 164.

[74] On the difference between Luther and Schartau, for example, see Ivarsson, *Predikans uppgift*, pp. 220-3, etc.

between death and life. This contrast goes right back to the Bible. In death I already experience the judgment which I can neither avoid nor lessen, and which affects the whole of my existence. Death does not come upon me instantaneously and suddenly, on a certain date, but draws near to me in everything which diminishes my vitality. It lies concealed in all the afflictions of life which come upon me, and reveal the wrath of God. We cannot expel death by religious experiences, or the performance of religious acts, but we can accept it in faith. In this willingness to submit to the afflictions of life we have a far clearer insight into personal guilt than in bewailing our sins, at any rate if we express our grief by complaining whenever misfortune comes. Our confession of sin is a sham if our troubles do not lead us to admit that they are ultimately to our good. The confession of sin will acquire new meaning for our day only when it is accompanied by a new willingness to suffer, and to suffer gladly; otherwise we shall retain the pretence of a confession of sin which has the form but not the substance. But this will involve a fresh discussion of the meaning of death and all that accompanies it.[75] It is not enough simply to call death the "power of destruction," and think of it as having been destroyed by Christ in His own Death. It is typical that this attitude is found most frequently in the theology which has nothing positive to say about the "Law." The Law and death belong together. Both have a work given by God to accomplish. Both are in God's hand and serve Him. They are in His left hand, it is true, as Luther said, but still in His hand.[76]

Death, as we stated earlier, is part of God's judgment of the humanity which has separated itself from Him. It is in turning from life that man seeks his idols. He must get life from some source, for he is so created, and the more eagerly he draws it from this source, the more closely he is bound to that which can neither create nor give life. Man ought properly to rule over things like money, honour, etc. for the only life these things have is what men give to them. To bow down to them

[75] Aukrust, *Forkynnelse og historie*, has shown that this is an urgent task for theology.
[76] Cf. Gustaf Törnvall, *Andligt och världsligt regemente hos Luther*, hereafter cited as *Andligt regemente*, Lund 1940, pp. 6 ff.

and worship them is idolatry and the utter destruction of human personality. But God's judgment ceases to be condemnatory and becomes quickening when it condemns and casts down what has severed man's fellowship with God, i.e. his false, usurping independence, and the need which stems from this of finding safety, assurance, and confidence in some other source than God Himself. To have this independence destroyed, so that even the inclination to worship the creature disappears, is grace; and it is the work of faith to accept as grace the apparent meaninglessness of this rejection of independence. The depth of human perversity is revealed in the fact that only death can achieve this shattering of man's sinful independence. He cannot do it by any resolve or act of will of his own. Only death can. For this reason death can serve the final and purifying Judgment.[77] Everything turns on the assent of faith to God's judgment, and the victory and freedom which are involved in this assent. Christ by His Death "has transformed death, so that it shall not hurt us."

It is important to define what constitutes this "transformation" of death. When a man has accepted the judgment of God, according to the Reformed doctrine of justification, and thereby abandoned his false independence and attained to righteousness, faith is not a quality in him which diminishes God's judgment. Yet God's character is such that He justifies the rejected. Man's transformation or change is dependent not simply on the fact that "faith" or godliness exists, but also on the fact that *God recreates*, and does so again *ex nihilo*. As soon as we remove the act of the Creator, we must begin to consider what we mean by "godliness," and conversion or change will then become a religious phenomenon within man. This is also the case when death is the bearer of judgment. If we allow death to lose its character of judgment and become "a friend," we are idealising man; and the agony of Jesus in Gethsemane— His shrinking from the "cup"—becomes incomprehensible.

---

[77] See II Cor. XII.7-10 where Paul rejoices over "weaknesses, insults, hardships, persecutions, and calamities" for the sake of Christ. Apart from this joy the period of martyrdom would be incomprehensible. In Church history, however, the period of martyrdom is one among many datable periods. As far as the individual is concerned, whatever the period to which he belongs, there will be times when he needs the joy of which Paul speaks.

Death is hell, and does not cease to be hell, and all the evil things that the Bible says about death, the enemy, remain true. But Christ descended into hell as victor. The transformation of death brought about by faith is simply the Resurrection of Christ.[78] Christ's Resurrection in turn means that God the Creator is victorious over all that has befallen men in the fall of Adam. Thus the single phrase, "Christ is risen," includes the whole of man's salvation and restoration. It is this God, the God who creates *ex nihilo*, on whom man lays hold when death looms before him. Death means wrath and not friendliness. But wrath upon "the old man," and upon that which has to die in order that "the new man" may come alive, is a wrath which serves God's new Creation. If the object of God's wrath had not fallen now, it would have fallen on the last day. Since it falls now, its very fall announces the Gospel, and man in faith assents to death, allows the Judgment to be passed upon him, forsakes his idols, and comes home. When all has been judged, the judgment is sufficient, and the events of the last time have already taken place. Faith, which puts its trust in God's recreating work in Christ alone, finds grounds for confidence even in death, judgment, and wrath.[79] Had Christ not died and risen, independently of my belief in His death and Resurrection, no such confidence would exist.

It is the presence of judgment in death and in the last day which allows faith to bring death and the last day together

---

[78] Since death is an intrusion into human life, it can be defeated only by some act within human life. Paul does not refer back to the primal Creation but always to Christ's Resurrection and its victory. Cf. John A. T. Robinson, *The Body*, Studies in Biblical Theology, No. 5, London 1952, p. 32.

[79] There should be no need to raise the question of the so-called "middle state" if we regard everything in man as having been condemned, yet trust that God is such that He raises the condemned. If, on the other hand, we believe that man is only partially condemned *coram Deo* and that a part of him is exempted from Judgment, we shall always need to have a "middle state." Whatever "Baptism for the dead" may have meant in early Christianity, it is unlikely that it implied faith in anything other than the Death and Resurrection of Christ. This was always what Baptism meant. It is typical that having spoken of Baptism on behalf of the dead Paul immediately goes on to express, as was commonly done in the New Testament period, the joy that he experienced in the presence of death and danger: "Why am I in peril every hour?" (1 Cor. xv.30), "I die every day!" (1 Cor. xv.31). To express such joy at the present day is to be regarded as psychologically abnormal—and this at a time when we are entering a cultural situation in which the Church badly needs this joy.

into a single reality, so that death contains and is itself the last day. Death is the uniquely personal and individual event. It may come upon me, without thereby affecting all other men. Judgment may remain for the world, but in my death judgment has already taken place. Furthermore, death is total. It leaves no part of me remaining. Therefore to hope that such a judgment as death may issue in life is to hope in the Creator who creates out of nothing, or (which is the same thing) to hope in the Resurrection of Christ. This hope "where there is no hope" and this faith in Him "who gives life to the dead, and calls into existence the things that do not exist" (Rom. iv.17 f.) may exist, as the example of Abraham proves, even before the Incarnation, as a turning away from visible idols in prayer to the One who is invisible and still to come.[80] This turning from idols may still be found in this form in the present day, when death is accepted as the end of all human striving. If the aspect of judgment in death and the aspect of judgment in the Last Day thus make it possible to alter Cullmann's interpretation, and allow each man in his own last day to experience something of *the* Last Day, its till does not follow from this that we can accept Bultmann's identification of death and the Last Judgment without making certain reservations and modifications. At each point in Bultmann's theology we have to ask the same question—when the existential interpretation centres everything upon man the hearer, does it not lose its character of Law and Gospel? Can my death contain the Last Judgment, if there is to be no Last Judgment after my death? Can my faith contain eternal life, if eternal life does not exist outside my faith? The power with which judgment works in me depends on the fact that it is a reality outside me, and similarly the power with which the Gospel works in me rests on events which have taken place outside me.[81]

If we connect death and judgment in the manner which we have just indicated, we shall be able to understand a little

---

[80] Israel refused to worship idols, "images." This refusal, which meant the rejection of the worship of the creature, was a faith in Christ before Christ. This was also expressed in the expectation of the One who was to come.

[81] Cf. Hellmut Traub, *Anmerkungen und Fragen zur neutestamentlichen Hermeneutik und zum Problem der Entmythologisierung*, Neukirchen 1952, pp. 21 f.

better what Cullmann means when he talks about the "extra" which salvation in the future will possess, but which it as yet lacks. "If the Spirit of Him who raised Jesus from the dead dwells in you, He who raised Christ Jesus from the dead will give life to your mortal bodies also through His Spirit which dwells in you" (Rom. viii.11). The Spirit is given to us now as a pledge or first-fruits, but in spite of the Spirit, the body is subject to corruption, and we still await a part of salvation which has not yet been realised—"the redemption of our bodies" (Rom. viii.23). There is only one point in the world at which the Spirit has obtained dominion over the body (a dominion which will be extended in the last age to include our bodies also), and that is Christ's Resurrection on the third day. Christ after His Resurrection is a spiritual body, while we on the other hand look forward to "the spiritual body" as something which is still to come (1 Cor. xv.44). In our case the Spirit strives against the intractable element in our bodies (Gal. v.17; Rom. vii.22-5), which prevents the full dominion of the Spirit. We are involved in an ethical conflict between good and evil, and victory for the good in this struggle is not perfect spiritual personality, but the resurrection of the dead. Our death lies on the line towards this goal. It is not that Cullmann is wrong in what he says about the body in this connexion.[82] On the contrary, he is quite correct in his main argument, which is confirmed at this point by what we have said above about *death* as the bearer of judgment and the Law. What is strange is that Cullmann can argue about the body and *life* in the future, while lacking the fundamental basis for the argument, which is to be found in the connexion between the body and *death* in the present.

Faith in our participation in the Resurrection of Christ is connected in the New Testament with faith in our participation in His death (see, for example, Rom. vi.5; Phil. iii.10 f.). The concept of the imitation of Christ finds its expression in following Christ into suffering and death, and thereby into life

[82] Cullmann gives his clearest interpretation of the future life and the body in *Christ and Time*, pp. 234-40. His unwillingness to discuss the relationship between the body and the Law must be due to his dependence on Barth. This dependence is clearly seen in several of his earliest works, e.g., *Königsherrschaft Christi* and *Earliest Christian Confessions*.

and resurrection, and not in imitating certain acts which He performed. This imitation of Christ in suffering is connected in the New Testament, strangely enough, with suffering under earthly "masters," "not only the kind and gentle, but also the overbearing," (1 Pet. 11.18). The reviling of Christ, when He stood before His earthly judges, and the wrath which He endured, are depicted as examples of what a Christian should be prepared to endure in his body (1 Pet. 11.21 ff.; cf. "and are beaten" in vs. 20): "For to this you have been called, because Christ also suffered for you, leaving you an example, that you should follow His steps." We have already dealt with the "wrath" in Rom. XIII, which is connected with magistrates, and clearly conveys God's judgment and is dispensed in His service (Rom. XIII.4).[83] It is quite clear that ideas such as these formed the basis on which the early Church developed its attitude to martyrdom and in general to persecution, for this attitude was based on Christ's own attitude to the earthly powers which sentenced Him to the Cross. For the early Church fellowship in Christ's death was a joyful thing, for it concealed within itself fellowship in His life. When hope reached forward to the participation by the body in full salvation, this did not mean that the body had now no sense, experience, or share, of salvation. What it did sense, experience, and share, however, was *death*—and death was the way to life. In our modern discussion of Luther's doctrine of the earthly government, one aspect of this doctrine of "government" is almost always pushed aside, viz. that which deals with the moment of death, the "cross" in the call of the Christian, the patient earthly suffering which, for Luther, was fundamental, and which he inserts into

[83] We should note that the counsel concerning submission to overbearing masters appears in the same context as the exhortation to obedience to "the emperor," "governors," etc. (1 Pet. 11.13 ff.). This passage corresponds directly to Rom. XIII.1 ff. Cullmann concedes that this latter passage refers to earthly authorities (*Christ and Time*, p. 196), but he does not connect it with the power of the Law. Even at this point he takes the second article as his starting-point by interpreting the authorities in terms of angelic powers. We may also add that the difference between the just and the unjust authority remains, even when the Christian suffers under the unjust authority. To suffer means to "give place" to the wrath of God, and not to avenge oneself (Rom. XII.19; 1 Pet. 11.13). The assumption is that when we "give place," God acts, whereas when we avenge ourselves, God refrains from intervening. The main problem is the nature of faith in God.

every statement which he makes about life under earthly government.[84] This aspect is probably remote from our modern period, which is concerned rather with a fellowshp of common interest, where each individual protects his own "rights," and a willingness to bear suffering is interpreted as morbid and disruptive of human solidarity. If, however, we lose this other idea from our modern consciousness, we are really disregarding an objective fact of human history which makes the periods of the early Church and the Reformation fundamentally different from our modern period.

We may define this difference in the following way. In these earlier periods God was seen to be active in Creation and in every event and circumstance which befell men. At the same time, however, a corrupt and evil force, hostile to God, was also seen to be at work. This force had gained so firm a hold upon man that only death could expel it. The Gospel of Christ's death and resurrection was preached in a world which God had created and continued to sustain, but in which sin was at work as an "enemy" (Mt. XIII.25, 28). When the whole content of faith is derived from the second article or from the Gospel as at the present time, this earlier conception is destroyed.[85]

Two points must here be added by way of conclusion. In the first place we have continually been forced to introduce into our discussion in the present section arguments which should really come later, and which can be fully developed only in a description of the work of Christ. Nevertheless all

[84] The fundamental difference between earthly and heavenly righteousness, the "earth of works and the cross" and the "heaven of faith," is described in particular in Luther's *Commentary on Galatians*. See, e.g., W. A., 40-1, pp. 213.30-214.21, 469.23-7.

[85] We should note that it is the derivation of the content of faith from the second article that is new in modern theology. The assumption here is that knowledge is the basic question, and that the revelation in Christ provides the knowledge from which all else is to be derived. In an earlier period the doctrine of the civil authorities was not, as is commonly supposed today, derived from the first article. The basic question then was not one of knowledge. Creation was the first work of God by which He dealt with all men. His work in the Incarnation did not bring this first work to an end, though He was now doing something new. The idea of the "Cross" in the Incarnation means, of course, that the second article has something direct to say about human life, just as the first article has. But there is never any question of derivation. It is not man's knowledge but the works of God which are central.

CREATION

these arguments have something to tell us about human life as it is without Christ. Death and judgment are active wherever the Conqueror of death has not come. In the second place, God's work of judgment as we have said, is only a part of His work in the world. God creates and gives in Creation, and recreates even in the world of death where Christ has not been preached. Birth, the giving of life, and bodily health, mean that God continues His work of Creation in spite of sin. We shall, therefore, devote our next section to this other aspect, viz. the relation between the Creation of the world and our birth.

CHAPTER III

MAN IN CREATION

The Creation of the World and our Birth

IN the first chapter of Part I, "Creation," we dealt with God as the One who gives life, and man as the one who receives life from God. In the second chapter we dealt with God as Judge, and man as the one who is subject to death, and the object of God's wrath. In both chapters our main subject of study was the relation between God and man. Both the *opus proprium* of God (the giving of life) and His *opus alienum* (His judgment) are directed at man. Our present concern in this third chapter, "Man in Creation," is with the different aspect of man's relation to the rest of Creation, i.e. his fellow beings and matter. We are now approaching the point where the meaning of Part II of the present work is becoming comprehensible.

At the same time, however, we must emphasise that in man's relation to Creation around him, it is God and not man who creates and sustains. Man's special position in Creation, and in particular his unique possession of dominion and government over the rest of Creation, is due to the fact that God has given him this position. God does not revoke this decree or change His will even when man goes against his nature and worships the creature over which he ought to rule, thereby putting himself into a position of constraint and bondage rather than of freedom. I have tried to express this sovereignty of God, which sets man in a purposeful relation to the world by the very fact of his birth and his living in the world, by putting this section on the Creation of the world and our birth at the beginning of the present chapter.

There will also be a further opportunity at this point of comparing Bultmann and Cullmann. In the comparison which we made in the previous section, our main assertion was that

the Judgment of the last day impinges upon the life of the
individual. Death is our confrontation with Judgment. The
reverse holds true of our birth. God's Creation at the beginning
is still continuing, and our birth means that God is creating
us.[1] The two extremities on Cullmann's long line, Creation at
the beginning and the last day at the end, are now drawn
together and combined in the "beginning" and "end" of the
individual, his birth and death. In this combination, however,
they are coloured in a way which Cullmann does not see by
"Law" and "Gospel". Death is combined with Judgment, and
the giving of life is filled with mercy and new Creation. By
bringing Creation and the last day into the life of the individual
we thus approach the position of Bultmann. To him Cullmann's
long line is mythological. God's works can never lie in a "redemptive history" which is separated from the Now of the
hearer. We must note, however, that man's position in the
world is to be seen in a quite different way from Bultmann.
Man's relation to the world around him is an independent
problem which requires its own theological treatment. In
Cullmann the Law has no role at all to play. When it appears
in Bultmann its function is restricted to that of my individual
judgment *coram Deo*. This is simply the "second" use of the
Law.[2] In his existential interpretation Bultmann's concentration on *my* existence pushes aside any idea of the positive
government of the *world* by the Law, i.e. the "first" use of the
Law. For this the question of *my* existence is not essential. The
Creation of the world and the Judgment of the world have
reference to more than my personal existence. Cullmann's line
with its events which are external to ourselves cannot be

---

[1] Cf. the section above, "The Creator and Life," Part I, chapter I.

[2] In one respect the civil use of the Law and the Last Judgment on all nations
coincide—it is the *world* that is to be kept pure and free of evil works. So also in
one respect the theological use of the Law and the preaching of the Gospel coincide
—in each it is the *individual* that God is confronting and his conscience that He is
addressing. In Bultmann it is the individual throughout who is the object of God's
works, and the idea of the world disappears. The Last Judgment, therefore,
becomes merged into the death of the individual, while the idea of future Judgment
is lost. In Cullmann, on the other hand, the individual disappears along with the
"*pro me*" character of the divine works. If there is any common ground between
Bultmann and Cullmann, it is that fundamentally they are both writing purely
New Testament theology. The Old Testament has no real part in their theology.

"demythologised" and then incorporated by the individual into himself. These events, rather, when rightly understood, are events which are preached, as Bultmann correctly says, to the individual.

First, however, let us consider some Old Testament passages which show that birth is one aspect of God's continuing work of Creation.[3] "Thou didst form my inward parts, Thou didst knit me together in my mother's womb. I will praise thee, for Thou art fearful and wonderful . . . Thy eyes beheld my unformed substance" (Ps. cxxxix.13-6). What was true of Adam holds good of every man: he is "formed from a piece of clay" (Job xxxiii.6). His living and breathing depends on "the breath of the Almighty" (Job. xxxiii.4). This is true likewise of manservant and maidservant. Anyone, therefore, who wrongs another stands mute when the Creator rises up and calls him to account: "Did not He who made me in the womb make him? And did not one fashion us in the womb?" (Job. xxxi.15).[4] "The hearing ear and the seeing eye, the Lord has made them both" (Prov. xx.12).[5] Hebrew has no single word for the "sustaining" of Creation, as if sustaining were a separate act which came after "Creation" in the narrow sense.[6] Life in the present depends on God's creating in the present, and if He removed His Spirit, life would vanish (Ps. civ.29). But in God's sustaining of Creation He does not take away His Spirit. He sends it forth and Creation thus continues. "When thou sendest forth Thy Spirit, they are created; and thou renewest the face of the ground" (Ps. civ.30).[7] These Old Testament concepts of God's creating of the individual and every creature reappear in the New Testament (Acts xvii.25; 1 Tim. vi.13).[8]

[3] On what follows, cf. Lindeskog, *Studien*, pp. 64 ff.

[4] Cf. Ps. cxix.73; Is. xliv.24; Jer. 1.5; Job. x.8 f., xii.10, xxxiv.14 f.; and also Ps. civ.27-30; Is. xliii.7.

[5] Cf. Luther's explanation of the first article: "I believe that God has created me and all creatures, given me a body and soul, eyes, ears, and all my parts . . ."

[6] See Eichrodt, *Theologie des Alten Testaments*, vol. ii, p. 78. Eichrodt considers that the term "*creatio continua*" is a suitable expression for this "sustaining" of creation. Cf. Lindeskog, *Studien*, pp. 64 f., where the same argument and the same expression are used.

[7] See also Johnson, *The Vitality of the Individual in the Thought of Ancient Israel*, pp. 95 f.

[8] On his point see Lindeskog, *Studien*, pp. 188 f., Gärtner, *The Areopagus Speech*, pp. 192 f., 198.

It is clear that the Bible does not think of God's work of
Creation as being connected with a primal cosmic foundation,
so that human beings were subsequently to be born according
to a predetermined order in Creation. This would render any
new creation by God unnecessary, and, as it were, take the
place of God on the horizontal level. The giving of life to new
creatures does not depend on powers which are lent to man,
and which continue independently of man's relation to God.
It is a direct new work of God, in which He repeats what He
did to Adam (i.e. man)—He moulds together clay and the
breath of the Spirit, and man receives life (Job. xxxiii.4, 6).[9]
A relationship to God is established in the very fact of human
birth. This may later undergo many changes brought about
by faith, Baptism, etc. All these are new relationships to the
God who created man in his physical birth. But we misinterpret
them all in a Marcionite direction if we do not keep Creation
(i.e. birth) as our starting-point. We cannot make the second
article our point of departure without dislocating the content
of faith.

If for a moment we connect the view of birth, which we have
here offered, with the description of death made in the previous
section, we shall have a total picture which is reminiscent of
Bultmann's demythologised theology. In Bultmann's theology
the events on Cullmann's long time line have been brought into
the life of the individual. If a man says that he believes in the
Creator, what he is saying is: "I believe that God has created
me." If he says that he believes in the Judge, he is saying: "I
believe that God is judging me." By faith he appropriates to
himself as much of these works of God as is of importance for
him. He cannot conceive of an act of Creation through which
the world came into existence long before his birth. Even if he
were able to do so, nothing would be more important for his
faith than that *his* life is in God's hands, and that he is created
by God. Nor can he conceive of some last day after his death
when all nations shall be gathered before a throne to be judged.

[9] On the allusion in I Cor. xv.45 ff. to Gen II.7 (clearly referred to also in Job
xxxiii.4, 6) and the use of this passage to denote the superiority of what Christ
has done, see Dahl, *Background*, p. 435. Even in the superior character of what
Christ has done, however, we find that there is a continuity in God's act of Creation.
God gives every man at birth the form of "the man of dust."

Even if he were able to do so, for him all judgment would still be centred on the judgment upon *himself*. Nothing would be more important for him than the fact that even now his judgment is taking place in the death which he is undergoing, and which incorporates him into Christ. It is a strength in Bultmann's Biblical interpretation that he is able to relate the content of the word of scripture to the most fundamental problems of the individual, and to rediscover in it the "*pro me*," which has disappeared in orthodoxy and its recent offshoots.[10] Not to be able to conceive of an event is one thing. To deny its possibility is quite another. In Bultmann demythologising is not simply an interpretation which brings the word of the Bible to the hearer and reveals the intimate relation of this word to the questions which he is asking. It is also a direct denial of assertions that the events described in the Bible have happened independently of and outside their acceptance by faith and their proclamation in the Church.[11] This means, however, that we have nothing in the Bible to which we can apply the words "*pro me.*" Judgment cannot be judgment unless there is something in my death which is other than biological extinction. The horror of death may be removed by a physiological explanation rather than the Gospel, so long as death does not conceal a judgment, at any rate any self-evident judgment, within itself. Life can continue and be renewed without receiving from the One who is sovereign Lord over me, provided that the whole world around me does not exist and is not renewed in this Creator. It cannot be denied that these events on Cullmann's long time line are distinct events of importance in their own right. If we deny this, faith loses the possibility of being faith. Faith must always be related to something which is outside itself, and draw, accept, and receive from that source. When I believe, I am always presupposing God's dealings with the whole world. This also means His dealings in the very beginning, before my birth, and at the very end, after my death. To affirm these dealings which God

[10] See Gerhard Gloege, *Mythologie und Luthertum*, Luthertum, VOL. V, 2nd edn. Berlin 1953, p. 155.
[11] Cf. Prenter, *Skabelse og genløsning*, pp. 395-8; Gloege, *Mythologie und Luthertum*, pp. 103 ff.

G

has with the whole world in particular statements of faith, without connecting them to the believing self—to deprive them, that is, of their *"pro me"* character—would be to misunderstand the significance of the confession of faith.[12] To deny that God has dealings with the world (i.e. with more than me personally) is to deny the very ground of faith, and ultimately to render impossible the *"pro me"* to which the Creed points.

It is a distinctive feature of the Biblical account of Creation that it places man and the world together.[13] In one way Genesis represents the external world as having been given to man, and not as existing for its own sake. The sun, the moon, the sea-monsters, the birds, and every living creature, are created to be used by man, who was put last into the world to "have dominion over all the earth" (Gen. 1.1-26). When man is created, he gets everything good "for food" (Gen. 1.28 f.). The beasts of the earth and the fowls of the air are given to man so that he may give a name to everything. This "calling by name" is man's dominion over the world around him, and his understanding of it, as having been given to him by God to serve his needs.[14] The whole of the "goodness" of Creation flows to man and waits to be used by him. God's goodness is expressed in the good things of Creation, and His giving of life in the sun, the rain

[12] At the time of the Enlightenment, when Biblical and dogmatic criticism denied miracles and at the same time the educational and disciplinary character of the Church was reduced to a mere façade, there was a tendency to demand a credal assent in which the idea of *"pro me"* had no real part. The ground for this, however, had already been prepared, e.g. by Melanchthon and orthodoxy. Cf. Henning Lindström, *Skapelse och frälsning i Melanchthons teologi*, Stockholm 1944, pp. 358 f., 400 ff.

[13] Cf. Rev. IV.11, XIV.7.

[14] See von Rad, *Das erste Buch Mose*, pp. 66 f. The peculiar position which the beasts have in relation to man in the Creation narrative, and which they retain in certain visions of the future in the Old Testament (e.g. Is. XI.6-9), underlies various chiliastic ideas which may appear fantastic to us, but nevertheless are deeply rooted in the Bible. Cf. Rom. VIII.19-22; Mk. 1.13; and see Leonhard Goppelt, *Typos*, Beiträge zur Förderung der christlichen Theologie, SER. II, VOL. XLIII, Gütersloh 1939, pp. 117 f. We should note that the beginning and end of Cullmann's time line, i.e. Creation and the Consummation, are both characterised by God's direct dealings with the cosmos (*Christ and Time*, pp. 109, 150 f., 187 f.). The world in which man lives is the same as it was before he came into being, and the same as it will be after he has ceased to be. Bultmann does not admit the events of redemptive history as independent acts, and interprets them existentially as God's dealings with me personally. This corresponds on the temporal plane to the disappearance of the civil use of the Law and of a positive interest in man's

(Mt. v.45), plants, and animals. This is only one aspect of God's work of Creation. As soon as man had been formed by the Creator, he was put in Creation to make use of the earth (Gen. ii.5 ff.). Man, that is, cannot live in obedience to God without living in the concrete relation to the world to which God appointed him. Man's goodness flows out to the world, and waits the opportunity of dealing with what God has created. In this way, viz. by man's use and dominion, the goodness of the Creator is manifested to other creatures.

By every birth a new man is added to the world which man has been given. Birth establishes a relationship to God, the giver of life, and to the world, the place where life is to be lived. Life cannot continue unless it is constantly created anew. Man bears his relationship to God about with him wherever he goes. Life cannot be lived except in the world which is created by God and given to man, and in which man has the responsibility of fulfilling certain functions which he has not freely chosen. These functions have been laid upon him by God, who created both man and the world. "Use" and "dominion" are to be distinguished in very many of the functions and activities which, however different, in one way or another mean the use of what is created and lordship over it. All this is included in the relation to God which is given at birth. The tendency to remove the world and one's neighbour from the individual's relation to God, and to base this relation on a specific "religious" experience, is quite comprehensible in those expressions of faith in which the Creation of the world has no essential part to play (e.g. mysticism). In Christianity, however, this tendency constitutes a denial that the two determinative sources of theological formulation from the very earliest period until the eighteenth century are Genesis i and the first article of the Creed.[15] However Christocentrically we may describe this "relation to

relationship to the world around him. For Bultmann it is in the *kerygma* that man is given his true existence. Here he is entirely on his own, isolated from the rest of Creation. It is strange that Bultmann can say this when the existentialism of Heidegger is so much against it.

[15] Cf. Prenter, *Skabelse og genløsning*, pp. 99-105. To constitute the New Testament as the point of departure is a recent—and degenerate—phenomenon in the history of ideas.

God," it is still a radical denial and destruction of the Christian faith.

The fact of the Fall and of death's dominion in the world in which God gives life and recreates, does not in the least lessen the area of contact which the Christian faith and fellowship with God have with the world. It certainly does not alter it in such a way that because of sin an essentially "unwordly" relation to God has to be established after the Fall. The new situation which arose through Adam's disobedience is bound up with the world in exactly the same way as his state of purity and innocence was at the beginning. The earth is cursed for man's sake (Gen. III.17; Rom. VIII.20), and the curse is expressed in the unreadiness of the earth to give man life: "In toil you shall eat of it all the days of your life." Creation is at enmity with man, and brings forth "thorns and thistles" for him (Gen. III.18).[16] This hostility towards man's life, and this death which expresses God's wrath, also afflict man from without. Like life itself, they come from the world in which man is set and in which God is active as Creator and Judge. The punishment which is in the woman's child-bearing and the sweat of man's face culminates in death, man's "return to the ground" (Gen. III.19). It is a phase in the inescapable relation which a man has with God, even although he may never speak about "God." Man does not freely choose this punishment, but carries it about with him from his birth, whether he wishes it or not. Man is born to die and to submit to the judgment which is involved in death. Birth means not only a renewal of the act of Creation, so that every man born after Adam begins by receiving life as he did. It also means man's entering into the world of death. Everyone, therefore, who is born is confronted at once with the necessity of having to taste death. There is no other escape from life except death. Death is a door through which only one can pass at a time, and until the last day it will remain the end-point of the life which begins at birth. Everyone, therefore, has within himself both the end of redemptive history and its beginning, Creation.

[16] Cf. Rom. VIII.19 and see Heinrich Bornkamm, *Luther und das Alte Testament*, p. 51. The curse may be alleviated, but it does not disappear. See von Rad, *Das erste Buch Mose*, pp. 100, 113, on Gen. VIII.21, IX.20.

When faith submits to the Judgment and is smitten by death, it is not harmed by the Judgment, but on the contrary brings life out of death, the life of Baptism and of the Resurrection of Christ. The Judgment affects only the "old man" who has to die, if we are not to perish. Although faith receives from God, it never exists in a vacuum as a purely I-Thou relationship to God which is separate from the world. The external world is always involved in our relationship to God.[17] Salvation was thus accomplished in a particular historic event—the trial of Jesus under Pontius Pilate. It is communicated to us by the external symbols of Word and Sacrament, and will likewise be fulfilled in an event which will involve all the nations of the world. To disregard the world is to cleave the Christian faith assunder at every point.

The "withdrawal" from the created world which is implied in faith's regard for God alone does not mean either flight from or indifference to the world and what it has to offer. The only things cast down by faith are idols. The object of idolatry is not usually something evil, but rather something good, something created by God. The fault is not in the world, but in man who worships the creature.[18] When faith brings the false worship of the creature to an end, it does not reject the creature, which is good, and has been given by God, but simply the idolatrous worship. Faith means that man now has dominion over the creature of which he previously made an idol. It means the unhindered control of Creation by man, and therefore new opportunities of serving his neighbour. It is a matter of crucial importance that for the Bible the one constant object of man's service is his neighbour, and not a group, nor even a people or family. For us today, on the other hand, a narrow individualism, which is unrelated to the world around it, passes into a collectivism, in which the individual is merged into a group or

[17] In all his theological writings Einar Billing concentrates on this point. Faith cannot be faith without being rooted in man's actual experience. See, e.g., *Vår kallelse*, p. 37 f.; *Försoningen*, p. 124; *Universitet och kyrka*, Stockholm 1923, p. 12 f.; *Herdabref*, p. 43 f.; and *De etiska tankarna*, p. 12 f. It is significant that Billing begins with the Old Testament.
[18] This is the basic idea in Rom. 1.19-25. Creation is good and the *locus* of God's revelation, but it is wrong to worship the creature. Faith in God and love of one's neighbour constitute a single reality. It is to "have dominion" over the creature and not to worship it, and to be free and yet to be at the service of the Creator.

organisation.[19] Particularly when birth is regarded as constituting the relationship to God, and as the extension of the act
of Creation, there is a tendency to let biological factors such as
nation and family communicate a specific "ethic of Creation."
The admonitions which we find in the Bible, even in the Old
Testament, are conspicuously free from any such collectivism,
and notably concerned rather with the neighbour—the needy,
the wearied, and even the stranger (i.e. the one who did not
belong to the people, but dwelt in the land, as Israel dwelt in
Egypt).[20] Collectivism is thus in this respect the failure to have
any real neighbour. It is a device for obtaining fellowship
apart from God, and for "creating" something (which in the
end means an idol, the only thing that man can create apart
from God). Collectivism does not recognise or accept the
fellowship which is given to us by the very fact of our living in
the world and having the neighbour God has given us.

The fact that the concept of Creation has been used in
recent years in support of certain given "ordinances" which at
the same time have also been maintained by collectivist
ideologies, has prepared the way for a modern school of
theology. This new theology has sought to find its basis in the
second article, which it has used as a weapon against this
theology of Creation, and at the same time against collectivist
systems in the sphere of politics. The distinctive feature of this
theological situation is to be seen in its unique association of
theology and politics. The theology which connected itself to
given ordinances inevitably bound the belief in Creation to
things that at times involved the worship of the creature. This
is contrary to God's purpose, which is man's free dominion
over creation, and when this is done, God's will in Creation
comes to be identified with the power which proceeds from the
collectivist group. If this group turns the belief in Creation into
a political concept, adopting its terms to further its own objects,
which may coincide with the objects of a particular party, the
theology which stands in judgment of all this, but which takes
the second article as its starting-point and regards knowledge
as the primary question, inevitably comes to make the Church

[19] Cf. Robinson, *The Body*, pp. 7 ff.
[20] See, e.g., Ex. xxiii.9 and cf. Billing, *De etiska tankarna*, pp. 128 ff.

a political factor, indeed the foremost political factor.[21] Perhaps the greatest danger facing the Church at the present time is that it may be misled by a false theology into making itself a collectivist group, one party against other parties. Such a disaster will occur when the Church fails to understand man as having already been put in the world by God the Creator, i.e. as already being where God wills him to be. He is there, even though hs misuses his position, and therefore needs to be freed from the evil which is in himself. As soon as we regard man's place in the world as being irrelevant from the point of view of the Church, the Church becomes a collectivist group with its own ideology. Its piety becomes destructive of what is human in man, and the ministry competes with the agencies of social service. If this ever happens, it means that the Church itself has become an idol. The Church on the contrary ought to be freeing man for service, and for free dominion over all Creation.

The life into which man is born is a life to be lived in the world in which the things of Creation can be used to support life and help it to continue. The relation to parents, children, or the other sex, is included in the relation to one's neighbour. This relation cannot, if worship of the creature is to be avoided and freedom allowed to prevail, be extended to an independent ethic based on another demand than that of love for one's neighbour.[22] Such a demand will always coincide with the demands of man's wishes in such a way as to fill the place of the idol. It will therefore become opposed in a particular situation to the love and freedom to which God appointed man in Creation, and for which He redeems him in Christ.[23] The life into which man is born is not life in a collective. The understanding of races and classes as strangers (and not as containing

[21] See Barth, *Rechtfertigung und Recht*, p. 40, and *Christengemeinde und Bürgergemeinde*, p. 24.

[22] Cf. Hillerdal, *Gehorsam gegen Gott und Menchen*, p. 307. For this reason the whole of the Law can be summarised in a single commandment: "You shall love your neighbour as yourself" (Rom. xiii.9; Gal. v.14; cf. Mt. vii.12). This does not in any way alter the double commandment of love (Mk. xii.29 ff., and parallels).

[23] The words about hating father, mother, wife, children, brothers and sisters, and even one's own life, relate to what we have here referred to as the situation of idolatry, i.e. the situation in which something that is good takes God's place. Cf. Lindsay Dewar, *An Outline of New Testament Ethics*, Philadelphia 1949, pp. 90 f., and also Lyder Brun, *Lukasevangeliet*, Oslo 1933, pp. 396 f.

"neighbours" in the same sense as other races and classes) is always acquired and secondary, and not innate. The "natural" interpretation given in Creation is in fact freedom from such ideological barriers. In Genesis the divergence between various languages and cultures which do not understand one another is represented as a result of human achievement and not as something created (Gen. XI.1-9).[24] The freedom in which man was created is conscious only of fellow men and nature, and does not make idols of or subordinate itself to any part of Creation. This freedom finds in the Creator its only object of worship, and looks on everything else in Creation as the good things given by the Creator for man to rule over. Since man's primary concern is with his neighbour, rather than with a collective, this will mean continual mobility and recreation of the good in the works to which man is called. Love of one's neighbour cannot be bound to particular social norms, for then it would not be the neighbour who was being loved, but rather the works of love would be restricted to the limits of the group.[25]

This trust which man has in God, and his consequent willingness to be at God's disposal for service to his neighbour, is the purpose of Creation, and therefore the purpose in every birth. When men neither trust in God nor display any willingness to serve their neighbour, they are under judgment. We have already dealt in an earlier chapter with the meaning of judgment in relation to God. In the present chapter our task is to define more closely what sin and creativity mean in regard to man's treatment of his neighbour and the rest of Creation. God's activity in Creation does not cease simply because man stands defiantly in opposition to Him. The primary event with which we have been particularly dealing in the present section is birth, God's continual fashioning of new life. Birth is in itself, as we have seen, a repetition of God's Creation, a renewal of the same act of Creation by which Adam came into existence (see, e.g. Job XXXIII.4, 6). God's Creation continues, in spite of men's opposition to God, and in His continuing Creation

---

[24] See Søe, *Kristelig etik*, p. 354.

[25] Cf. Løgstrup, *Den etiske fordring*, p. 57. The need of our neighbour may require that we do something for him that has never been done before, and that does not therefore conform to any previous method. Our neighbour implies a factor which breaks through accepted convention and law.

God uses men, and their opposition and unwillingness do not
prevent Him from using them.[26] We shall be dealing in the
two remaining sections of the present chapter with this double
aspect of man's status in Creation. In part man retains a certain
power over Creation, so that he is able to have a certain
control over it in freedom. In part, however, he is disobedient
to God's will for him in relation to his fellow men and the good
which God has created. Therefore when God forces him to do
His will he is brought into a relation of compulsion and bondage
to his neighbour and to the work which he is given to do on
earth.[27]

"Dominion" and Freedom

We have seen earlier that in order to be able to give a description of the destiny to which God appoints man, we need to
have some picture of the world or external Creation. Man is
put into the world to have dominion over the animals and over
the whole earth (Gen. 1.26, 28). He gives names to all creatures,
which exist to serve him (II.18 ff.).[28] Man is appointed to have
dominion over the work of God's hands; all things have been
put "under his feet" (Ps. VIII.7 f.).[29] When God establishes the
covenant with Noah He renews His decree for Creation concerning the replenishing of the earth (cf. Gen. 1.28 with IX.1),
and says that all creatures are now delivered into man's hand,
and that every moving thing that lives is to be for food for him
(IX.2 f.).[30] Fear and dread of man shall therefore be upon
every beast of the earth (IX.2). Although God's command to
till the soil may have been easier to obey before the Fall and

[26] It is a common Biblical idea, to which we have referred earlier, that God uses
even evil powers for the accomplishment of His purposes. See, e.g., Is. x.5-15; Acts
IV.24-8; II Cor. XII.7-10 (on the messenger of Satan). Cf. Ragnar Bring, *Dualismen
hos Luther*, Lund 1929, pp. 264 f., 316 f.
[27] This element of compulsion appears in Luther's doctrine of the earthly
government. Cf. also Olsson, *Luthers socialetik*, VOL. I, pp. 114-45.
[28] Cf. Sven Herner, *Di Natur im Alten Testament*, Humanistiskt vetenskaps-
samfundets i Lund årsberättelse, 1940-1, VOL. II, Lund 1941, p. 70.
[29] The meaning of "man" here is indefinite. Even though the term refers to the
king or to some person who is specifically said to "rule," it is still the restoration
of Creation which is involved in his rule. On the connexion between Ps. VIII.7
and the New Testament, see Lindeskog, *Studien*, pp. 230 f.
[30] Cf. Walther Zimmerli, *I Mose I-XI*, VOL. II, Zürich 1943, pp. 107 ff. The new
factor that entered the unsullied Creation was discord and death.

the cursing of the ground, and more difficult to obey afterwards, it is valid both before and after. Man as a created being is inescapably related to the soil he has to till (II.5, 15; III.23; cf. V.29).

Similarly we have seen earlier that man's independence does not prevent God from using him. God can do good even with a wicked instrument. He allows the desire for power or influence to serve the good. No man can remain in possession of a position of power without in some way exercising a positive and beneficent influence upon the lives of those around him. The words, "You meant evil against me; but God meant it for good" (Gen. L.20), have an application far wider than the limits of the story of Joseph.[31] We do not need to minimise man's wickedness in order to leave a place for divine goodness. Human wickedness, even when it is complete, can still serve divine goodness, and even in its ignorance and utter blindness do the good which God wills to be done (Acts IV.27 f.). Only so does God continue to be God—otherwise He would be dependent on men's goodness and powerless to deal with men's wickedness. He is not, and He continues to govern the world in spite of men's selfishness. Men seek their own advantage every day, but in doing so they incidentally promote the welfare of others. The will of the Creator runs like an undercurrent beneath the stream of human works, and is not disturbed even when the surface is ruffled. Of course, a man does not become good just because he is used by the Creator for His purposes. Man's relation io God means sin and wrath, and therefore the destruction of his life. Just as the pure man in the primal Creation was put into Creation to have dominion over it, so too man in his impure and broken condition is lord over Creation (Gen. IX.1-7). He is lord over Creation, even though his dominion is now exercised in strife and judgment and against an unhelpful ground which brings forth thistles and thorns, and which therefore forces him to toil by the sweat of his face.[32]

I propose to deal with this dominion which man exercises in

[31] Cf. Gen. XLV.5-8.
[32] See Zimmerli, *I Mose I-XI*, VOL. II, p. 106, and cf. Gen. III.17 ff. God's "change of mind" in Gen. VIII.21 does not reverse His cursing of the ground, though it lessens it. See von Rad, *Das erste Buch Mose*, pp. 100, 113.

conflict and under opposition in two stages. On the one hand we may say that man does not have dominion over Creation, or have it "under his feet." The wrath of God comes against man through the creature, and the ultimate result of wrath is death in one form or another. Man finally breaks down under some external injury which destroys him.[33] This is a sign that he no longer exercises dominion, and does not realise his purpose in Creation.[34] I do not propose at present to take up the problem of man's bondage and constraint in relation to Creation in the present section, but will leave it until later. On the other hand, however, we may also say that in spite of sin man still has dominion over Creation, and has it at his disposal for the purposes of his good or evil deeds. This is to say that man, in comparison with other creatures on earth, exercises a comparative dominion. Even in his relative powerlessness he still has a power over other creatures which they do not have over him. No animal, or tree, or any other creature, for instance, however strong its opposition to man may be, and however it may resist man's attempts to domesticate or train it, uses man in the same sovereign way as man makes use of all that is created. In that part of Creation where nature is "red in tooth and claw," and where life can be maintained only under the threat of death or injury, where hunting and slaughter are inevitable and conflict rages, God has put the fear of man and the dread of man "upon every beast of the earth, and upon every bird of the air, upon everything that creeps on the ground and all the fish of the sea." They are all delivered into man's hand (Gen. ix.2 f.). At the same time God has protected him from violence: "Whoever sheds the blood of man, by man shall his blood be shed: for God made man in His own image" (Gen. ix.6). "For your lifeblood I will surely require a reckoning; of every beast I will require it and of man; of every man's brother I will require the life of man" (Gen. ix.5). Man, therefore, in spite of sin is still lord of Creation. The creature bears no rule over man.[35] It is this particular aspect of our problem, man's dominion and

[33] See the sections above, "Sin and Wrath," and "The Last Day and our Death," Part I, chapter II.
[34] Cf. Dietrich Bonhoeffer, *Schöpfung und Fall*, 3rd edn., Munich 1955, p. 45, Eng. trans. *Creation and Fall*, London 1959, p. 54 f.
[35] See Zimmerli, *I Mose I-XI*, VOL. II, p. 110.

freedom in relation to Creation, that I now propose to take up
for further discussion. Both aspects, however, man's dominion as
well as his bondage, his freedom as well as his constraint, are
to be regarded as belonging to the subject described in the
heading of our present chapter—man in Creation.

The prehistory described in Gen. I-XI deals with the whole of
humanity, and not just with Israel especially. It deals also
with the basic crafts and occupations which maintain all
human society (see, e.g., 1.28, II.15, III.16-19, IV.2, 20 ff., IX.
20). The basic function in all human work is to bring both
inanimate nature and living creatures into man's control, for
only by exercising such a dominion can man continue to live.
A particular occupation is the means of benefiting others as
well as the one who is occupied in it. Although work such as
farming, stock-raising, smithing, building, and so on, occupy
those who are involved in them from dawn to dusk, we do not
normally think of them as belonging to the province of "ethics."
We tend rather to assume that ethics has some other province.[36]
In this respect we are quite different from many of the earlier
writers who took Creation seriously, notably Luther. Luther's
doctrine of vocation had as its central affirmation the assertion
that earthly works such as these, continued in men's daily
occupations, are given by God and are the means of rendering
service to our neighbour. They are, therefore, also the means
of rendering the service which God has also commanded us to
give in Christ. The Incarnation purifies and perfects Creation,
and accentuates the commandment which God has already
given in Creation.

It is remarkable how closely these earthly works are connected with the work of God which is described in the first
article, viz. His Creation of life. Human life (i.e. created life)

[36] The main interest of ethics, at least since the 19th century, has been with a
law or imperative which treats the actions involved in such work as ethically
irrelevant. This has been connected with a concept of autonomy or self-deter-
mination in regard to law which directly contradicts the Biblical concepts of
Creation and Law. More recent theology has criticised this concept of autonomy
on the basis of the Bible, but it has still begun essentially with the *Gospel* and a Law
derived from the Gospel. The work which men do in their occupations is thus still
irrelevant. There can be no place in Christian ethics for the works which all men
do, whether or not they have faith, and whether or not they have heard the Gospel,
if the Gospel is put before the Law.

needs food, and God gives us daily bread when the soil, for instance, yields its harvest. The harvest requires to be gathered by human hands. It has to be cut, milled, and baked. Numerous trades and occupations are involved in bringing bread to the family table. In the same way human life needs clothes to protect it against the cold, and God gives us clothes when the sheep, for instance, gives us its wool. Here, too, numerous other trades and occupations are involved. The wool has to be sheared, carded, spun, woven, and so on, before the garments can be worn.[37] The reapers, millers, spinners, and weavers, do not become good by attending to their own business. Some of them may be the essence of respectability, and others the worst of rogues—but they are doing the things which lead in the end to the victory of life over death, to the preservation of life from death by hunger or cold. This preservation of life is the work of God, who has created it in the womb and keeps it alive by the work of men's hands. It is a work which is turned outwards beyond itself, and which primarily benefits someone other than the doer, and is therefore in some sense a work of service. Whatever may be the case in the present, the main point is that the man who is involved in these occupations enjoys substantial freedom in what he does. He has a certain control over Creation. He deals with matter in a particular way, and in doing so, reveals his dominion over it. Sin has not destroyed man's freedom and dominion, at any rate in this sphere. Although in comparison with men the creatures are pure and uncorrupted, yet unlike men they do not have this freedom to control their environment.

If we understand dominion and freedom in this basic sense, it will be evident that even those who are in bondage to Creation and make idols of it, e.g. the covetous or miserly, still have command over the things of Creation. Man's dominion does not free him from making idols. On the contrary, it forces him in sin to do so. His dominion consists solely in this,

<hr>

[37] These examples are taken from Luther's sermons on vocation, and he in turn takes them from the Biblical passages which deal with God's creation of the world. Cf. W. A., 15, pp. 368.3-369.5 (an exposition of Ps. cxxvii, with illustrations from Genesis), W. A., 17-1, p. 418.1-3 (sermon on Mt. vi.24 ff.). Other examples are ore in a rock or other hidden wealth of the earth. These also are given, but must be sought and shared through human work. It is thus that God's gifts come to men.

that he *can in fact* make idols, and having done so he then bows
down before them as his own work. In Deutero-Isaiah's attack
on the makers of idols, one of the main points stressed by the
writer is man's freedom and power in regard to trees and metal.
To worship bread "baked on its coals," or "roasted flesh," or
to "fall down before a block of wood" (Is. XLIV.19) is monstrous
simply because man is free, and yet bows down to worship it.[38]
It is the same with the miser who worships money, and the
lovers of ceremony who worship glory and honour. They all
submit themselves to man-made products and beg life from
them. Money and honour are marketable products only among
men; before God they have no significance or power. Even
though we may be in bondage to these idols and lack the
distance from them demanded by true freedom and lordship,
we can, however, achieve and enjoy honour and riches, just
as the maker of idols in Deutero-Isaiah was able to manufacture
his idol with skill and artistry. This power, which includes the
demand for freedom from all worship of the creature and for
perfect lordship, still exists in everything that man does. It
disturbs his idolatry, and reminds him that his slavery is unnatural, and that he ought to be lord of Creation.[39] Man does
not possess such freedom without faith in God, and never
possesses it fully before death.

Faith is a growing towards this natural condition which man
will attain only in eternity. Christ is the pure man who in His
own person achieves what Adam was created to become; but
when He does so, He achieves something higher than the
innocence of the primal Creation. He achieves it by being
victorious in the temptation in which Adam was defeated.
And when He forces His way through to victory in His final
temptation, the Cross, He enters into a dominion in which He
is for ever raised above the power of temptation, viz. the
Resurrection and His seat at the right hand of the Father (see
Heb. i-v).[40] This means that Christ is raised above Adam when
He restores what Adam destroyed. Even in his primal purity

[38] See Is. XL.19-24, XLI.6 f., XLIV.9-20, XLVI.6-11.
[39] Cf. Bonhoeffer, *Creation and Fall*, pp. 52 f.
[40] In the same way "Christ being raised from the dead will never die again"
(Rom. VI.9). This was not true of Adam, however, even before the Fall.

Adam was confronted by temptation. Christ, however, is not confronted by temptation, for "when Christ had offered for all time a single sacrifice for sins, He sat down at the right hand of God" (Heb. x.12).[41] He is, therefore, able to give to His own a dominion which is greater than any possessed by man at any time before the Fall.[42] Those who belong to Christ (and not only Christ Himself) will also share, in the resurrection of the dead, in the freedom from falling which Adam even in his purity never had. This is the freedom from the possibility of falling and therefore of death (Rev. xxi.4, xxii.5). What is to be revealed in the resurrection of the dead will not be different from what Adam was destined to attain. The Fall, Adam's defeat and disobedience, had no part in God's decree and purpose from the beginning. Redemptive history deals with the healing of *man*, since it was man, and not the whole of Creation, who violated the will of God. Man must be restored in order that God's Creation may become whole and perfect again, for the injury lies in man, and not in the creature.[43] On the contrary, the rest of Creation groans and awaits the time when man shall finally become pure again, and be able to regain his rightful place in Creation (Rom. viii.19 ff.).

Creation itself is "purer" than man. Sin does not exist on the face of the earth, but in the heart of man. We do not find sin in Creation, as though matter belonged to some "lower" order of Creation than ourselves. Sin is within us. It comes out of us to Creation. Sin is "from within" (Mk. vii.14-23). The Biblical word about salvation refers only to man, and not to the rest of Creation. When the Word became flesh, it became man (Jn. 1.14). When the apostles go out to preach "to the whole Creation," it is to men they preach (Mk. xvi.15); and when death is destroyed, it is men who rise (1 Cor. xv.50-7). This does not mean that Creation itself is evil. On the contrary,

---

[41] In spite of the position of power which He has already gained, Christ has still "to wait until His enemies should be made a stool for His feet" (Heb. x.13). The New Testament is characterised by this note of victory, and frequent references are made in these passages to the dominion, rule, and power to subdue, which were given to the first man, Adam. Cf. Lindeskog, *Studien*, p. 230 f.

[42] Cf. Luther's *Commentary on Genesis*, W. A., 42, 48, pp. 30 f.

[43] Cf. Rom. xiv.14; Tit. 1.15; and Luther's exposition of Ps. ii, W. A., 40-2, p. 203.6-11.

the acts of redemption are continually directed at man, for it was man who fell at the beginning. It is therefore man who lacks purity. The Creation around man is purer than he is, and constitutes no problem in the world which was made by God. What does constitute a problem is man, who lays hold on the things of Creation and corrupts their proper functions by greed, theft, envy, and lust. All of these are consequences of his idolatry. The Creation around man is lower than he is, i.e. he ought to rule over it, rather than be ruled by it, but although it is lower than he is, it is pure. Man is higher than Creation, and this has made his fall the greater. He cannot control his sinfulness. For this reason man discovers in Creation a greater purity and wholeness than exists in himself. This is of great importance in relation to the dominion which man still has, even in a limited way, and in spite of the sin in his heart, over the rest of Creation.[44] It is particularly difficult to state here how man does continue to rule over Creation in spite of his condition, all the more so as his sinfulness is expressed in his idolisation of something in Creation which in itself is good. Man himself in his worship of the creature brings his sinfulness with him, and bows down to the creature which he ought rather to have at his command. Although his attitude of sovereignty over Creation does not absolve him from his sinfulness, we may still speak of a specific form of freedom and dominion over Creation which is undestroyed by human sin.

We can see this freedom and dominion only if we consider his acts in isolation from man. In our discussion of these questions we are usually forced to turn too quickly to the problem of the goodness of the agent of these acts, and in doing so are compelled to make a dichotomy in man himself. We then measure man *coram Deo* by an absolute standard, and find him evil, but measure him *coram hominibus* by a relative standard, and find that he is (at any rate relatively) good. In so far as he is relatively good, he can be used as an instrument of God. This would mean that we were then regarding man as having no connexion at all from his birth either with Creation, or

---

[44] Cf. Løgstrup, *Den etiske fordring*, pp. 124 f., 161 f., 189, 275. If the earthly "order," to use a current term, is impure, this is due to men, either to me personally or to others. Sin is distinctive of men, not of outward circumstances or conditions.

with God's creative power. Man would then be an independent part of Creation, to be judged differently from Creation. When man, even in his sinfulness, "has dominion" over Creation, it is not, properly speaking, man who "has dominion," but God, who in man is continuing to create. Nor would it be man who was being judged, but man's acts, which are then conceived of as lying in the field of force between God and Creation, and which may in themselves be good, even though *coram hominibus* the man who does them is not himself good.[45] When God allows a child to be born by means of a man and woman, the birth of the child is not in any way conditional on any personal goodness possessed either by the man or the woman. Even in adultery and fornication it is God who fashions the foetus, and even though the man and woman hate and quarrel with one another, they are still acting as the servants of God in the acts of conception and parturition.

In the same way stock-raising and farming, which are mentioned in Genesis immediately after the Creation narrative, are life-giving works which continue Creation. Unlike conception and parturition, however, they are brought about by making use of another created thing. They are brought about by man's exercise of dominion over something other than man —over "every plant yielding seed which is upon the face of all the earth," and over "everything that has the breath of life." Man was appointed lord of all these. Man in Creation was commanded by God, first, to "be fruitful and multiply," i.e. to submit to the process of birth, but also to "subdue" the earth (Gen. 1.28). The first of these two commandments passes immediately into the other. Conception and parturition merge into "dominion" and manual toil. All of these have a goodness which has nothing to do with any ethical quality in man, but is present and operates even when man is evil, cruel, and presumptuous, even in Cain's descendants, even in the corruption which existed before the flood. By that very fact it proves that it is a divine goodness which stems from a command of God, and depends wholly upon it. Man himself is not made the object of ethical judgment, but only his works, which are

---

[45] See the section below, "The First Use of the Law," Part II, chapter II.

H

the expressions of his dominion, and ordered by God.[46] The goodness which is inherent in any manual occupation in which men may be involved is of the same kind as the goodness which is inherent in conception and parturition. It is a goodness which is independent of human thought. Yet man is not passive. There is in a measure a correlation between the sex act and the daily toil or occupation in which men are occupied. In the sex act the lover is wholly taken up with orgastic joy. In any manual skill there is a comparable joy experienced in the sensation of technical mastery. There is a sense in which the worker may cleave to his task and find his joy in it. All these human activities take place in the field of force between God and Creation, and may be used by God for some other purpose than man himself has in doing them. The power which activates them is the power of the Creator, and however eagerly men may throw themselves into their performance, they are in fact God's dealings with the world—birth, feeding, finding shelter, etc. Man has freedom in doing them. That man is an instrument for the work of the Creator does not mean that he ceases to have any choice in what he does. Throughout the whole of Genesis men are repeatedly in situations in which they have to choose—to choose themselves wives, for instance—and in such situations they have full freedom of choice. The one thing neither men nor women can do is to withdraw from the given relationship to the other sex which is established by their very manhood and womanhood. The two sexes are always related to one another[47] and must choose what this relationship shall be; but neither can choose in the way that God did when He made male and female and determined the pattern of the sexes.

[46] As soon as men's works are judged in the light of the question, Are they good or evil in the sight of God?, we see that it is man himself who is being judged. God judges Adam (Gen. III), Cain (Gen. IV), and the whole human race (Gen. VI. 5 ff.). But those whom God judged were parents, or performed the tasks which God gave men to do in Creation and in which they exercise "dominion." The fact that they have been judged does not mean that they have ceased to fulfil these functions which God has commanded. But they meet with stronger opposition in those areas in which they ought to have dominion (Gen. III.16-9, IV.12, V.29). Cf. the next section, "Bondage and Constraint."

[47] Cf. Barth, *Die kirchliche Dogmatik*, VOL. III, PT. II, pp. 344-9, VOL. III, PT. IV, pp. 181 f. The two sexes always live in relation to one another. There is no human life above or beyond this necessary relation, any more than there is human life without dominion over nature.

Throughout the whole of Genesis, too, men are continually in situations in which they have to choose, for instance, work to do and places in which to live. Here too they have perfect freedom of choice. Whatever their choice may be, they still live somewhere on earth and still exercise a measure of control over their environment, otherwise they would become a prey to the elements or to the animals. Man can live and move only under and within the decree of God for the human race. But his freedom makes different types of work possible. The pattern of human life is at the one time the same for every man and different for every man. The freedom which all men possess will be expressed in different ways, but the choice which all men have to make is merely a choice of means, and is never one of freedom to create, or of birth, or of beginning. All men can choose *how* they are going to exercise control over a given part of Creation, but none can choose in the way that God did when He created man and determined the uniform pattern of Creation.[48]

Man's freedom is thus freedom to use what God has created. Since what man has at his disposal to use (or abuse) has been given by God, and not created by man himself, man is limited at the same time as he is free. There can be no summer until the winter is ended, no day until the sun has risen, no harvest until the soil has borne fruit. When the Creator bestows all this upon man, He gives him life and also freedom of action. At the same time, however, He determines the limits of man's action. Man can control and "exercise dominion" over what is on the earth only by laying hold of what is already there, and not by creating life by himself. "While the earth remains," God declared after the flood, "seedtime and harvest, cold and heat, summer and winter, day and night, shall not cease" (Gen. viii.22).[49] These are the conditions in which all human life is to be lived. Human toil can succeed only by accepting these changes, by taking what opportunities it may, and by using what God has already created. The freedom which is

[48] To be born means to have received life and to live in relationship to God. Cf. the section above, "The Creator and Life," Part I, chapter I, and the previous section, "The Creation of the World and our Birth," Part I, chapter III.

[49] See also Gen. ix.8-17 on the rainbow as the sign of the covenant between God and "every living creature," and cf. von Rad, *Das erste Buch Mose*, pp. 110 f.

given to man in the rule which he bears over Creation is a freedom which is restricted to the time or occasion proper to his activity—for example, the harvest can be brought in only at the time for harvest, and so on. It is a freedom which man can exercise only within certain confines and limits. God is the God not just of man, but also of the world, and He gives every man his appointed place and time in which to reveal his lordship over Creation. Even so, God still retains the oversight of the world. Men express their dominion over the world in the field of force between God the Creator and the world which He has made, but this does not deprive Him of His own creative freedom. On the contrary it establishes it. In the exercise and expression of his dominion in regard to the world, man is free. He can never create life from himself. He has to be given it. He cannot bring into being, but uses what is already in existence.[50] The Creator uses man's activity in the world as the instrument of His own government of the world.[51]

The imposition of these limits on man is implied in the terms "dominion" or "lordship," which state the nature of man's relation to Creation and show him his proper place within this Creation. Whatever freedom man may have in the exercise of his dominion, he is at the same time a servant of the Creator. The more he exercises his dominion, the more he obeys.[52] This

[50] The frequently recurring expression "times" or "hours" (*Stündelein*) in Luther's doctrine of work is a direct interpretation of certain Old Testament passages, and is also included in his explanation of the terms "have dominion" or "bear rule" in the Creation narrative. The work which men perform in the world from day to day and year to year reveals their absolute freedom to use the things of Creation in the accomplishment of their work, but their freedom is limited to this. It is typical, for example, that Luther can give a broad picture of this freedom, as though there were no obstacles to man's dominion, and yet in the very next moment he can say: "Here a death-blow is struck at man's free will!" Man's freedom to work is restricted to the place to which God has appointed him, viz. the world. He has no freedom of initiative against God, and if he tries to create anything, it becomes a tower of Babel and falls. See W. A., 20, pp. 58.21-59.22 (*Notes on Ecclesiastes*) and W. A., 33, pp. 404.9-412.12 (on Jn. VI-VIII).

[51] Cf. the section below, " 'Government' and Mercy," Part II, chapter I.

[52] Cf. Wilhelm Caspari, "Imago divina," in *Reinhold-Seeberg-Festschrift*, ed. W. Koepp, VOL. I, Leipzig 1929, p. 208. When a monarch or ruler sets up his "image" in a particular place, he exerts his power by means of the "image." He does not exercise this power by himself, but by setting up the image. (Caspari's whole essay offers a great deal of material to illuminate our understanding of Gen. I. 26 ff.).

appears most strikingly in the description of the biggest and technically the most successful enterprise which we find in Genesis, the building of the Ark. This operation saved all living creatures, men and animals, from the flood, which put to death "everything in whose nostrils was the breath of life" (Gen. VII. 22 f.). By it a new and purer beginning was made possible for all flesh. This action, which preserved life, and was simply a continuation of God's creative activity from the beginning against destruction and sin, is a graphic demonstration of man's obedience to God's command (Gen. VI.22, VI.7, etc.). It also revealed man's dominion over Creation and his superiority over the animals. In the story of the flood the animals are powerless, and were saved only by co-operating with a particular human plan. This is the nature of man's dominion. When men exercise their dominion, other lives are saved than their own. The exercise of man's dominion preserves the life which God has created, but even when man does so exercise his dominion, he is not carrying out any plan of his own, but that of the Creator Himself. Man's actions take place in the field of force between God and the world.[53]

Genesis also provides us with examples of how man may use his power over Creation against the will of the Creator, notably in the story of the tower of Babel. When man's purpose is not to serve, but to "make a name for himself" (Gen. XI.4, "Let us make us a name"), his purpose is a worthless one. There is a direct parallel between the self-will which attempted to build the tower of Babel and Adam's disobedience at the tree in the Garden of Eden.[54] In both instances the act of self-will was possible, because man had the power to do what he wanted with Creation. In both, the act of self-will led to destruction: bodily destruction, i.e. death, in the case of Adam, and the downfall of the tower at Babel.[55] Here we also see the restriction which is placed on man's control of Creation. This restriction makes it necessary in describing man's relation to his

---

[53] See especially Zimmerli, *I Mose I-XI*, VOL. II, p. 101.
[54] On the wider context, cf. von Rad, *Das erste Buch Mose*, pp. 127 f.
[55] In regard to the building of the tower of Babel, see Zimmerli, *I Mose I-XI*, VOL. II, pp. 217, 231. The co-operative interest group or collective is quite a different thing from the God-given relation to one's neighbour.

environment to use other terms than simply "dominion" and "freedom." Man's relation to Creation is also characterised by bondage and constraint.

Bondage and Constraint

The transition from the pure and uncorrupted Creation to the Fall is represented in Genesis as one of momentous consequences and change. Man's relation to God is altered, and he has to hide himself from God. His relation to his fellow creatures is also changed. He blames others for his own guilt, and falls a prey to envy, and yields to the temptation of murder. Finally, his relation to the earth itself is altered. Man was created to have dominion over the earth, to rule over it, and to subdue it. Now he is in bondage to the earth. He finds an antagonism in God's Creation, and no longer a bountiful co-operation. He has to labour by the sweat of his face for a scanty livelihood.[56] Finally, in death, he loses the whole of his dominion over the earth, and returns to the ground from which he was taken (Gen. III.19). This return to the earth over which he was appointed to rule is a sign that man's dominion over the earth is now broken.[57] Man now performs the first half of the command which God laid upon him, to be fruitful and to multiply, under the same bitter conditions as he performs the second, to subdue the earth. The sorrow which is multiplied to woman when she brings forth children corresponds to the sorrow multiplied to man when he seeks to sustain the life of the children who are borne to him (Gen. III.16, 17 f.).[58] In their need, neither the man nor the woman is free, or displays true dominion. They fulfil and obey, it is true, the command which God has given to them in Creation, but they do so in constraint and bondage. The woman is driven by desire to her husband: "Your desire shall be for your husband" (Gen. III.16). The man is forced to seek his daily bread: "In the sweat of your face you shall eat bread" (Gen. III.19). This compulsion both for the man and the woman is spontaneous, but is created by God.

[56] Gen. III.16-9, IV.12, etc.
[57] Cf. von Rad, *Das erste Buch Mose*, p. 75 f.
[58] *Op cit.*, p. 75. See also Bonhoeffer, *Creation and Fall*, p. 87 f.

Since the Fall, God's Creation is continued with the help of a compulsion which man is not able to avoid.[59]

We have seen earlier that man in Creation, independently of his sin, and even before the Fall, is limited in his freedom. He is able to choose his relationship to the other sex, but he cannot choose a life which transcends the created and essential relationship between the sexes. This limitation, which refers to the first half of the command which God gave at Creation, refers also to the second half of the command, man's relation to the world around him. He is able to choose his trade or occupation, and to choose the means by which he will express his lordship over Creation, but he cannot withdraw himself from the connexion with the created world which was established at his birth. All choices are choices of means, and not of beginning or birth. No one can choose in the way that God chose when He created the world, and thus established the relationships in which we are involved. Our freedom is a freedom to use what God provides, i.e. to use what we find in the world around us. This freedom is also a limitation, for it is connected with a particular place and environment which is to be "used." This was man's situation in the pure and undestroyed Creation.[60] In the present section, however, our immediate concern is not so much this, as the specific situation of constraint in which man finds himself as a result of sin.[61] This new status of bondage is profoundly illustrated in Genesis in the account of the cursing of the ground, and its "resistance"

[59] What is said in Gen. i-iii is true of all men, whether or not they are Christians. The passage does not add to man's existing knowledge, nor does it initiate faith. Every man is already in the situation described in Gen. i-iii, independently of knowledge or faith. When the early Christian Gospel was preached, it was preached to men of different nations whose situation was precisely that of Gen. i-iii. So when Christ undergoes temptation, crucifixion, and death, and is finally raised, it is because the universal human condition is that described in Gen. i-iii, and because this is an unnatural condition. Perhaps the only thing Gen. iii is telling us is that our life is unnatural, while only Christ's is natural and free. But even in our unnatural condition God continues to create, to use, and to constrain us, with an eye, as it were, on the One "who is to come."

[60] Cf. the section above, " 'Dominion' and Freedom," Part I, chapter III.

[61] Cf. Paul Althaus, *Gebot und Gesetz*, Beiträge zur Förderung der christlichen Theologie, VOL. XLVI, PT. II, Gütersloh 1952, pp. 14 ff. Althaus uses the term "Gebot" to describe the state of the pure, primal Creation, though we have not done so above. The most important thing, however, is that Althaus makes Law and sin correlative concepts.

to man as expressed in the growth of the thorns and thistles, in the sweat of the man, and in the pains of the woman in childbirth. All these are different aspects of a new and additional limitation upon man which did not exist at the beginning. This constraint and bondage is laid upon man when he first sins. The freedom and dominion exercised by man are not, of course, completely broken by his sin. He continues to conceive and beget children, and to exercise a dominion over Creation which no other created being has over him.[62] Nevertheless he performs the command which God has given in Creation in bondage and constraint. It is this aspect of man's bondage in relation to the world which we are now considering in the present section, and which forms part of the general theme dealt with in the present chapter, viz. man in Creation.

We may summarise all that we have to state in this section by saying that man's bondage is a bondage in his external relationships. It is expressed in relation to the world in which he lives, and is a consequence of the primary fact that man's faith in God and his attitude of receptivity have been dislocated. In the chapter entitled "Creation and Judgment," we have already dealt with this dislocation in man's relation to God which has put him in bondage to God. Now we are more particularly concerned with man's bondage and constraint in relation to external Creation. The new situation in which man is held captive is a direct result of the dislocation of his relation to God. It is important that we should follow this order in what we have to say. We shall then be in the position of being able to understand how the "government" of the Law develops in Creation, and impresses itself upon man as a constraining force, because his will is opposed to that of the Creator. The Law is the creative will of God, in so far as it is contravened by man.[63] The world does not cease to belong to God when man falls. It is still the Creator's world, and even yet much takes place in the world which proves that the will of the Creator is opposed to human sin. These events, which as it were block man's evil will, put constraint upon man as long

[62] Cf. Zimmerli, *I Mose I-XI*, vol. ii, pp. 109 f.
[63] Cf. Althaus, *Gebot und Gesetz*, pp. 7-11, 14-21. The reign of the Law ends when the Last Judgment takes place.

as he wills what is evil, and raise a barrier against his evil deeds. This barrier at one time checks the external expression of his evil will, and yet at the same time contains the promise of new Creation and victory in his conscience by the Spirit and the Gospel, and in his body and in the universe by the Resurrection of the dead and the Last Judgment. In our present discussion of the constraint which man experiences in the form of the resistance which he encounters in the world, we have now come very close to the subject with which we shall be dealing in Part II.

In Genesis this opposition to self-willed man appears as the "resistance" of the ground. This resistance of the ground to man is a consequence of his broken relation to God. The ground is cursed and ceases its spontaneous supply of man's food solely because man has fallen into disobedience: "Because you have listened to the voice of your wife, and have eaten of the tree . . . cursed is the ground because of you" (Gen. III. 17).[64] The cursing of the ground extends to man's daily work, and makes it different from what it would have been if the ground had never been cursed. It makes man's work harder, less productive of results. Above all it exhausts his powers, and indeed even kills him: "In the sweat of your face you shall eat bread, till you return to the ground, for out of it you were taken" (Gen. III.19).[65] The same resistance from the ground is to be seen again in the account of the second "Fall" in Cain's murder of Abel (Gen. IV.1-16): "When you till the ground, it shall no longer yield to you its strength" (Gen. IV.12).[66] Sooner or later all men fall before the onslaught of illness, accident, or simply the failure of their natural powers. In each case death witnesses to the punishment inherited by humanity, and the failure of their dominion over Creation. It is a sign that God's original purpose for man has not been accomplished in his life. The resistance which man encounters springs from the very source over which, were he to fulfil the command

[64] Cf. Rom. VIII.20. In the New Testament the hope that the curse may be lifted is hope in the return of Christ.

[65] Cf. von Rad, *Das erste Buch Mose*, pp. 81 ff. Work is thought of as a burden.

[66] Cf. Gen. V.29. On God's "change of mind" in Gen. VIII.21, see von Rad, *Das erste Buch Mose*, pp. 100, 113. The primal cursing of the ground is not thereby abolished.

given by God in Creation, he should properly rule and exercise dominion. When man sins his unnatural condition is seen not only in his immediate relation to God (if we can separate this relation from his relation to his neighbour and the world around him), but even more obviously, and indeed glaringly, in his relation to his God-created environment. Here too it is seen as an unnatural *bondage*—as the failure of his dominion, and his submission to the external forces which press upon him.[67]

After the flood, according to Genesis, man is in a new situation. God, as it were, accepts the ineradicable nature of sin (Gen. VIII.21), and allows Creation to continue in its condition of strife and killing (Gen. IX.1-17). All creatures are now delivered into man's hand, i.e. man is now for the first time permitted to slaughter them (Gen. IX.2). His rule over the lower Creation is now based on their fear of him (Gen. IX.2). A warning is also given: "Whoever sheds the blood of man, by man shall his blood be shed." It is man himself who is charged with the responsibility of executing this judgment, for it is man who is given the commission to punish the shedder of blood.[68] This was the basis of the Reformed doctrine of "earthly government," as a power entrusted by God to man for the purpose of preventing violence and ensuring peace. This power was not entrusted to Israel, but to the whole human race, to all those who survived the flood. Therefore it exists among all who live on the earth as a God-given means to peace.

This new situation, in which the power of sin is a given part of man's condition (Gen. VIII.21), and in which the possession and use of force as a means of securing peace is also given to man (Gen. IX.6), does not mean that the primal Creation is totally destroyed. God's command in Creation is repeated (Gen. IX.1, 7). In spite of the cursing of the ground and the universal fear of man by "every beast of the earth," man still possesses a dominion over the other creatures which they do not have over him. Nevertheless man lives in a world in which

---

[67] Cf. Bonhoeffer, *Creation and Fall*, pp. 54 f.

[68] Cf. Mt. XXVI.52 and the other important passage which deals with the "sword," Rom. XIII.4.

his unnatural condition is only too apparent, and in which God has given him the commission of preventing the unnatural conditions of murder and sin. Man's possession of power given to him by God to prevent murder is at one time an expression of his special position in Creation, and also a witness to his depravity. The "earthly government," which God has established in the world, did not exist in the pure Creation, but is a government of conflict, and exists only because of sin and hostility.[69] It is of the nature of the conflict of the earthly government with sin that it cannot eradicate sin, but can simply block its progress and prevent its outward occurrence. When, therefore, the administration of civil justice succeeds in repelling injustice, we have a foretaste of God's final destruction of His enemy in the eschatological period.[70] After the Last Judgment the power of the Law will cease, and no longer have any function to fulfil.

In the situation which came about after the flood the nature of the relation between men in society necessitated the possession and use of force. When men begin to devise mischief, they come in conflict not only with the resistance of the ground, but also with the God-appointed resistance of their fellow men. We must notice here that God's appointment of force in human society means that men feel the pressure of this constraint from two directions. In the first place there is the constraint of human justice as and when this is administered against them. In the second place, they themselves are forced to administer justice against others, for God appoints certain men to mete out punishment on His behalf. This double constraint affects all human society without exception, and Genesis states that it does so in accordance with the will of God.[71] In the early Church the statements in Genesis on the state of

[69] See Zimmerli, *I Mose I-XI*, pp. 131-6.
[70] Cf. *op. cit.*, pp. 113 f.
[71] What is said of the covenant with Noah in Gen. ix applies to the whole of mankind, as we see explicitly stated in the account of the rainbow as the sign of the covenant: "It shall be a sign of the covenant between me and the earth" (Gen. ix.13); "This is the sign of the covenant which I have established between me and all flesh that is upon the earth" (ix.17). The covenant with Noah is not a covenant between God and Israel. The particular history of the Chosen People has not yet begun. The prehistory in Genesis says something about all mankind. The rainbow is the sign of the covenant between God and all men.

affairs which existed after the flood were interpreted to mean
that the fear of men (i.e. the administrators of civil justice)
produced at least an external righteousness after man's direct
relationship to God had been destroyed in the Fall. This
doctrine is thus no innovation made by the Reformers, but
had been formulated in a non-Christian environment by the
Church as early as the second century as an interpretation of
the function of the pagan authorities (it had also appeared in
Paul, Rom. XIII).[72] This basic order is to be found among all
peoples, for without it life is impossible. The Creator continues
His work of creating and sustaining even in the midst of man's
bondage.

The fact that this bondage cannot be finally destroyed is
due to man's false worship of the creature (Rom. 1.25-32), and
his lack of trust in the God who creates. Man could be lord
of Creation if he did not worship the creature, but his idolatry
is such that to worship the creature means to submit to the
creature. Man, therefore, is unable to stand over it and subdue
it, and so re-establish the *distance* between man and the rest
of Creation which is the expression of his lordship. Even though
man is aware of his unnatural condition, he is incapable of
escaping from it. He is conditioned by a compelling instinct
for self-preservation and looks to the creature for his support
and security, thereby making an idol out of it. Here we see
an illustration of man's God-given nature, for he was created
to *receive*—but to receive from the Creator.[73] Since in the Fall
he has broken his relation of trust in God, he now discovers
God's wrath, rather than His mercy. In his idolatry man clings
for his security to something in Creation that is intrinsically
good, for it has been created by God, but he clings to it as
though it itself had power to create. Thus his estrangement
from God grows wider (for he has put idols in the place of
God). So does his estrangement from his neighbour (for he
cannot give freely to others as long as he clings to that which
is created), and from the earth (for he cannot rule over the
earth as he ought to by nature, as long as he bows down to

[72] See, e.g. Irenaeus, *A.h.*, v.xxiv (Stier. ibid.) and the section below, " 'Idealism,' " Part II, chapter II.
[73] Cf. Vajta, *Theologie*, pp. 6 ff.

worship it). Man's alienation from God, his neighbour, and
the world around him, does not mean that he has no longer
anything to do with the world which God has made. On the
contrary, he continues to live in the world, and the things of
Creation around him are purer than he is himself. God continues to create and to show His handiwork all around man.
When man opposes the will of God, God's will becomes hardened into opposition to man, and stands in the way of his
self-will. The means which God has appointed to check man's
sinfulness, as described in Genesis, operate on earth in accordance with the decree of God. But this decree was made only
after the Fall. In the New Testament the disappearance of
this divine opposition is an inseparable part of the hope which
looks forward to the eschatological future, in which evil will
no longer be a reality.[74]

One of these "enemies," which according to the New Testament will in the end be deprived of their power, is death, "the
last enemy," to which even Christ Himself submitted (1 Cor. xv
26). Death is one of the forces which oppose man, and came
into the world through man's sin (Rom. v.12). In stating this
truth, the New Testament is pointing back to the story of
Adam in Gen. ii and iii. It is pointing to the primal act of
disobedience which has since affected all men everywhere, but
which is reversed in all who hear and accept the Gospel of
Christ, to whatever race or culture they may belong. In death,
the earth, over which man ought to rule, receives him back
to itself when his power fails and he "returns" (Gen. iii.19).
There is thus a double interconnexion between sin and death:
the power of death depends on sin, but the power of sin also
depends on death. The necessity of self-preservation which
forces man to seek idols, springs from the threat of death, and
from man's fear of the threat of death (cf. Heb. ii.15).[75]

[74] Rom. viii.19 ff.; 1 Cor. xv.24-8.
[75] Cf. Michel, *Der Brief an die Hebräer*, pp. 85 f. We must remember that death
is unnatural, because it was not a part of man's condition at the beginning. Man
alone of all Creation is aware of death as a threat. The references in the New
Testament to the hostile "powers" which are destroyed by Christ's Resurrection
become comprehensible when understood from this point of view. For Christ is
man, and when He defeats death *man* is rescued from the "powers" whose whole
power consisted in their subjugation of man. When one man finally lives according

Death is used by God against fallen man.[76] It has a part in
the "government" which God has established for the purpose
of procuring at least external righteousness on earth. The
power of avenging murder, entrusted by God to man in the
covenant which He established with Noah after the flood,
means that death can in fact serve God's purposes, in so far
as it acts as a check on evil (Gen. ix.6). The forces which have
been called into being as a result of man's sin—the opposition
of the ground which ends in man's death (iii.17-19), and the
human courts of justice which employ force and even death
against man's infraction of the law (ix.6)—do not put man
outside any relationship to God. On the contrary, even when
he encounters these forces man is dealing with the work of
God, for this is God's world, and these are the manifestations
of His wrath. God's wrath is directed against evil, and in this
sense promotes life. It is a manifestation of severity, it is true,
but it is intended by God as a means of allowing life to
continue.[77]

Since human society as we know it is characterised by
idolatry, any Christian ethic which identifies the demand made
by the Law with the demands which are made by a collectivist
group, is in obvious danger of concealing human self-assertion
and endeavour under a kind of "divine ethic." The demand
which God makes is expressed in relation to one's *neighbour*.
This relation, however, may well be spoiled or corrupted by

to God's decree in Creation—*lives*, and does not die—the power of the enemy is
broken. If, on the other hand, we regard death as natural, we shall not understand
how the proclamation that Christ rose from the dead can be the good news of
salvation for the whole world. The account of the Creation of Adam and his
disobedience forms the background of the New Testament Gospel.

[76] God uses one of His enemies, death, in order to defeat sin, another of His
enemies. The problem in the second use of the Law is the putting to death of the
old man. This is where Baptism comes in.

[77] Cf. Zimmerli, *I Mose I-XI*, VOL. II, p. 132; von Rad, *Das erste Buch Mose*, p.
110. These passages from Gen. 1 form the Biblical basis of the later doctrines of
earthly government. Because of the tendency of modern theology to work with the
New Testament rather than with the Bible as a whole, these Old Testament
passages are seldom discussed. If, however, we make them the basis of our discussion, there can never be any problem about the universal application of the
Law and earthly government. The prehistory of Gen. 1-xi is descriptive of mankind. The experiences of one particular nation, Israel, shed light on the condition
of the whole of mankind.

the action of a collective group, whether it be an interest group, an arbitrary State, or even a bad family. There are vast numbers of collective or group influences such as these which are able to determine the course of action or habitual choice which I as a person make. There is, however, no normative pattern of human conduct which is unaffected by the demand of love for one's neighbour. The collective group is always in danger of becoming a macrocosm of individual egoisms, and at the same time of becoming just a "friendly society." Then it will become little more than a collective egoism which attempts to conceal its true character in a self-interested caring for other members of the group. Any position can thus be mis-used—father, mother, worker, politician, priest, and so on—but we must continually stress that if any of these positions are abused, it is something *good* which is being abused. We shall shall not be able to deal with these problems unless and until we revive the Biblical doctrine of *vocation*, i.e. a doctrine of human work and occupation understood in the light of man's actual situation of conflict, in which the categories of abuse as well as use will be useful to us. Protestant ethics has either shown a relative indifference to existing social structures, or has accepted them too uncritically. It has less frequently com-bined a positive interest in man's position in the world with a comprehensive criticism of the development of the power of collective groups. In attempting to formulate a truly Biblical doctrine of man in Creation, we shall find our best starting-point in the positive statement that Creation around man is purer than man is himself. The negative side of this statement is that man by his worship of the creature is continually perverting his very administration of that which is created by imposing false patterns upon it. We must maintain both the positive and negative sides of this statement if we are to avoid falling into a rigid theology of orders.[78] Bondage and

[78] The main question is always whether or not the Gospel should criticise the existing order. We shall return to this question in the section below, "Preaching and the Law," in Part II, chapter III, and more particularly in my projected work on Gospel and Church where I shall deal with the subject in greater detail. In criticism of Friedrich Gogarten's *Politische Ethik*, Jena 1932, we can say that in his analysis of the state (e.g. pp. 62, 117, etc.) he develops man's "bondage" (*Hörigkeit*) without emphasising the recreative function of the Gospel even on the

constraint afflict man outwardly in accordance with the will of God, but cannot be identified with any coercive force of the State to the exclusion of criticism of such force. Nor can they be identified with bondage to a particular collective group which is in conflict with other collective groups.

Now that we have reached the end of the present chapter, it may be appropriate to make certain general statements in regard to the prehistory of mankind of which we read in Genesis, and to which we have referred several times in the foregoing sections. It is true to say that the first chapters of Genesis are late literary products which represent the experiences of Israel. In its early chapters Genesis represents the universalisation of the experiences of Israel in its limited history, i.e. the expansion of particular historical experiences into the universals of Creation, the Fall, and the other parts of man's prehistory. The God of Israel was also the Ruler of the world, and must therefore, the writer concluded, have dealt with the whole of humanity in the way described in these narratives. In its essential features, its freedom as well as its bondage, all human life has been created and determined by the God whom Israel worshipped.[79] At the same time, of course, this means that human life in its full extent is to be interpreted in the light of God's dealings with Israel. It is important to note that what Genesis is interpreting is in fact the situation of *man*, and not just of Israel. It is incorrect to state, if we are being faithful to the Biblical texts, that the Bible does not offer us any basis on which to make statements about man in general. On the contrary there is a great deal in the Bible which tells us about man, and it is no accident that this was put in the first few pages of the Bible. Nor is it accidental that both the Apostles'

level of works. Since Gogarten's position is based on a particular interpretation of Luther, it should be pointed out that Luther does in fact recognise an earthly government, but he is also aware that the Gospel calls on men to display "new works" in regard to their neighbour, and that these works are the direct product of the Gospel when it has been accepted. Luther thus rejects the simple alternative of "Law or Gospel" or "Gospel and Law" in favour of a slightly different metaphor. See Ivarsson, *Predikans uppgift*, pp. 69-163, where these problems are discussed in the light of passages from Luther which are seldom quoted.

[79] See C. H. Dodd, *The Bible Today*, Cambridge 1948, p. 113.

Creed and the Nicene Creed speak of Creation as the first
act of God which precedes everything else that God does for
man.

It is important, moreover, to notice that human life as
represented and interpreted in the early chapters of Genesis
is not different from all human life, in all peoples, cultures,
and at all times. What we find there expressed are the human
circumstances of conception and birth, love, work, and death.
These primary realities are established by God, and are the
spheres of activity of His love and His wrath. One of the fundamental errors in certain systems of natural theology is their
"religious" character. This is revealed in their assumption
that there is a "religiosity" in natural man which has to be
sought out, as if human life itself bore no relation to God,
and the history of religion were a kind of preparation for the
birth at Bethlehem and the cross at Golgotha. All this is alien
to the Bible itself, which mentions the names of certain tribal
gods only in passing, and never does so in order to show a
point of contact but always to point to an error.[80] The only
conceivable "preparation" for Christ's birth and death is the
primary fact of human birth and death. Birth and death have
a particular meaning, and point to the receiving of life and
judgment from the hand of the Creator.

When the Gospel of Christ's birth, life, death, and resurrection is preached, it is always preached to men who have
behind them the story which is recounted in Gen. I-III. Creation
is repeated in every birth, the Fall in the egocentric attempt
made by every man to guarantee his own safety. The condemnation of the Law is felt by all men in the bondage and
constraint in which they are imprisoned. When the Gospel is
preached to men, it leaves it to them to interpret their life in
this light, and to say with the penitent, "I am God's lost
Creation: I believe—help Thou mine unbelief!" It is left to man
himself to make this interpretation. He may refuse to acknowledge that his life is given and wasted. The Gospel then has

---

[80] Even Acts XVII.23 is no exception to this. In his Areopagus speech Paul
follows the usual pattern of missionary preaching in describing God as Creator,
and treats the idolatry of the Gentiles as something from which there is now the
possibility of conversion. See Gärtner, *The Areopagus Speech*, pp. 236 f.

I

nothing to say to him. There is a unity between man's prehistory and the Gospel, and when man accepts the Gospel he always accepts this prehistory. Or, to put it in a different way, the assent of faith to the second article is dependent on assent to the first article.[81]

[81] See the section above, "The Trinitarian Creed," in Part I, chapter I. The Creed and the Bible both follow the order of redemptive history in their structure, as would any account of God's saving works or hymn of praise.

PART II

LAW

CHAPTER I

THE CREATOR AND THE LAW

The Old and New Testaments

In taking up the discussion of the relation between the two Testaments, it is not our intention to deal with the problem in general and from every conceivable aspect. We have limited ourselves to that aspect defined in the title of the present work—Creation and the Law. In our treatment of Creation and the Fall we have already discussed the threatening and constraining aspect of God's will as this affects all men on earth after the Fall. We must now relate our conclusions to the Old and New Testaments as the two parts of the Biblical writings. In doing so we shall direct our attention to the discussion of Creation and the Law in modern theology, in particular in that of the Barthian school. In Swedish theology, it is Einar Billing who will merit our particular attention.[1]

It cannot be said that modern theology has reached a well thought out view of the Old Testament Law. On the one hand those commandments which occupy a dominant place in the Old Testament Law, such as the Sabbath law, the prohibition of images, etc., are here misinterpreted to a greater or lesser degree. At the same time, however, many forms of modern theology assert that the sequence of events between the election of Israel and the giving of the Law are of vital importance from the systematic aspect, and therefore it is demanded that the modern theological concept of "Law" should be faithful to the Old Testament. But in particular, modern theology is not clear why in actual fact the institution of the Law in the

[1] Billing's reinterpretation of the idea of vocation is really a piece of Old Testament theology, with the Exodus from Egypt, i.e. the forgiveness of sins, coming first. Each individual interprets his own history prophetically in the same way as the prophets interpreted the history of Israel. See Billing, *Vår kallelse*, pp. 37 f.

Old Testament is rejected today. By and large modern theology does reject the Law, although its rejection is concealed in the fact that it picks certain laws almost haphazardly from the Old Testament, because they suit its case, but without any real reason for the choice.

Earlier theology, on the other hand (and here again we see the integral connexion between the early Church and the Reformation), had a quite clear answer to these questions, and knew why the Old Testament Law was to be regarded as obsolete after Christ had completed His work of redemption. But it was also able to assess what was the positive value of certain Old Testament commandments. This was *their correspondence to the natural law*.[2] If we reject the concept of a natural law, then the Law of the Old Testament becomes an insoluble problem. The problem of the multitude of Old Testament regulations can be simplified only by starting with the concept of an unrecognised demand which is operative in human life itself and experienced by all men. It is no solution of the problem to begin, as sometimes happens, by asserting that all the relevant statements about the Law are to be found only in the New Testament, and then proceed to tag on an essentially meaningless "Old Testament" to what is then assumed to be the authoritative New Testament writings. We must read the Bible from the beginning to the end, and in that order, just as we must take the Creed from the first article to the end, and in that same order.

This means that the primary fact is the divine self-giving in Creation. Thus far the goodness of the Gospel precedes the Law. But this also means that the opposition of sin to God is a universal condition which in all human life comes into conflict with the will of God in Creation. Thus far the Law is universally relevant. This means, further, that Israel was elected by God against the background of the total depravity of the whole human race, and that in this election, long before the Law was given to Israel (Gal. III.8-18), the promise of salvation,

---

[2] Cf. Olsson, *Luthers socialetik*, vol. I, pp. 32-5, and as regards the early Church see Irenaeus, *A.h.*, IV. xxii-v (Stier. IV. xii-xv. 1). Irenaeus sees the Decalogue as an expression of the natural Law which is written in the heart and not primarily in the Bible.

viz. the content of the Gospel, was already given (Gen. xii.3). Abraham was chosen in order that in him all peoples should be blessed, and the extension of this blessing to include "all nations" comes also in the world mission of early Christianity, when God's acts within the narrow frame of the people of Israel were accomplished through the death and resurrection of Jesus.[3]

If the election of Israel represents the same will to give and to redeem as the divine act in Creation and the Incarnation, the Law of Israel is a concrete form of the will of God to constrain and to judge. This finds expression in what we have called the "unrecognised demand" experienced in all human life, which in Israel "consigned all things to sin," in expectation of the Gospel of Christ (Rom. iii.19 ff.; Gal. iii.22 ff.).

We are unable to define the many relationships involved in judgment and grace by using either of the two formulae "Gospel and Law," or "Law and Gospel," alone. To express the complete relation we require a more detailed and diversified description. The simple expression "Law and Gospel" may often be interpreted as little more than the conjunction of certain prescribed "ordinances" ("the Law") and the *kerygma* ("the Gospel"). Creation is then assigned to some past time, and the ordinances regarded as a surviving product of the past act of Creation.[4] In such a case, however, we lose all idea of God's continuing Creation and reforming of the world. And since we have completely lost the "dynamic aspect" of Creation, we also lose *the* dynamic aspect which is the transformation by the Gospel of human life in the attitude to one's neighbour. The Gospel proclamation of Christ as the gift of God involves also the proclamation of Christ as the example of men, and of "new works."[5] Now if we isolate this latter aspect, and derive the commandments exclusively from the Gospel, we may invert the formula and use the phrase "Gospel and Law." But here again we have destroyed all connexion with the Bible, for in this case we have not only lost the idea of God's Creation

---

[3] See Cullmann, *Christ and Time*, p. 118. See too Billing's profound analysis of "election" and "covenant" in *De etiska tankarna*, pp. 134-58, 351 ff.

[4] See Prenter, *Skabelse og genløsning*, pp. 211 f.

[5] See Ivarsson, *Predikans uppgift*, pp. 113-33.

continuing outside the proclamation of the Gospel, but also
all possibility of speaking about a "natural law" given by God,
and of God's sustaining and governing of the world by the
demand of the Law for good works. The Gospel in consequence
is given a legalistic twist, and made the source even of political
order.[6] There is an already existing unity in our Bible which
holds together Creation, the Fall and the revelation of God's
will to the whole world at the beginning, the election of Israel
and the subsequent giving of the Law, the Gospel of Christ,
and the eschatological expectation of the epistles. This internal
unity prevents us from treating the Bible as a source-book of
theological catchwords or dogmatic formulae.[7]

It has been possible, however, for certain interpreters to use
the exegesis of the Old Testament in support of one of these
catchwords, viz. "Gospel and Law." Interest in the origin of
Israel's belief in God makes it natural to stress the significance
in Old Testament exegesis of the idea of election, which is the
obligation laid upon Israel as a consequence of God's saving
work among His people.[8] But this focusing of attention on the
development of a particular ethic as exhibited especially by
Israel means that we are concentrating on something which
from one point of view is alien to Israel, and shifting attention
from Jahveh to a people who were characterised by their belief
in Jahveh. In addition, there is also the fact that the prehistory
of Gen. I-XI, which deals with the whole of humanity and not
particularly with Israel, is a late literary product, which was
conceived on the basis of Israel's own experiences.[9] The combination of these observations of literary criticism and the
obvious interest in the origin of different religions, which is
typical of the whole of our culture, has succeeded in eradicating
the question of the significance of the text of the Old Testament in its present sequence—Creation first, then the Fall,

---

[6] Cf. Barth, *Christengemeinde und Bürgergemeinde*, p. 24, and also *Rechtfertigung und
Recht*, pp. 32-40.

[7] See here also Edmund Schlink, "Gesetz und Paraklese," in *Antwort*, Zollikon-
Zürich 1956, pp. 323-35.

[8] Cf., e.g., Søe, *Kristelig etik*, pp. 60 f.

[9] Dodd, *The Bible Today*, pp. 112 f.: "The story of the Creation in the first
chapter of Genesis is . . . subsequent to the work of the great prophets, and it arises
out of it."

and then the history of Israel. This order is significant, and indicates a universal emphasis in the history of Israel. And this stress on all people of the world is later to be seen clearly in the latter part of the Bible—the New Testament—in which the dimensions of prehistory are recovered (cf. Acts xiv.16, xvii.26; Mt. xxiv.14, xxviii.19; Rom. xvi.26). It is once again "all the nations" who are involved, and to whom the Gospel is to be preached. But these nations to whom the Gospel is to be preached are, like all the nations of the prehistorical period, at one time both the creation of God and the enemies of God. When the tower of Babel had been destroyed, all the nations lost the capacity to understand one another. But when the Spirit was poured out at Pentecost they all heard the preaching of the Gospel in their own tongues, and were conscious of their unity in listening to this preaching (cf. Gen. xi. 7 ff., and Acts ii.5-12).[10] But this is still only the beginning. Soon there will come the gathering of all the nations before the throne of Christ (Mt. xxv.32) and the united song of all peoples and tongues (Rev. vii.9).

When the Gospel is preached today, the same situation exists as when it was first preached. Everyone who hears the Gospel is at the one time both created and fallen. We all belong to the humanity whose origin and fall is described in Gen. i-iii, and whose salvation is intended when the New Testament *kerygma* is proclaimed.[11] The unity of the Bible is to be found only in the fact that it is *now* being preached. The one who hears the Gospel holds together in his own person the first and last sections of the Bible, for it is *his* history which is narrated on the first pages of the Bible, and *his* future which is described on the last pages. He is the one addressed in the proclamation of the Gospel, which is the voice of God speaking to *him*. The Old Testament depicts a humanity which, represented by the peculiar people who were chosen by God for the salvation of all, can merely await the outpouring of the Spirit. And *we* are this humanity. It is to us that the Spirit comes now by the Gospel. It is also from this perspective that the complicated

---

[10] On the connexion between Acts ii and Gen. xi see also Zimmerli, *I Mose I-XI*, vol. ii, pp. 232 ff.

[11] Cf. Odeberg, *Skriftens studium, inspiration och auktoritet*, p. 26.

commandments of the Old Testament are to be seen in their
true meaning. Fundamentally this confusion of detail in the
Old Testament commandments is the confusion of the demands
about us which call for our obedience, without being able to
purify us. These demands, however, bind us inflexibly to the
Creator, who has the future in His hand and who is able to
use even death and apparently meaningless fear in His service,
purifying, and putting to death, in order to raise from the
dead.[12] Man's continuing refractoriness belongs to the situation
of the Law. The content of this Law is marked by the fact that
it acts as a continual rein on evil. Death is an integral part of
the work of the Law, in which death retains its hostile sound.
When God destroys, He is doing something that is really
contrary to His will. The content of the Law cannot therefore
be derived from the Gospel, which by its very nature is always
opposed to Law and judgment, just as Christ's Resurrection
reverses His death.[13] But just as the way to the Resurrection
lay inevitably through Golgotha, so the way to the purity which
is given in the promise of the Gospel passes inevitably through
our death to sin. And this death becomes "good" in reference
to the life which is thereby given. The goodness of God's
"wrath," and therefore the goodness of the Law, can be understood only when we finally attain *life* in the vision which will
be given in heaven.

The unity of the Bible thus consists in the fact that from
beginning to end it is the same God who is at work. The act
of Creation does not end, but continues, and has both the Law
and the Gospel in its service. Both the pedagogical work of the
Law and the regenerating work of the Gospel aim at realising
God's decree for Creation, and making man into the "image
of God," i.e. making him like Christ, who is the "image
of God." Involved in this are our death and resurrection,

---

[12] When Irenaeus speaks of the Law as having been given to "slaves," and as
being adapted to them, he means that the Law has a divine function to fulfil in
mortifying man's refractoriness, but also that the Law can be criticised from the
point of view of the "natural laws," which are the same as the commandments
of Jesus, and which are given to "free" men. See *A.h.*, IV. xxiv (Stier. IV. xiii). The
same thought occurs in Luther when he speaks of love as "supreme over all laws."

[13] We find this even in Barth, *Evangelium und Gesetz*, pp. 27 f., though the derivative attitude and cognitive aspect of Barth's writings are predominant.

viz. our submission to Baptism.[14] The difficulty of understanding the Bible lies in the fact that we are now immediately involved in the work which the Bible is accomplishing
in us. We are neither in the purity of the primal Creation nor
that of the Resurrection. Because, therefore, we are intimately
concerned in the events described in the Bible, and therefore
unable to see them in their true perspective, we must have
recourse to faith on the basis of a preached word. There are
no limits to the use which God in His power can make of
unexpected and even recalcitrant means in order to serve life—
"a messenger of Satan to harass me" (II Cor. XII.7-10), expulsion from the fellowship of the congregation (I Cor. v.4 f.).
or the tyrant's murder of the only pure One (Acts IV.27 f.).
We must bear this full extent of God's power in mind when
we come to ask how the events of Israel's history were able to
serve and prepare the way for the Gospel of Christ. We must
also bear it in mind when we seek into God's works in our own
life. Otherwise we are wilfully restricting the work of God to
the few poor demonstrations of piety which we evidence, and
in which we usually find no God at all.

If we ask what were the specific demands that were laid upon
Israel, the answer must be the primary demand and the first
of all the commandments, to have no other God than Jahveh,
to trust in no other, and not to make any image (Ex. XX.1 ff.;
Deut. v.6 ff.). In these commandments Israel was bound to
the invisible God, and at the same time set free from all
worship of the creature. Even isolated cultic commandments
and purity regulations become significant when regarded from
this perspective as the means of protecting and safeguarding
Israel, and preventing its turning to alien cults. Beneath all this
was the assurance that Israel was worshipping in its image-free
acts of worship the one Creator, who also rules the other nations,
and is Lord of Pharoah, and therefore powerful to save from
Egypt, Lord of Assyria, and Lord of the kings of Persia (Is. x.
5-12, XLI.2 ff.). God's lordship of history stems from the fact

---

[14] Cf. Gen. 1.26; Col. 1.15; Rom. VIII.29; II Cor. IV.8-14; Rom. VI.3 ff. We
may also include here I Cor. v.5 and also II Cor. XII.7-10. Both these passages
deal with the continuing struggle against sin, but with resurrection and life in
view.

that He is the One Creator God (Is. XLI.4 and *passim*). The
direct consequence of this as far as Israel and man is concerned
is that all idolatry is to be shunned (Is. XL-XLVI).[15] The concentration on a single righteousness and mercy towards one's
fellow men which we find reappearing both in the proclamation
of doom in the prophets and in the institution of the Law in
Israel, stems from the same reality, viz. the fact that God is
the God of the world and of all men. The commandment about
the "stranger" as deserving of care and protection was framed
with reference to Israel's life in Egypt (Ex. XXIII.9), and the
demands made by the prophets often stem from the same
source.[16] But Israel's deliverance out of Egypt is not the only
work on which right and righteousness in regard to one's
neighbour can be justified. God's creation of all men is the
primary ground of universal righteousness. If anyone violates
the rights of another, he will stand mute when God appears to
call him to account: "Did not He who made me in the womb
make him? And did not one fashion us in the womb?" (Job
XXXI.13ff.).

Earlier in our analysis of the account of Creation and Rom.
1.18-32, we have maintained on several occasions and in different contexts that faith in God, dominion over Creation (i.e.
freedom from worship of the creature), and service of one's
neighbour are not disconnected concepts, but integrally related.
No one of them can be realised independently of the others.
Together they constitute a single reality, seen from three
aspects. If their unity is broken at any one point, it is broken
at all three points. No one part can be realised unless all three
are realised. *But the relation to God is the source and starting-point
of all three.* This is so in Gen. I-III, where the whole of Creation
is dislocated and disobedience to God begins, as well as in the
New Testament where faith is the source of man's healing.
The Old Testament has no essentially different view. The
demand for faith and trust in Jahveh, denial of all idols, and
righteousness and mercy towards one's neighbour, is central.
It is a critical factor in regard to the many detailed regulations,
as we see especially in the preaching of the prophets. In this

---

[15] See also, e.g., Ps. XCVI.5.
[16] Cf. Billing, *De etiska tankarna*, pp. 104 f., 130.

the prophets refuse to admit that sin is to be found only outside Israel. On the contrary, Israel herself is corrupt at heart. From one point of view this is the essential thing in the history of Israel. The prophets point to the fact that it is Israel which is being disciplined, Israel which will perish. This is the prophetic message—the nation is progressing steadily towards catastrophe, and Jahveh (who is the God of Israel) moves as steadily towards victory and the accomplishment of His will.[17] Such a view as this is possible only when "the first article," as it comes to be called later, viz. faith in God as the Creator of heaven and earth, underlies our relation to God.[18] To persevere to the end of the journey which ends in death without making any graven images is to be in Gethsemane, to receive the cup of death in the assurance that in this God's will is done for the world. From here there spring Resurrection, world mission, the raising up of apostles in every corner of the world, and the eager expectation of the gathering of all nations before the throne of God. From the beginning the world was included within this design, even though it was not affected by it.

The primary demand upon Israel to let God be God led to the dissolution of Israel. This was accomplished when Christ, the only righteous One and the last of the Remnant, was crucified. The old idea that the Law was fulfilled in the death of Christ is an unspecified element in the doctrine of the Atonement which we shall discuss in my projected work on Gospel and Church.[19] Christ was "made sin" for us (II Cor. v.21) and thus there was a possibility of conflict between His will and God's when He set "my will" against "Thy will" in Gethsemane, but did so only to stress that "what I will" and obey is death through "Baptism" (Lk. XII.50). We are all baptised into

[17] Cf. Hartmut Schmökel, *Jahwe und die Fremdvölker*, Breslauer Studien zur Theologie und Religionsgeschichte VOL. I, Breslau 1934, pp. 67 f., 109 f., and A. Causse, *Israël et la vision de l'humanité*, Etudes d'histoire et de la philosophie religieuses VOL. VIII, Strasbourg and Paris 1924, pp. 38-58.
[18] The belief in Israel in God as the God of the whole world is older than the account of Creation as a literary product. See Eichrodt, *Theologie des Alten Testaments*, VOL. II, pp. 47-57. Eichrodt argues that Israel's belief in Creation must be "very primitive," since it could be traced in every aspect of Israel's thought, and constituted the main difference between the Israelite view of God and the world and that of its surrounding tribes.
[19] Here we shall be able to return to this subject in fuller detail.

Christ's Baptism. This constitutes the Church. But when
death comes upon us, in spite of our having been baptised,
and we are left on the earth because we are still in Adam's
body, this also means that the Law has still a work to accomplish in us. We enter the old covenant when we hear the Gospel
preached to us. We cannot put the Old Testament behind us
and regard only the New Testament as our "Bible." We live
by the whole Bible. Everything in the Bible relates to us and
speaks to our condition, from Genesis to the Book of Revelation.
The Old Testament is in the Bible, not simply so that we shall
understand the New Testament, but that the Old Testament
itself may address its word to us.[20] Connected with this is the
fact that the Law still continues to exercise a certain proper
restraint upon us. Christ comes to us daily in the preaching of
the Gospel from without as news comes to us, and as He came
to Israel when He was born and began His work on earth.[21]

The fact that the Law "puts to death" is sometimes interpreted as a by-product of its primary function, which is to
legislate concerning right behaviour in society, or to protect
and preserve life. But the Law "puts to death" precisely when
it demands the required behaviour in society and protects life.
If we find it difficult to relate these two ideas, this is basically
because we fail to see how the Law is regulative in all human
life. In other words, we fail to see the Law in its connexion
with prehistory—the Creation and the Fall. We therefore
argue simply on the basis that the majority of men are free
from the Law, though some take it seriously (in which case
certain good works follow), while others, still fewer in number,

[20] There is a tendency in certain theological quarters to disregard the fact that
the Old Testament has a word to speak directly *to us and to our condition*. There are,
of course, many reasons for this—the dominance of the history of ideas as the basic
theological view, the tendency to dismiss Creation and the Law, and the lack of
interest in the exposition of scripture as a theological problem.

[21] Luther frequently emphasises this point, especially in his *Commentary on
Galatians*: "For as Christ came once corporally at the time appointed, abolished
the whole Law, vanquished sin, destroyed death and hell; even so He cometh unto
us spiritually without ceasing, and daily quencheth and killeth those sins in us"
(W. A. 40-1, p. 537.31-4. Cf. *op. cit.*, p. 550.20-31). The purpose of the Church
year, rightly interpreted, is continually to promote and advance this "coming"
of Christ. We have a good example of this in the early hymns and prayers of the
Church, which do not confine the events of redemptive history to the past, but
make them directly related to our present condition.

are condemned by the Law as guilty (in which case the Law "puts to death"). This pietistic interpretation of "tribulation" lies very deep in popular theology, and at the present day is the dominant one.[22]

God's will to chastise, but also to give life and to sustain, which according to Gen. III and IX was the consequence of human sin, and issued in the covenant after the flood, is so deeply implanted in all human life and so fundamental, that all life is lived only under this divine decree. Daily toil, the punishment of the murderer, and conception and birth are all part of it. Death too is part of it. God uses death in His government of the world (Gen. IX.5 f.) in order to protect life, and preserve it by means of death. This will of God is operative among all peoples. But God elects Israel alone out of all the nations to be the well-spring of the word of life for all the world. This was still the intention of God in giving Israel the Law and the commandments. And when finally the word of life was given to all the nations in the early Christian missionary preaching, they were addressed as being self-evidently created and no less self-evidently as sinners. They are one with the humanity of mankind's prehistory, created but fallen, and are subject to the same chastising will of God as Israel.[23] The distance between Abraham and Christ is now removed, for Abraham's election took place in order that "all the families of the earth" should be blessed (Gen. XI.3). When the Gospel is preached to all the world, Abraham's election is fulfilled (Gal. III.8). God's wrath is manifest among all nations, and the Gospel is preached to all nations (Rom. I.16-32).[24] When

[22] According to this pietistic interpretation of tribulation the Christian has already experienced the "mortifying" work of the Law at his conversion, but not after this. On the difference between Luther and Schartau at this point see Ivarsson, *Predikans uppgift*, pp. 220-5.

[23] It is for this reason that in the missionary preaching of the New Testament the Gentiles are called to repentance and offered the forgiveness of sins. For this reason too the early *kerygma* speaks of the Creation of the world. The reference to the Creator is particularly common in the missionary preaching of the New Testament. See Lindeskog, *Studien*, p. 180; Gärtner, *The Areopagus Speech*, pp. 229-37.

[24] The point which Paul stresses in Rom. I-III is that Gentile and Jew are in the same position. Both are guilty in the sight of God (Rom. III.9, 19). It is in the same context that Paul states that God makes Himself known to all men through His works (Rom. I.19 ff.), and that those who are outside Israel have what the Law requires "written on their hearts" (Rom. II.14 f.).

the distance between Abraham and Christ is removed, the difference between the laws of Israel and those of other nations ceases to be decisive. The difference remains, and is to be emphasised in the proper context, viz. where the object is to state Israel's "precedence" (Rom. III.1, IX.4 f.). But against the background of God's intention in creating man and of the "new Creation" in Christ, the difference disappears: "There is no distinction; since all have sinned and fall short of the glory of God" (Rom. III.22 f.). The Law stops every mouth, and brings the whole world under the judgment of God (Rom. III.19 f.).[25]

Israel's history has also something to teach us directly. If it is true that the New Testament Gospel is always preached, even at the present time, to those who are in one sense under the judgment of the Law, and if the Bible is both the "Testaments," and not the New Testament by itself, then we must interpret the two Testaments together, and allow the contribution of Israel's history to have its proper place. There are, however, only a few modern theologians who have dealt with these and similar problems. One is the Swedish scholar, Einar Billing, who has dealt systematically with prophecy in the Old Testament and its connexion with the New Testament, and has laid special stress on the history of Israel.[26] One of the most original contributions made by Billing is the parallel which he draws between the major prophets and Jesus. By their preaching of God's election of Israel, Billing holds, the prophets held God's grace before the *people*, but failed to offer it to the *individual*. But Jesus by the forgiveness of sins offers such a point of new beginning in the individual's "exodus" out of Egypt.[27] In Billing's theology the prehistory which deals with humanity in Gen. I-XI has no part to play. What is of importance to Billing is the history of Israel, seen throughout in the light of the Exodus.

On the level of the individual, the disappearance of the prehistory means the disappearance of the interpretation of the

[25] Cf. G. Bornkamm, *Das Ende des Gesetzes*, pp. 25-33.
[26] See, e.g., Billing, *De etiska tankarna*, pp. 85, 185, etc. The Law comes in between God and Israel increasingly as Israel loses sight of God's working in history (see pp. 156 f., 197 ff.).
[27] See Billing, *Försoningen*, pp. 22, 75.

Creation of the individual in birth. Moreover, the concentration on the basic and "primitive" human labour which is wholly concerned with the support of the created life also disappears. It is true that Luther's doctrine of vocation has a central place in Billing's theology, but he also explicitly states that we cannot give works the negative, "ascetic" interpretation which Luther gave to them.[28] According to Billing the concept of vocation must be supplemented by a prophetic interpretation of our personal history, in which each of us must individually undergo what Israel corporately underwent. Our starting-point, therefore, is the forgiveness of sins, interpreted as our personal "exodus" and election.[29] This means for us, as in the history of Israel (as Billing sees it), an "evangelising" of work. For Billing the Law is a labour only when we cannot interpret it prophetically. The Law, he holds, has no independent position alongside the Gospel, but is to be seen as an independent factor only in periods of theological weakness, e.g. in Judaism, and particularly when we cannot evolve the true concept of "vocation." Billing thus dismisses any idea of the Law, judgment, and wrath as being inspired by God's active will. He fails to make it clear that God's mercy is hidden behind a hard "government," and that His *opus proprium* and His *opus alienum* (the Gospel and the Law) are mutually opposed.[30]

"Government" and Mercy

It is precisely this relation between judgment and mercy which we propose to examine more closely in the present section. Here too, however, we are unable to deal adequately with all that is involved in the unity of judgment and mercy and the

[28] Billing, *Luthers lära om staten*, VOL. I, Uppsala 1900, pp. 87 ff., and *Vår kallelse*, pp. 14 f.
[29] See Billing, *Vår kallelse*, p. 37: "In the forgiveness of sins we experience our own Exodus out of Egypt. By this we know that God will bring us into His eternal kingdom. Whatever events may befall us on our journey thither, we know beforehand that their innermost purpose is to bring us closer to this goal. Deep in each of them there lies embedded a new intimation of grace. We are to excavate this hidden gold from our own little history just as the prophets did from the history of their people."
[30] Cf. Gustaf Wingren, "Om Einar Billings teologi," in *S.T.K.*, 1944, pp. 292 f.

K

tension between them. As in the previous section on the two
Testaments, so here we must let the chapter heading "The
Creator and the Law" act as the limiting factor in our discussion, even though this may mean having to exclude certain
important problems. The conflict between judgment and grace,
for instance, is an integral part of the doctrine of the Atonement,
but is not dealt with here. Our immediate concern is only with
the conflict between mercy and judgment which marks the
administration of God's "government" on earth, in which
force is employed to ensure peace and quiet. One of our tasks,
therefore, is to attempt to see the distinction between this
"government" and the Gospel—and also the distinction
between it and the commandments which stem from the
Gospel. Another is to see the unity between the two, as far as
it can be seen, or at any rate to point to where the unity can
be found.

The commandment concerning the shedding of blood insti-
tuted by God after the flood sets force against force (Gen. ix.
5 f.). If any man sheds another's blood, his own blood will
also be shed. The intention of this commandment is the
maintenance, and not the destruction, of life.[31] God entrusts
to certain men the power to punish as need may arise so that
life on earth may not be extinguished. The context in which
the particular commandment was given is that of the in-
eradicability of sin in the human heart (Gen. viii.21). But
even though sin is ineradicable, God will never allow it to
destroy the human race (Gen. viii.21, ix.8-17). The whole
purpose of the covenant described in Gen. ix is the prevention
of murder and the maintenance of life on the earth. A part
of this covenant is the establishment of justice by the use of
force—the earthly "government" as appointed by God. From
the beginning man was set on the earth to make use of that
which is created, and thereby to be lord of it. Even before sin
entered the world, this status implied for man not just freedom,
but also limitation, and his limitation consisted in the fact that
he could merely use, but not create. For God, man's limited
freedom to "have dominion" over the world implies His

[31] Cf. Zimmerli, *I Mose I-XI*, vol. ii, pp. 103-53. Even when we separate the
different sources of scripture, this unity still appears in the prehistory.

continuing rule over Creation which He Himself has made and man uses. God "governs" the world which He has created by means of the man whom He has placed in the world. This "rule" over the world takes other forms when man falls into sin, but does not cease or disappear. In the exercise of His rule in the world God makes use of human power, administered by human reason. But this power itself rests on God's decree to maintain life on earth, and consequently on His continuing will to create, even in the teeth of human opposition.[32] This creative will of God is His *love* and self-giving, even when men resist Him and harden their hearts against Him.

This is also Luther's view of the earthly government.[33] When the Sermon on the Mount forbids us to resist evil by force, it is commanding us, says Luther, to love our neighbour. To employ force for its own sake is to set oneself over the wicked neighbour, even though he is guilty. But it is characteristic of civil office or "government" that it never considers its own ends. When a judge punishes harshly, it is not he himself who has been wronged, and if it is, he has no right to judge his own case. The judge is not representing his own personal reaction to the offence, but the reaction which God wills to be produced by any violation of His commandments. The judge is merely the instrument of God in effecting His will.[34] God then uses human hands and voices in order to check the course of evil, just as He uses the judge or soldier to protect and benefit even the judge's or the soldier's own fellow beings. It is this same power, love of one's neighbour, which in *my* case compels me to abandon all use of force, but for my neighbour's sake compels me to take up arms to defend and "serve" him. This distinction between works of "service" and works for their own sake becomes inevitable as soon as we admit, for example, universal military service. We find it again even today in discussing the right of a Christian who is also, let us say, a soldier, policeman, or magistrate, etc., to use force, even although the

---

[32] Cf. Gustaf Aulén, *Church, Law, and Society*, New York 1948, pp. 37-92.

[33] Cf. Franz Lau, *Luthers Lehre von den beiden Reichen*, henceforth cited as *Luthers Lehre*, Berlin 1952, pp. 49-53, and also an earlier work by the same author, "*Äusserliche Ordnung*" *und* "*Weltlich Ding*" *in Luthers Theologie*, Studien zur systematischen Theologie vol. xii, henceforth cited as *Luthers Theologie*, Göttingen 1933, pp. 132-41.

[34] Cf. Werner Elert, *Das christliche Ethos*, Tübingen 1949, pp. 536 f.

terminology of the doctrine of "government" is often rejected.[35] In fact, we display greater kindness towards our neighbour and interest in his well-being in the apparently unloving use of force, than in refusing to take up arms for his protection. We shall be able to justify the use of force only by these arguments, but we shall also be true to the substance of the Reformed doctrine of government which assented to the use of force for the protection of one's fellow men. Thus the mercy of earthly government is God's own mercy.[36] It is God who is active in earthly government, and civic officials are simply His instruments.

The mercy which is actively present in the Law applies also to the one who is called upon to perform the works of the Law. The statement that "vocation is the Law" or "service is the Law" cannot be separated from the general doctrine of Law as being in part good, in so far as it mediates God's mercy, but in part also the "alien work" of God, functioning with greater severity than He would have displayed towards man, had man not opposed Him in sin. The Law is the "hardened" will of God—but it is still the same divine will which God revealed in His pure gift in the primal act of Creation. Now, however, His will is opposed by that which must die—sin, the devil, and the "old man." Man may undertake in obedience to administer the hard and disciplinary function of the Law upon his fellow beings without being untrue to the command to love his neighbour. Indeed love demands this. We may often doubt the goodness of what we do in thus administering the "hard" aspect of the Law. If so, we need to be convinced again of the truth that such disciplinary functions are essential for the good of our neighbour, and are pure and good because they rest on God's appointment—there is no guilt attached to the performance of this earthly duty.[37] The strange thing is that even though this function which we have described is absolutely essential for the preservation of life, and men and women in society assume and desire that it will be fulfilled,

[35] An interesting example is the analysis of the use of force in Paul Ramsey, *Basic Christian Ethics*, New York 1951, pp. 166-84.

[36] Cf. Törnvall, *Andligt Regemente*, pp. 54-8.

[37] See Ivarsson, *Predikans uppgift*, pp. 149 ff., on Luther's social preaching.

yet all of us tend to expect someone else, but not ourselves, to be responsible for it.

The Law thus protects both the administrator of the Law, and the one for whom it is administered. In the case of the latter, it guarantees freedom from unlawful violence, while the former, on the other hand, fulfils his work of protection of the innocent in obedience to the command of God. In one sense, however, the Law also protects the criminal himself, preventing him from wrongdoing. The evil intention of the criminal actively affects and corrupts the life which he enjoys as a creation of God. A light streams into our world both from the first pure Creation and from the eagerly-awaited Resurrection from the dead. If any man in the act of guilt detects even so much as a glimmer of light from either source, sufficient to convince him of his guilt and make him cease, it will be God's love and not His vengeance upon evil which has turned him from his evil intention. We tend sometimes to regard the continuing power of evil in separation from eschatology, and must constantly alter our misconception in the light, for example, of the concise and clear passage which deals with the "protection" of the Church in 1 Cor.v. Here expulsion from the congregation, a purely negative and punitive measure, serves ultimately, and is intended to serve, as a means of procuring the salvation of the one who has been excommunicated (1 Cor. v.5). This text is one example among several. With the Fall, a hostile element entered the world. This will be expelled from the world only at the division and separation in the Last Judgment.[38] God's love is active, even though it is not universally recognised, in the period between the entry of evil and its expulsion which we call human history.

In the midst of this period stands the Cross. In this it is hardest of all to discern the love of God, since the Crucified One was innocent, and yet had to die in accordance with the will of God. And yet from another point of view we see the love

---

[38] Cf. Pierce, *Conscience in the New Testament*, pp. 68-71. "Wrath," which is experienced by man both in external punishment and in his conscience, aims beyond itself at its own abolition. For this reason wrath will disappear when the Last Judgment, the "last" of the many judgments, has taken place. The present experience of wrath contains hope of external freedom from wrath in the future (cf. 1. Cor. v.5, XI.32).

of God most clearly in the Cross, since the Crucified was
not sent to condemn the world, but to save it, and brought a
new commandment—"Love your enemies"—which He Himself fulfilled in His prayer for those who crucified Him. He had
no desire to punish them, or even to oppose their designs. The
hard and punitive attitude which the Law takes in regard to
evil, and which we include in all that we mean by "government," is totally different from the attitude of Jesus on the
Cross. How then can the attitude which is displayed in the
exercise of earthly government express God's mercy, if it bears
no resemblance to the clear revelation of God's mercy which
we have been given in Christ? This is the problem, and it will
not be solved either by denying that our exercise of "government" partakes in any way of the character of mercy, or by
eliminating the difference between Jesus's attitude of patient
submission to force and the severity displayed by "government"
in its treatment of violence or oppression. In both cases the
mercy of God is active in different ways. The difficulty arises
when we are confronted in our own lives by the necessity of
having to adopt one or other of the two attitudes. That we shall
have to face such decisions is beyond doubt. There are quite
clear commandments which enjoin our imitation of Christ at this
point, even in our daily work or "vocation" (see, e.g., 1 Pet. II.
18-23), so that it is impossible to escape the dilemma by
eliminating one or other of the two attitudes.[39]

We shall never come to terms with the problem if we think
of the two attitudes as being alternatives, of which individuals
are required to adopt one or the other. The first thing which
we must say is that they are both given states. The existence
in human societies of force used in the service of peace and
security is not something devised at a particular time or in a
particular situation, but is to be found among all peoples
without exception. There is no period in recorded history in
which the use of force in such a way is unknown. The mercy
which is expressed in this earthly government of which we are
speaking is not human mercy, but God's, just as the mercy

---

[39] On the demand of the New Testament for an imitation of Jesus, cf. Gustaf
Wingren, "Was bedeutet die Forderung der Nachfolge Christi?" in *Theologische
Literaturzeitung*, 1950, pp. 385-92.

which is evidenced in the alternation of sun and rain is His, and not ours. The existence of these manifestations of mercy precedes any choice of ours, and constitutes the condition of human life—we should be consumed if the Lord's mercies were not new every morning (Lam. III.22 f.). Each new morning we are made alive again. Just as the Creation of the world issues in the strict order which God has appointed for the protection of human life, so we are born into the conditions of this earthly government by which in fact we are defended, disciplined, and nurtured on every side. To participate in human society in which evil is ineradicable is primarily to receive that which God has given, and not to fulfil a certain "ethic."[40]

Similarly, what Christ bestows on us in His work of redemption is primarily a gift. He has not established a kingdom in which death is defeated and sin no longer stands as an obstacle between God and man. Had He done so, He would have ended the unnatural situation which was brought about by Adam's fall, and which the Law opposed in its constraining and threatening aspect. Christ's kingdom becomes a reality in the preaching of the Gospel and the administration of Baptism. Both these acts remove the judgment which is upon man and restore to him his freedom as a child in Creation. But Christ's kingdom is still in process of extension, and continually brings new men and women into participation in His death and resurrection, in order finally to establish with power the life eternal. The fact that death is still before us is a reminder to us that we have not yet attained, but are still "on the way." We are moving out of the old kingdom, in which the Law hangs over men as the expression of God's merciful government of the world, into the new kingdom in which the final Judgment has already taken place, and death itself is ended. We enter the old covenant, and hear in the Gospel that Christ is coming each day to us with the kingdom that is to come. This coming kingdom is already pressing upon us, but the old kingdom of the Law still co-exists with it. Here we must hold the Law and death together, otherwise we shall "moralise" and thus alter the difference between the two kingdoms into a difference between two kinds of ethic. To say that the old kingdom still

[40] Cf. Løgstrup, *Den etiske fordring*, pp. 161 f., 275.

remains is to say that death still rules—it is not yet destroyed (I Cor. xv.26). Since there are some alive who have not tasted death, the kingdom of the Law is not yet ended, and therefore fear and temptation continue to hold sway.[41]

It is of no avail to try to abolish the rule of the Law by human means. Only the resurrection of the dead will end this power given to the Law. In the meantime it continues to rule over the whole earth in the strength of God's own will. We cannot wrest an ethical attitude which we find in Jesus and make it regulative in the world. There is no greater objection in saying that we must await the termination of God's "hard order," or employ force for the purpose of trying to forestall the onslaught of evil, say, in war or murder, than there is in saying that even after the Resurrection of Christ we are still liable to death. The man who has received the Gospel of Christ in faith now knows that he is going out of this world, and that when death strikes, it comes bearing hope, and will not destroy him. This very hope gives birth to new works and new freedom in this world of Law and death. The man of faith does not cling apprehensively to life, and has no need of taking thought for it. Here, as elsewhere, we see that freedom from idols and trust in God expresses itself in a readiness to seek the good of others, but also in what we may call the Christian's "invulnerability" —the supreme mastery of life, even with all its cross accidents, or (to use our earlier term) the free "dominion" over everything in life, even in suffering and desolation (see II Cor. xii.9 f.).[42] Where this sovereign freedom exists, the harsh government

[41] There are two reasons why theologians of the present day find it difficult to see the universal application and effect of the Law. In the first place they do not regard an elementary demand such as that of "maintaining life" as worth noting. In the second place they reduce the concept of sin correspondingly to a superficial level, making it refer to certain specific acts and separating it from its connexion with death. As long as we isolate sin from the basic fact that death prevails, we shall fail to see that it is a "power" in the Biblical sense. There is only one way of "breaking with sin," and that is through Baptism and the resurrection of the dead. In this way new works, different from the works of the Law, are produced, but these themselves do not accomplish the break with sin—on the contrary, they *are produced*, while the "Exodus" from the power of sin *has already taken place*. See Rom. vi.1-22, and cf. Prenter, *Skabelse og genløsning*, pp. 507-10, 530. One of the most valuable parts of Prenter's book is his continual reference to Baptism.

[42] On the freedom of the Christian as "incipient total freedom," see Elert, *Das christliche Ethos*, pp. 310-13.

exercised by the Law no longer appears as a merciless institution which the Christian must avoid. On the contrary, faith sees far more clearly than unbelief the mercy which is in God's harsh and punitive resistance to sin, and is willing to submit to the retributive function of the Law, without which life could not continue. It is precisely because the thread of mercy which runs through all the Law is revealed to the man of faith that he is free to alter in part, or even, when the good of his neighbour demands it, at times entirely change any part of it.[43] The Christian has something which the world cannot reasonably be expected to have—a willingness to suffer even injustice. In this willingness to suffer, far more clearly than in anything else which he does, the power and freedom of the new and eternal kingdom are revealed to him.

Thus the earthly "government" does not require the same unvarying obedience or course of action at all times and in every situation. Since God's "hard order" put power into men's hands after the flood (Gen. ix.6), the administration of divine right now lies in the hands of idolatrous men. It may in consequence be distorted throughout the earth and changed at men's whim. This is simply to say that as soon as we speak about earthly government, we must also bear in mind the possibility of its abuse.[44] However disgracefully a tyrannical father may behave, he can never stop marriage from being of divine institution, or prevent God from using this appointed institution as a means of creating life, and even from using the bad parent himself as his instrument. So no abuse of the power which was entrusted to man after the flood can annul the fact that God uses for good what man misuses for evil.[45] The

[43] Paul rejected circumcision, though Jesus did not. Jesus's freedom in regard to the Sabbath Law (Mk. ii.23-8) is expressed in Paul as a freedom in regard to another one of the many demands made by the Law, viz. circumcision (Gal. v. 1 f.). Our faithfulness to this freedom can be expressed at the present day in a third aspect of which the New Testament does not speak. See Ramsey, *Basic Christian Ethics*, pp. 63, 75. There is no essential difference here between the demands of the Old Testament and those which are made upon us in society. Christian freedom *may* express every demand in a different way.

[44] Cf. Törnvall, *Andligt regemente*, pp. 225 ff.

[45] Luther's parallel applies here: Is there anything more misused than the light of day or the darkness of night? Yet both of these are good, both are God's, and will remain such, whatever use men may make of them.

impression that the Gospel (and the commandment which proceeds from the Gospel) is absolutely incompatible with the Law and the right which God appointed in the world usually arises from the identification of this Law and right appointed by God with an actual and often arbitrary group or collective which has acquired the administration of government, and now misuses it. Criticism of the ruthlessness of the collective, however, is not excluded by the doctrine of the divine institution of the earthly government. On the contrary, it is an organic development of this doctrine.[46] Just as the divine institution of the family sharpens the demands on the family, and makes it impossible for us to stand by idle if we see family life destroyed in any society, so the divine institution of the earthly government does not mean that the obligations which are laid upon those who are charged with its administration are lessened, but rather increased.[47] The existing structure of the earthly government must continually be re-examined and criticised, otherwise its harsh regulations will continue unchanged. Undeviating allegiance to an outmoded and rigid order of government can often be as lacking in love and consideration as calculated ill-will. The order of earthly government must always be flexible and elastic, if it is to be of use.

However we may seek to modify the Law in the world, there still remains an indelible difference between the order of earthly government at its best on the one hand, and, on the other, the attitude of Jesus—the proper object of our imitation—to evil. This difference is not to be explained away, but remains as a testimony to the fact that we live in a world in which evil is opposed to God, and in which therefore something must *die* before the kingdom of the Resurrection appears. What we are here concerned with is the necessity of death in the old kingdom, the kingdom of the Law. In the pure and sinless Creation death had no power. In the eternal kingdom to come it will

---

[46] Søe, *Kristelig etik*, pp. 383-6, quotes several Biblical passages in criticism of magistrates. These passages, however, do not contradict Luther's doctrine of the earthly government, as Søe maintains.

[47] The hatred of father and mother (Lk. xiv.26) belongs to a situation of abuse or idolatry. On its compatibility with a positive view of the family, see Dewar, *An Outline of New Testament Ethics*, pp. 90 f.

be abolished for ever. But here on earth death retains its power in accordance with the will of God. As long as sin remains, death has all power against it. Jesus alone of all men has made His way out of the kingdom of death, fulfilled the Law, and established the eternal kingdom in which neither Law nor death are to be found. This "attitude" of not resisting evil, but suffering unjustly, is one aspect of His Crucifixion and His willing offering of Himself for the purpose of establishing the new kingdom. We cannot isolate this aspect of His Crucifixion and make it into a binding rule for human societies, but it can be expressed anew, in fellowship with Christ, by any man who is willing to suffer and die, and thus leave the old kingdom of the Law. If this willingness to suffer and die lacks true jubilation and gladness, despite the agony, it is a hypocrisy. The joy experienced by the martyr Church when confronted by death clearly reveals how "Jesus's attitude to evil" can be realised in this world of Law and death. If, for instance, a man who is assaulted refuses to use a gun against his assailant, but sends for the police, his conduct may be faithful to the appointed use of the Law in regard to force, but does not represent the attitude of Jesus to evil. The imitation of Jesus in action is only one aspect of our total imitation of Him in His death and resurrection.[48] We may "imitate" Jesus in solving a particular social problem. If we do, the kingdom of God is being extended. Soon all human societies will be ended. Only in the Spirit does the individual know when his imitation of Christ is real. If it never becomes a reality in the life of the Christian, there is something vital missing.

We have seen above that the history of Israel culminates in the destruction and downfall of Israel, which was finally achieved in the death of Jesus as Ebed Jahveh on the Cross. What we have just said about suffering and death as the central part of the Church's imitation of Jesus is organically related to this. The New Testament stands in contrast to the Old Testament, and grows by way of the death at Golgotha out of the soil of the old, in the same way as the new mercy which is

[48] Cf. Eduard Schweitzer, "Der Glaube an Jesus den 'Herrn' in seiner Entwicklung von den ersten Nachfolgern bis zur hellenistischen Gemeinde," in *Evangelische Theologie*, 1957, pp. 7-17.

commanded by Jesus stands in contrast to the earthly government appointed by God. At the same time, however, it develops in suffering and martyrdom against the background of the earthly government. Neither of these processes can be understood as long as we fail to discern the *transitory nature* of all that God does and man experiences. The history of Israel and "our own history in miniature" (to use Einar Billing's phrase)[49] extends between the Fall at the beginning of the Bible and the Resurrection at its end. Israel's actual history takes place between the primal act of God in the Creation of the world, and the unfulfilled act of God in the Consummation.[50] The history of each individual Christian, beginning with Creation (i.e., birth), lies between the same two divine acts.[51] Part of the history of Israel was the "Baptism" to which Jesus submitted in His death, and which points forward to the new kingdom. This same Baptism appears in our own history as a promise of a coming transformation. All that we have to endure until the resurrection of the dead is simply a development of what is given to us in Baptism, and of this, death is a part. We live in a particular situation in which the element of hostility to God which is present both in the world and in me personally is continually being expelled. It is this that constitutes the transitoriness of our position.

Einar Billing begins with Exodus, our "exodus from Egypt," and not with Genesis[52], and maintains that there is an unbroken connexion between the Old and New Testaments. Our own "vocation" is, he argues, a miniature of the history of Israel, although he does not regard death as being of primary importance. Because of this, he often tends to allow the idea of the "Cross" in vocation, so frequently discussed by Luther, to disappear, and he adopts instead a much brighter picture of human work. For the same reason he is able to make Baptism central in his theology as few others have done in the twentieth century, seeing infant Baptism as a sign of God's prevenient grace. He

---

[49] Billing, *Vår kallelse*, p. 37 f.
[50] See Cullmann, *Christ and Time*, pp. 117 f.
[51] See the sections above, "The Last Day and our Death," in Part I, chapter II, and "The Creation of the World and our Birth," Part I, chapter III. In both these sections there is a discussion of Bultmann and Cullmann.
[52] Billing, *Vår kallelse*, p. 37, and *Försoningen*, pp. 22, 75.

has failed, however, to see its integral connexion with death, and has thus allowed it to become little better than the initiation ceremony of a folk Church.[53]

All this is closely connected. The contribution made by Billing to European theology is among the most original and methodical of the present century. Billing himself was a pioneer in the attempt to relate the content of the Bible to the modern situation. But like all such pioneers and interpreters, he was in danger of being infected, or at least influenced, by the society in which he lived. In Billing's case it is something of the safe seclusion of the study we seem to detect—almost, if we may use the term, a kind of bourgeois clerical culture, an idyll which was to be rudely shattered by the Biblical writings themselves. Our modern society will likely shatter our own comfortable security by discords similarly disturbing. This makes it all the more important that we should attempt again to relate the scriptures to our modern situation, as Billing did to his. If we do, we shall run the same dangers as he did, and perhaps misinterpret the scriptures in our attempt—but the attempt must still be made.

If our present social order develops in such a way that the split between the Church and State widens, we shall find that the New Testament will speak to us with greater clarity and authority than at an earlier period in European politics. In the first place, the writings of the New Testament originated in a situation in which there was a vast gulf between Church and political government, but in the second place they also declare that in the future this gulf will be even greater. For the New Testament this widening gulf was itself a sign that the coming of Christ was not long delayed (Mk. xiii.3-29).[54] Where the split between the Church and the world grows wider, there is also great danger for the Church itself, and it becomes all the more difficult to discern God's mercy in the earthly order. It also becomes all the more easy for the Church

[53] The Swedish is "folkkyrka," which can be translated "State Church," but Billing has strongly criticised this latter term. The Swedish is therefore rendered by the vaguer phrase "folk Church." It can sometimes be said that infant Baptism is a consequence of the idea of a folk Church, based on the concept of universal and prevenient grace. See, e.g., Billing, *Herdabref*, p. 62.

[54] Cf. Cullmann, *Christ and Time*, pp. 160, 163.

to isolate itself, and make itself a sect, and to regard the world
outside the walls of the Church as being outside the area of the
divine activity. In such a situation as this, Billing's concept of
a folk Church, admittedly in a new form, may well come to be
re-expressed and constitute a better pattern for us than when it
first emerged.

The early Christian Church, even though it was persecuted
by the earthly powers, could still regard them as appointed by
God and as the "ministers of God." This simply means that
God's mercy is to be found in the exercise of power, even when
it is abused. This view of "government" is true and faithful
to the New Testament in all cultural situations[55] and, if we
lose sight of it, we are losing an essential element both in
scripture and in the Creed.

[55] The basis of the belief that the civil authority is "the servant of God" is not
any question of the usefulness of the civil authority to the Church. If it were, this
belief would differ from time to time, and sometimes be right, sometimes wrong.
The belief, however, is based on the conviction that human life is impossible apart
from an authority which exists to punish wrong. It is also based on the conviction
that in Creation God has armed the civil authority with power to put down dis-
order, and that He has done this universally among all peoples. This is the significance of Gen. i-ix. Cf. Zimmerli, *I Mose I-XI*, VOL. II, pp. 135 ff.

CHAPTER II

THE FIRST USE OF THE LAW

Our Neighbour and the Law

IN using the term "the first use of the Law" we are adopting the terminology of Lutheranism. This was also true of our use of the term "government" in the previous section. Luther himself, however, although he made a distinction between a "civil" or "political" use of the Law on the one hand, and a "spiritual" or "theological" use on the other, did not refer to the civil use as the first use, or the spiritual as the second. This terminology developed later in connexion with the dispute in regard to a suggested "third" use of the Law. To be faithful to Luther, we must simply make a distinction between the civil or civic use of the Law and the spiritual, without saying which is first and which second. In the present work, however, I am not attempting to reproduce Luther, and therefore propose for convenience to call the two following chapters by the titles "The First Use of the Law," and "The Second Use of the Law," respectively. As soon as we begin to ask ourselves the question, "What does the Law do in the *world?*", we at once find that we are dealing with the first use of the Law. The Law is operative in the external world. It produces works which would not have been produced had it not demanded their performance. But the Law also reveals *coram Deo*, or in the conscience, what the heart of that man is like who "performs" what is thus demanded of him and so renders at least superficial obedience. This work of the Law is invisible in the world.[1] It is still, however, the essential work of the Law. It is the work of the Law before God in man's

---

[1] Cf. Ragnar Bring, *Die paulinische Begründung der lutherischen Theologie*, Luthertum VOL. XVII, Berlin 1955, p. 28.

conscience. This is the judging and guilt-revealing function of the Law. Here we see the second use of the Law.

When we thus define the meaning of the use of the Law, it is quite obvious that we have already discussed both uses in our interpretation of Creation. God's demand that men should continue to "have dominion" over Creation is part of His continuing Creation of the world. His wrath and judgment are evident in Creation, even when the man who is forced to undertake the performance of these works is evil, disobedient, and hostile.[2] I have already laid the basis of our discussion of the two uses of the Law in what I have said above in dealing with Creation, and do not require to cover the same ground in the four sections which follow. I propose rather to stress certain neglected aspects of the doctrine of the Law which are of great importance for systematic theology.

The first point with which we are concerned in the present section is the doctrine of our neighbour. In two passages Paul summarises the whole of the Law in a single commandment, "You shall love your neighbour as yourself" (Rom. xiii.9; Gal. v.14). It is at first somewhat strange that, unlike the Synoptic Gospels, Paul does not summarise the Law in the two commandments to love God and to love one's neighbour (Mk. xii. 28 ff.). But the difference between the Pauline and Synoptic summaries of the Law is really insignificant, if we bear in mind the point of reference in either case. Even in the first of the Synoptic Gospels Jesus can also summarise the whole of the "Law and the prophets" in the "golden rule" (Mt. vii.12) in which the need of those around us is the decisive factor in our attitude to them.

The important truth is that love of one's neighbour is in fact the same thing as love of God, and this in turn is the same thing as man's free dominion over the things of Creation. By man's act of sin in the Fall all three aspects are lost. The sinner who separates himself from God the Giver, to stand in false isolation from Him, also separates himself from his neighbour, the one who receives, to stand in false isolation from him. Fear of "losing one's life" is a part of unbelief (in relation to God)

---

[2] See the sections above, "Sin and Wrath" and "The Unrecognised Demand," in Part I, chapter II. The work of the Law is also dealt with in Part I, chapter III

and suppresses any willingness I may have to give of myself (to my neighbour), and forces me to bow down and cleave to some part of God's good Creation (in idolatry). These are not three separate sins, but one sin, seen from three aspects—my relation to God, to my neighbour, and to the world.[3] Now when the Bible sums up all the demands of the Law in love for one's neighbour, it is not isolating one of the three aspects of sin, but stressing all three equally, as many passages show. But when it summarises the Law as love of one's *neighbour*, it is stating something about the power of the Law to compel all men to act on their neighbour's behalf. We are not here concerned with what the Law demands, or the extent of its demands. At any rate this was not the problem of the Reformers. What we are concerned with is rather the power of the Law to enforce its demands, to succeed in getting something done, even though what is "done" is not entirely what it demanded.

This was for Luther the main aspect of the civil use of the Law. Luther had no interest in whether man has wisdom, knowledge, or insight. The whole of this problem of epistemology, which dominates theological discussion at the present time, was dealt with fairly summarily and in passing by him. It did not seem to be a problem of any particular importance. Nor was he interested in whether man becomes good or righteous when he is forced into obedience of the external commands of the Law. He was quite sure that man does not, but he did not attempt on the basis of this conviction to begin with man, his sin, and his powerlessness. God has created the whole world, and not just man; and the world, and not just man, is the chosen area of His gracious activity. The first use of the Law refers primarily to the world. It does not refer primarily to man, who is active (even under constraint) in the

[3] We can see this unity of thought when the New Testament speaks of covetousness as *idolatry* (Eph. v.5; Col. iii.5). Since the covetous man does not believe in God, he has to assert his own power against the Creator. He does so on the grounds of his possessing something, even though what he possesses is merely created and given. This will to possess shuts him off from his fellow men and renders him incapable of giving. The fact of his being shut off from God as well as from his neighbour is in itself idolatry, and this worship of the creature is filled with fear of loss and death. What the covetous man cannot do is to rule over the world.

world, or to his purity or lack of it. As soon as we raise the
problem of man, however, we are at once involved in the
second use of the Law. Here too the Law has an important
task to fulfil, viz. the condemnation of man. But in the world
and in the courts of law, it is not the evil of the human heart
which is the essential thing. It is man's deeds against his
neighbour. The power of the Law to enforce a certain pattern
of conduct in human society is connected with the fact that
the whole of the Law in all its demands is to be found in the
needs of one's neighbour. It is an outward expression of human
society, and we either accept it or reject it, "know" it or are
ignorant of it. No man can evade the pressure of the Law upon
him to act in a particular way because of the need of those
among whom he lives.

We notice at once how the civil use of the Law proceeds
directly from the fact that God is *Creator*.[4] He has created the
whole world, and cannot remain a passive onlooker while evil
and death become firmly entrenched in the world. He sets up
a barrier against the onward course of evil, and restricts its
effects. Various social institutions such as the police force, the
judicature, and so on, have each been given their allotted task
from God. To understand the connexion between these earthly
ordinances and God's continuing Creation we must try to see
two things: first, it is men's evil deeds which are punished and
prevented by these earthly ordinances; but second, in their
actual prevention, the whole life of society is preserved. Life,
which comes into being as a direct act of God, cannot continue
unless God continues to create it anew each day. The defensive
and protective activity of earthly government against anything
which injures life, such as murder, or theft, and so on, is also a
life-giving and life-preserving activity. Even when it is necessary
to use force to prevent injury to life, it is the Creator's force
which is operative and the good of the neighbour which is
being safeguarded. Indeed, to take up arms in defence of one's
neighbour is an act of love.[5] The same holds good of all
peaceable occupations which help to furnish the necessities of
life, such as shoes, and clothing, and so on, or deal with the

[4] Cf. Aulén, *Church, Law, and Society*, pp. 84-92.
[5] See Lau, *Luthers Lehre*, pp. 49-53; Ramsey, *Basic Christian Ethics*, pp. 166-84.

transport, sale, or distribution of such commodities. Here too the direct connexion between birth (i.e. Creation) and the growth and protection of life is quite clear. Even cultural, artistic, or scientific work can also serve a community. It may be difficult to detect this purpose in the work of the artist or the scientist, as it is difficult to see how we can talk about "loving one's neighbour" when the soldier shoots him. But just as the soldier realises the possibility of a meaningless war which will benefit nobody, but injure many—and knows that if he were to refuse to take up arms that possibility would become a reality—so likewise every artist is well aware of the possibility of creating something which is of no significance or use. The artist's picture or the writer's book belong to the world. But, of course, it is also a universal experience that months and years of lonely and isolated work for the artist or writer may still be allied to a strong sense of fellowship with all men and with all Creation. This feeling is not misleading to the artist, but keeps him true to his vocation.[6]

We have been comparing many different kinds of human activity, and have thus disconnected the first use of the Law from too narrow an association with politics. Whenever the Law demands the performance of good works, we are dealing with the first use of the Law, and of "earthly righteousness," to use Luther's phrase.[7] It does not matter whether these works have been performed in politics, family, school, art, science, or the administration of justice. It is the works themselves with which we are concerned, i.e. the first use of the Law. In every one of these activities, however, there is a constant temptation to misuse one's position for purely selfish

[6] The purpose of all human work is man's continued "conformation" to the destiny which has been appointed for him in Creation. This purpose will be finally achieved only in the life eternal, but there is nothing that man can do which may not serve this end and promote his "conformation." Cf. Lau, *Luthers Theologie.* p. 47.
[7] See Luther, *Commentary on Galatians*, W. A., 40-1, pp. 45.24-47.14. Luther's distinction between the two "righteousnesses," the earthly righteousness of works and the heavenly righteousness of faith, is the one with which we are particularly concerned here. This is not to deny that Luther can be one-sided in connecting the civil use of the Law with the action of the earthly authorities. This is one respect in which we should decline to follow the Reformer, for our society is quite different from his. Cf. Wingren, *Theology in Conflict*, pp. 105 f.

ends. We can understand how real a temptation this is only when we realise that this "abuse" ("*abusus*" was Luther's term, while "*usus*" signified man's proper use of the gifts of Creation) never affects the individual alone, but always affects others with him. If it affected the individual alone, there would be no real temptation. When men are tempted, it is always to do something that appears to be good. The difficulty, however, consists in the fact that, like me, all my neighbours are also idolaters, and the evil that I do pleases them, if not directly, then derivatively. Service of one's neighbour is not a kind of ready-made programme with a list of items which we are to perform for his benefit. The factor of sin enters in, and so we find that whenever we do attempt to do good to our neighbour, all kinds of voices around us plead with us to do something different. Thus if the only rule which we have for doing good to our neighbour is that which promotes his advantage, we shall be left vacillating as haphazardly as though we had no rule at all.[8]

But it is only in appearance that this is so. The gradual discovery that the regulative factor in ethical decision is our neighbour and his good means something quite practical. It means that we are directed outwards towards the world. The goodness which exists in anything that we do for our neighbour's sake is the Creator's goodness, mediated to him by a human act. God has created him to live, and life is continually given to him by another's goodness. The human instrument is caught up into the activity of the Creator, and because God's activity is directed towards the *world*, those who are the instruments of His goodness are also directed towards the world. The works are done "for man's sake, do you not hear, for man's sake!"[9]

[8] On the contrast between the *opus Dei* and the *opus diaboli*, see Törnvall, *Andligt regemente*, pp. 223 ff. This contrast cuts right across the two "governments."

[9] This quotation from Luther is to be found in Ivarsson, *Predikans uppgift*, p. 125. Ivarsson's treatment of Luther is unique among writings which deal with the Reformer in repudiating the individualist aspect of his theology. In this connexion Ivarsson's section on Luther's political sermons is of the greatest interest, because the passages which he quotes reveal how Luther regarded man before and in dependently of the preaching of the Gospel as being in fellowship with the Creator and his fellow men. Man's works are a part of this relationship which is established at birth. No other post-Reformation preaching succeeded in preserving this total view.

But since it is not always easy to see from moment to moment how we may best benefit our neighbour and avoid doing him harm, a great number of our decisions in such matters is lifted from us as a result of some previous decision that has been made. Most of the things we do each day, week after week, at our place of work, in the home, in the shop, have already been chosen for us by others long ago. By and large it is purely accident or custom that has determined such things for us. But at some time or another, someone chose them, and in so doing rejected other possibilities after hesitation and even conflict. To accept military conscription, for instance, or taxation, or compulsory education, etc., is to accept something which has already been decided, and the decision to do these things may have caused at the time a good deal of trouble. But it was others who undertook this trouble, and we have "entered into their labours." We do not choose what we do every single minute of the day.[10] Indeed, we cannot so limit our daily activities, for every moment we are involved in some relation or other to our neighbour, even when we are not conscious of doing so, and even when our neighbour remains anonymous.[11] The important thing is that at some time someone chose to adopt this particular course of action in a situation of struggle or temptation in which he might just as well have chosen to act in a different way. This might in fact have been more to his advantage. But whatever the choice, it is always open to us to accept it or reject it.

It is fairly obvious that within limits any acts which we perform for the benefit of our neighbour are forced upon us by various social pressures. The Law is embodied in these pressures,

---

[10] Cf. Prenter, *Skabelse og genløsning*, p. 211 f. Prenter does not accept the so-called "orders of Creation" (*Schöpfungsordnungen*) as being divine institutions, but acknowledges them as freely chosen "pacts" which have a historical existence, and which are thus essentially variable. This is what we mean by the works of the Creator. The act of Creation is not limited to a single beginning, but is still going on.

[11] The relationship to one's neighbour is always a double one. Not only am I under obligation to act on behalf of my neighbour, but I must also accept the actions of other men for me. These in turn are the instruments by whom God preserves my life. If it is asked, "Who is my neighbour?" (Lk. x.29) on the assumption that "my" neighbour is the object of my good deeds, it can be answered, "You are the neighbour" (Lk. x.36), the subject who does the good deeds.

and as social conventions alter, so does the form in which the Law is expressed. Most of our daily conduct, even the conduct of those who are Christian, is forced upon us (under normal circumstances, at any rate) in this way. At the same time, however, the actual demands which are made upon us are subject to the judgment of the word of scripture. At the period of the Reformation, for instance, when the doctrine of the civil use of the Law was being formulated, Christian men and women were continually being confronted with conflicting decisions in which they had to choose one course from another. Thus there was developed the concept of the possible "abuse" of their official position by the existing powers of government. The ruler was no different from other men, in that he was tempted and, like them, needed to be guided and criticised. Whatever theological view we may have, this at least is a self-evident truth.[12] But it is quite a different thing to conclude from this that the Church is the only true originator of political activity. Such a suggestion has been made by Barth, but is possible only if we put the second article before the first, make knowledge the central problem of theology, and on this basis argue that the sequence is first "Gospel" and then "Law."[13] If we do this, however, we thereby deny the faith which the Church has held for two thousand years in God's work in Creation, and which has now become altered in the twentieth century of the Church's life.

To those who accept the view of Barth, the word "neighbour" presents some difficulties. The basic meaning of the word is "the one who lives near to me." It implies a relationship between demand and act which may be made clearer through Christ, or the word of scripture, but is not thereby established. It is established, rather, in Creation, i.e. when we are born into the world of human need. N. H. Søe, who follows Barth in this regard, conceives of the relation to one's neighbour as having

---

[12] Cf. Wingren, *Theology in Conflict*, pp. 98, 165. See also the section below, "Preaching and the Law," in Part II, chapter III. A detailed criticism of the actual demands cannot be given here, but will be discussed in my proposed work on Gospel and Church.

[13] See Barth, *Christengemeinde und Bürgergemeinde*, pp. 21-5. Barth's argument here is based on the view which he advanced earlier, e.g. in *Evangelium und Gesetz*, and *Rechtfertigung und Recht*.

been established through the word of the Gospel.[14] According to Søe, my fellow being becomes my neighbour only when I have acquired full insight into the meaning of Creation.[15] Here again, however, the acquisition of knowledge and insight is made of greater importance than the works of God. This attitude is perhaps comprehensible as a reaction against the misapplication of the first article in an earlier idealist and anthropocentric period. It does not, however, correct this misunderstanding. In fact in its attempt to modify an anthropocentric misinterpretation it is still very much man-centred, although in a negative way, being concerned with the lack of knowledge in man. Whatever this concern with man may mean, it is God in His sovereignty who has created the world, and who preserves it in spite of death. He does so by compelling men to act in such a way as to guarantee the continuance of life, even though they may be unaware of what they are doing, or lacking in love for others. But still they continue to do what God wills to be done, simply because they must, and because they stand under the Law of God. If we are not to lose sight of the sovereignty of God, it is necessary to accept the older definitions of "neighbour" which have previously been accepted. These do not imply any natural theology, but in fact reaffirm a belief in God the Creator and in the work of Creation as the first work of God.[16] To allow the first article of the Creed to stand first simply means that Creation took place first, and not that we gained a full and clear knowledge of God when we were created. If clarity is to be the determining factor in arranging the order of the articles of the Creed, we should properly begin with the Consummation, when we shall "see face to face."

If the preaching of the Church is to constitute any criterion of judgment in regard to the multifarious demands which

[14] Søe, *Kristelig etik*, pp. 166-71.
[15] Cf. *op. cit.*, p. 170, where Søe gives his own definition—"The word concerning Jesus Christ and the glory of God in Him alone makes my fellow man my neighbour"—with the quotations from Luther and Calvin to which Søe refers in footnote 14 on the same page. Søe frequently maintains that the Word gives knowledge of goodness, and that it alone provides such knowledge. See, e.g., his *Religionsfilosofi* p. 15 and many references.
[16] Cf. Prenter, *Skabelse og genløsning*, pp. 104-8.

158 L A W

press upon men daily, it is important to see clearly the centrality of the concept of neighbour in the Bible.[17] We can perhaps see this most clearly in what the Bible does not say. For instance, we find no attempt in the Bible to lay down general commands about speaking the truth in the abstract, however frequent these may be elsewhere. What we do find is a commandment which is to be fulfilled in a particular way. "You shall not bear false witness *against your neighbour*" (Ex. xx. 16; Deut v.20). When the Bible enjoins the truth and forbids lies, it does so *because of the neighbour*. The words which we speak produce some effect or other in the society in which we live. The reason for Paul's command to speak the truth is well-nigh incomprehensible to our individualistic consciousness: "Therefore, putting away falsehood, let every one speak the truth with his neighbour, for we are members one of another" (Eph. iv.25).[18] If this is incomprehensible, it is almost certainly because the idea of the individual as being an integral part of the life of his fellow men as they are of his, has practically disappeared from our consciousness. Instead, we think of ourselves primarily as individual units with a private relationship to God which is established in the performance of certain religious acts, in consequence of which we can then enter into an individual ethical relationship with others. But any such purely individualistic attitude renders a true critical evaluation of the many demands which are made of us every day quite impossible.[19] The Church cannot make itself a collective over against other collectives in the world without destroying itself. Nor can it extract individuals from their existing earthly solidarities into an artificial ecclesiastical relationship which estranges them from the world in which they live. The Church must respect the existing relationships of those outside, and recognise that these are divinely appointed. To "come into the

[17] See Ramsey, *Basic Christian Ethics*, pp. 60 f., 153-90. Ramsey quotes several examples from the New Testament and regards Luther's doctrine of vocation as being true to the New Testament at this point.

[18] In this connexion the introduction of the neighbour to justify a minor digression from the truth is more frequent today (the whole problem of the "white lie" is usually expressed in this form). This might be held to prove that truth itself is non-ethical, and that only a "softening down" of the truth is social.

[19] Cf. Robinson, *The Body*, pp. 8 f.

Church" does not mean that we have to exchange neighbours or alter the God-appointed relationships already in existence. But the virtual loss of the doctrine of the first use of the Law makes it difficult to retain this attitude of respect for the world.[20] The less the Church respects the world for what it is, in other words, the more the Church feels it has to interfere in the world and regulate it, the more legalistic its attitude becomes, and the more it loses what characterises it as the Church, viz. the Gospel.

We have just mentioned the danger of legalism which the Church faces when it becomes involved in the world. This legalism is destructive both of the Gospel and of the Church. But the danger cannot be evaded simply by adopting a purely passive attitude in regard to earthly concerns, or by simply preaching the Gospel without displaying concern for the problems of the Law.[21] Suppose, for instance, the conflicting claims of medieval feudalism and national socialism are both defended on theological grounds. Now if the Church rejects the Bible as the criterion by which a false theology of society is to be distinguished from the true, and instead advances *reason* as the sole means of judging such problems, then it is guilty of a wrong "involvement" in the world.[22] It is not this, however, which makes the Church legalistic, but its involvement in two separate and distinct spheres, the Church and the

[20] Cf. Løgstrup, *Den etiske fordring*, pp. 122-32.

[21] When Aukrust, *Forkynnelse og historie*, p. 345, says that what is of decisive importance in the preaching of the Gospel is not the method but the content—not *how* it is preached, but *what* is preached, viz. the Resurrection of Christ from the dead—he is clearly dependent on Bultmann, despite his forthright criticism of this scholar. As we saw earlier, Bultmann has little positive interest in the first use of the Law or the world. But if preaching has no immediate reference to the Law or any direct doctrine of the first use of the Law, it is really an escape from outward Creation. If, on the other hand, we treat the problem of the Law seriously in the context of the proclamation of the Word, it becomes a matter of great importance *how* it is preached. Preaching which assumes a rule of Law in the world also assumes as self-evident that its form will alter according to the period or situation. It must continually change in order to be the same in its work of freeing men from the oppression of the Law.

[22] This is not to deny that when a man is freed from false worship of the creature (and therefore from unbelief), his reason is also freed to give him greater insight and to allow him to exercise his dominion over Creation better. But this is a quite different position from that of Biblicist or Christocratic ethics, or the ethics of natural law. Cf. Olsson, *Luthers socialetik*, VOL. I, pp. 76-92.

world, at the one time. To stress the doctrine of the first use
of the Law means not only to affirm that the world belongs
to God, but to reject any other *religious* interpretation of the
world. For where it is denied that the world is God's world,
the attempt is soon made to regulate it by some other "religious" standard. To criticise one legalistic, religious standard
does not mean putting another one in its place. It means
rather allowing the world to stand freely in its own right and
be subject to its own critical standard. The first use of the Law
does not solve any problems in advance. What it does do is to
allow men to enter into a situation in which ultimately the
solutions to particular, concrete, and individual problems will
come as it were "from moment to moment."[23] Daily we enter
into new relationships with others, each with their own demands
upon us. Life, as God has created it, is not created and done
with, but is continued and renewed in ever-changing situations.

The settlement of these difficulties, which provide the means
of benefiting others, is not solely, or indeed primarily, the
achievement of those who are Christian. The motive and
inducement in serving one's neighbour does not in fact need
to be love. It is easier to govern in a society in which there is
an equitable distribution of goods and in which there is no
real need, than it is in a society where hunger is liable to breed
revolution. Stern treatment of petty dictators and profiteers
is often a better protection for the oppressed than love for them.
Since the constraint of the Law, which forces all men to do
what it demands, stems from actual need and not from any
altruistic feelings in the heart, the Law retains its power of
compulsion, even when love for one's neighbour is non-existent.
Our neighbour, simply because he is our neighbour, puts us
under obligation to him. The multitudes of our fellow beings,
each with his different requirements, bring into being a process
of service which continues life and gives life to the many. If we
have disconnected human conception and birth from the work

---

[23] On the term, cf. Luther, *Sermons on John*, W. A., 33, p. 406.10-24, and for a
discussion of the subject see Østergaard-Nielsen, *Scriptura sacra et viva vox*, pp. 39-45.
The expression is quite common in Luther. It is of great importance to bear in
mind that the primary factor in the first use of the Law is its dynamic and not its
cognitive aspect.

of God, it is quite natural that we should also disconnect this process of service from God. In other words, if we reject the first article, we shall also automatically reject the first use of the Law.[24] Conversely, if we give the first article its proper place, i.e. leave it at the beginning, we shall recover the first use of the Law, and the second use of the Law will follow logically.[25] The first article of faith and the first use of the Law belong together.

But Creation at the beginning was Creation in Christ. Before He came in the flesh, man was created and destined for Him. This does not mean that the doctrine of Creation can be derived from the Gospel of Christ, crucified and risen. It means that God's work of Creation is continued in His work of Redemption, and that this work of Creation is perfected in the Incarnation and the fulfilment of God's mighty works which are described or awaited in the second and third articles. Just as the Creation of the world and of man is Creation in Christ, so also the first use of the Law is a work "in Christ." We cannot derive the first use of the Law from the Gospel. What we are concerned with is not derivation, but a work which continues even when its premises have ceased to be valid. But the constraining work of the Law also involves tribulation, judgment, and "wrath" (Rom. XIII.4), the meaning of which is revealed only in the Gospel of Christ. This "wrath" brings a "death" upon man, which, even though it is swallowed up in Resurrection and victory, still remains even in the fellowship with Christ which is created by the Gospel and Baptism.[26] The new life, therefore, which comes into being when the old man dies and the new is born, involves also a service of one's neighbour in which the first use of the Law is found to exist concurrently with freedom of action.[27]

---

[24] See Søe, *Kristelig etik*, pp. 203-6, and the arguments with which he dismisses the civil use of the Law.

[25] See Ivarsson, *Predikans uppgift*, pp. 71-5.

[26] On "wrath" see Pierce, *Conscience in the New Testament*, pp. 66-74. The death in Baptism is Christ's death, but it is made real in us through that which puts us to death. We cannot separate the death in Baptism from the physical death of the individual, any more than we can separate the hope which the individual possesses of Resurrection from the actual death which he experiences.

[27] Cf. the important section in Ivarsson's *Predikans uppgift*, pp. 144-58, on preaching and conscience.

"Idealism"

The term "idealism" is used here to cover a multitude of views and theories of life which, although they have no basis in any existing law, in fact determine human behaviour either negatively or positively. It should be noted that in taking up the discussion of these various theories in the general context of the first use of the Law, we are primarily concerned with their effect in fostering or hindering the service which men are called upon to render to their neighbour. It is unimportant, therefore, whether these views can be deduced from the New Testament, or the Bible, or indeed from any other historical source. In particular, we must add, the question of their philosophical validity is quite irrelevant. Nor is it of fundamental importance (and we ought, perhaps, to stress this particular point) whether these various theories consciously define the neighbour as the one who is to be benefited by acts of service, or the acts themselves as being morally essential. In the end this will lead to an individualistic ethic which makes the perfection of self and not the need of the neighbour its central concern, and which spiritualises the performance of acts of service into inclination, in spite of the fact that the constraining or restraining work of the Law does have some kind of effect in what we do, or fail to do, for our neighbour. By concentrating on this effect, we are treating the theory in the same way as Luther regarded the earthly ruler. Any power or influence which the ruler wielded was independent of his acquaintance with scripture, and independent of whether his personal attitude to the actions which he took coincided with the publicly acknowledged *usus civilis* of the Law. The ruler is the instrument of the Law, even though he himself does not understand it. Similarly, an ethical theory which has taken root in a particular environment in which it exercises a universally acknowledged pressure, may be an instrument of the Law, even though the doctrine of the Law is nowhere explicitly mentioned in the theory itself. If we are thinking of the effect in this sense, it makes little difference whether the theory itself is clear or not. An attitude of intuitive sympathy is as effective in this case as any consistent theory.[28]

[28] Cf. Wingren, *Theology in Conflict*, p. 101 f.

We should note here by way of introduction some other parallels between ethical theory and the earthly ruler. In the first place the category of "abuse" is appropriate to both. In the Reformed doctrine of earthly government the action of the ruler is not accepted as a *good* action without further qualification. This interpretation is one of the many modern misunderstandings of the doctrine, and cannot be derived from the doctrine itself. We have a double starting-point—first, belief in God as the Creator, whose work of Creation is not relegated to some past time, but, as countless Biblical passages state, is still continuing throughout the world, wherever life comes into being; and second, the conviction that the work of God's "enemy" is also continually destroying His work of Creation. In his own person the earthly ruler either uses his position well, or he abuses it. Here, as in every other human occupation, all degrees are possible from willing service to inhuman wickedness. A characteristic part of this older doctrine of earthly government was the belief that an evil ruler is less to be feared than the absence of any authority at all. Civil disturbance, which produces indiscriminate bloodshed and gives free rein to evil, is a worse disaster than a corrupt governor.[29] We are not, therefore, concerned with any question of "ethical right" in the government, but simply with the fact that there is a latent tendency to evil in all men which can still be held in check even by rulers who are ethically corrupt.

In the same way even ethical theories which in some respects are objectionable act as a check upon the capriciousness which lies hidden in all men. Here again we discover that these theories exhibit every possible degree of morality from utter inhumanity to simple, human goodness. In the mission field, for instance, it may perhaps be worth considering whether it would not be more disastrous to attempt to eradicate a non-Christian way of thinking which may be theologically objectionable, but which

[29] Cf. also Løgstrup, *Den etiske fordring*, pp. 104-6. We may perhaps understand this fear of disturbance a little better when we hear a small child express relief at having got a "strict" teacher at school. Why? Because a child's fear of the teacher takes the place of a fear of being put at the mercy of his fellow pupils, and for the weak child a firm teacher is an advantage. The principal fear in the 16th century was not of oppressive authority but of the wielding of arbitrary power by individuals without the deterrent of punishment.

is at least indigenous to, let us say, the Africans or Asians, and capable of acting as a cohesive force in a way that a pre-conceived "Christian" way of thinking would not. If we try to see what fundamentally the "first use of the Law" is about, viz. that it is quite simply about the preservation of life, we may come to realise that to a far greater extent than we in the West are generally aware, we employ a great number of highly doubtful ideas, rules of solidarity, and preconceptions about honour and merit, and so on, for the protection of our own life and our neighbour's life. It was against the background of the basic relationship, however, that the doctrine of the first use of the Law was originally formulated. To put it crudely, the fundamental question was, "How are we to avoid being killed?" This in turn was based on the positive form of the question, "How can we guarantee life?" No answer was possible to either of these questions which did not speak of God the Creator.

In the second place *fear* (whether of the ruler or of these "ideal" conventions) was as decisive a factor in impelling the one who rendered obedience as his voluntary endorsement of the demand. Fear, as a factor in the *usus civilis* of the Law, was not, according to the Reformers, a wrong impelling force, but a good and useful one.[30] We must always remember that the intention of the first use of the Law is that the *works* that men do shall be good, not that those who do them shall become better. Those who originally formulated the *usus civilis* of the Law were thinking primarily here of fear of punishment in terms of the existing earthly law, and of fear of eternal punishment. In comparison with the situation four hundred years ago, modern legislation leaves a far wider area of life untouched. There are far greater liberties today than there were in the sixteenth century. But there are other factors than law which influence man's daily conduct. One of these is *fear*—fear of losing status or prestige or fear of social exclusion. The pattern

---

[30] The positive doctrine of fear is based directly on Rom. xiii.3 f. This interpretation is the correct one. It is quite clear that in this passage fear is represented as something which compels men to do certain acts and restrains them from certain others in accordance with the will of God. The fear here mentioned is fear of the Gentile authorities. Neither the civil government nor the subjects need to be Christian for the work of God in Creation to be done.

of human activity and behaviour is largely determined by our fear of men's judgment or condemnation.

Our criticism of these conventions must be based on two quite distinct Biblical grounds, as it was during the sixteenth century. We must begin by recognising that in fact these conventions force men into a way of life in which the neighbour is of vital importance. It is not the purpose of the Bible to provide regulations for human society. Even the early Church had no such intention for scripture.[31] God uses even our social conventions as the means by which we serve our neighbour. To disregard the rules of solidarity which prevail in a particular environment is to disregard forces which check and restrain the human tendency to evil, and therefore to despise God's Law and Creation. To affirm these conventions, however, does not mean to overlook their inadequacies, viz. the harm which men suffer on account of them. But to criticise something is not the same as to confuse it with something else, or to want to put something completely new in place of what we disapprove. A "Christian ethic" which rejects or alters natural rules of solidarity is wrong from the Christian point of view.[32] It does not follow from this, however, that these multifarious demands are to go uncriticised. There is also a social fear from which men need to be freed, not only through preaching the Gospel of the forgiveness of sins, but also by demanding "new works" by which men may break out of the strictures of their prevailing environment. That which is "natural" in the sense of *unfallen* can never exist as a given order, but is always something to which action must approximate, otherwise we should now be living in the sinless purity of Creation. The situation in which man has free dominion over Creation, without turning it into an idol, and freely serves his neighbour without restricting his service to a narrowly defined collective, is always a matter of

[31] Cf. C. H. Dodd, *New Testament Studies*, pp. 129-42; Dahl, *Background*, p. 439 f.

[32] Cf. Løgstrup, *Den etiske fordring*, pp. 125 ff. Where Løgstrup is weak is in his understanding of the critical function of the Gospel in relation to the prevailing order. This is connected with his failure to treat the first use of the Law correctly. When Løgstrup does discuss this, he does not do so in the part of his book in which he deals with the radical demand of the Law, but in the small section (pp. 69-120) in which he treats the "social norms." It is clear that Løgstrup regards these norms as being variable, but he is little concerned with how the Gospel fulfils its critical function in relation to them.

striving and not of attainment.[33] One does not need to be a Christian to admit that one is working for social reform.

We may pass over certain other parallels between prevailing social conventions and what in the sixteenth century was called "earthly government." Before going on any further, however, we must give at least a cursory glance at a purely historical fact. It is often said that the Reformed doctrine of the rule of the Law throughout the whole world is possible only when the rulers themselves are Christian. If this were so it would just mean that the function of civil government was simply an expression of the New Testament Law, and that the governing authorities were primarily members of the Christian congregation, who submitted themselves to the judgment of the Word. To maintain then that their civil function is an expression of the Law of God would mean, as the protagonists of the "Gospel and Law" formula hold, that the Gospel is the source of the Law. If this interpretation were correct, it would mean that the Reformed view of the rule of the Law throughout the whole of the world would be untenable in a situation in which the Christian Church was surrounded by a wholly pagan environment, or in which the New Testament Law was rejected by those in authority, and obedience to the "Law" of God was limited to an insignificant group of Christian believers. The presupposition in this argument is that the early martyr Church before Constantine was in a situation quite unlike that of the Reformation, and that the Churches in our own day are gradually coming into the same position as the early Church in relation to its environment.

Let us consider here two writers from the second century, each of whom has something helpful to say to us in this regard —Justin Martyr and Irenaeus. Both stressed that what Christ gave to the world was something radically *new*. Justin declares[34] that God has shown the whole human race what righteousness means, and has condemned murder, fornication, and adultery as sinful. Even those who commit such sins show by their treatment of others who do them that in their conscience they do not approve of them as good or righteous. The whole human

---

[33] Cf. Ramsey, *Basic Christian Ethics*, pp. 349-51.
[34] Justin Martyr, *Dialogue with Trypho*, xciii.

race therefore stands under the curse of the Law. No one is innocent before the Law, which hangs over all men.[35] The work of Christ is not to give a new Law, but to free men from its curse, and this liberation from the curse of the Law is the new thing which the world cannot procure for itself apart from Christ. Irenaeus on his side directly connects Creation (i.e. birth) with God's setting of "kings" on the earth: "For by the law of the same Being as calls men into existence are kings also appointed, adapted for those men who are at the same time placed under their government."[36]

The natural laws, which Christ in His Incarnation confirmed and accentuated, but did not exchange for others, were not given at Sinai, but at Creation, and work in the heart of every man.[37] Neither natural law nor earthly rulers can "recapitulate" man, and restore him to the purity of Creation before the Fall. In the incarnate Christ alone is man's restoration and salvation accomplished. Man's liberation is something which the world cannot procure for itself apart from Christ. When men are forced to serve one another, this is a different work of God. It may be performed even by men who are not free, but who, forced into service of their fellows because of fear, are at least "to some extent" righteous.[38] For Irenaeus there is a parallel between this and the fact that even apart from the Gospel men can beget children. When a man conceives or begets a child, God is creating through him, even though he is evil.

To suppose that there is any real contradiction between the Reformation and early Christianity on this point is due to a failure to consider the relevant statements in the writings of the early Church. We then assume that identical statements from the sixteenth century are really a misinterpretation, containing as they do what we suppose to be a fundamentally anthropocentric

[35] *Op cit.*, xcv.
[36] Irenaeus, *A.h.*, v. xxiv. 3 (Stier. ibid.).
[37] *Op cit.*, iv. xxiv-vi (Stier. iv. xiii-xv).
[38] The interpretation of Rom. xiii.1-6 which we find in Irenaeus is almost exactly the same as we find in the 16th-century doctrine of the earthly government. On the basis of Paul's own statements Irenaeus makes *fear of other men* the fundamental force which compels men to act properly. See, e.g., *A.h.* v. xxiv. 2 (Stier. ibid.). Irenaeus argues that when men cast off the fear of God, God lets them "restrain one another" by means of human laws.

M

and quite modern doctrine. This doctrine sees the State as constituting in itself an ethic in virtue of its biological structure, while it sees the individual as being hereditarily endowed with altruistic instincts. The Reformed doctrine of government was quite different from this. The tendency today is to ignore the early Christian doctrine and romanticise the statements of the Reformers. What we should rather attempt to do is to hold together the statements from the second century (which were formulated under pagan rulers and in a non-Christian environment) and those of the sixteenth (which were formulated under Christian rulers and in a Christian environment), and see both as together constituting the most likely exegesis of the Biblical texts.[39] But we must add that we shall understand both the second century and the sixteenth only as we recognise how fundamental are the demands which are made in all human societies, and how closely they approximate to the primary demand for the support and continuation of life. These demands stem from and are attributable to the basic fact of human birth. We today find difficulty in thinking of birth as a purely human act, and prefer to classify it under ethics.[40] Strangely enough, this does not lead us to think of it rather as a divine act, for which the Creator is praised in the first article. The modern Gnostic says that birth is simply a natural phenomenon, thus denying the fundamental article of the Christian faith. He then comes into conflict with the doctrine of the first use of the Law, and fails to discover the real meaning of the works which all men are forced to do by the demands which are made upon them.

When, however, we subject the concept which we have here referred to as "idealism" to critical examination, we discover that it gives rise to certain theological problems which are not found in the simple and everyday claims made by those set over us. The demands which are made by idealism are part of an ideological framework and a quasi-religious attitude to life which is alien in content to the Christian faith, and which

[39] See also Caird, *Principalities and Powers*, pp. 22-6, 49.
[40] It is difficult to define the proper sphere of ethics in this way without from the first excluding the belief in Creation in defining our limits. The concept of "works" must be central for such a definition to be acceptable.

consequently abolishes faith and the Gospel, if it is acknowledged as "Law." The acceptance of the Gospel demands
getting rid of an attitude to life which is defined by the ideal
of the development of personality, and which recognises Jesus
as being merely one of several "religious geniuses," or perhaps
the "ideal man." This idealism is hostile to Christianity, rather
than its ally on the level of the Law. If it is not premature to
say so, we may state that in regard to the *usus civilis* of the Law
there is only one question which we are to ask—Does idealism
make men better or worse *in their outward works on behalf of their
neighbour?* If we fail to ask this question, and set the Gospel
instead in opposition to idealism, this is a proof that we are
dealing simply with a disembodied Gospel, and that we have
lost the double concept of "Law *and* Gospel" from our thinking.[41]
The relatively non-committal position taken by evangelical
Christianity in regard to contemporary culture is connected
with its general neglect of the doctrine of the Law. It is possible
to adopt a particular position in regard to modern culture only
on the basis of the Law, and this position is one both of affirmation and negation, i.e. it involves a positive acceptance of
the expressions of human solidarity, while at the same time it
maintains a critical distance from them. The popular move-
ments of the last hundred years in temperance, education, etc.
have not had the association with the evangelical Churches
which might have been possible if the first use of the Law had
been a living doctrine within these Churches.[42] The concentration by theology on an unrelated and disembodied Gospel
without reference to the civil use of the Law has meant in
practice that the Churches have become collective groups in

[41] To think that the problem of preaching is unimportant, or to maintain that
we can preach the Gospel without making changes from one generation to another,
is clear proof that we have excluded the Law from our theological picture. The
Law of necessity involves a change in our proclamation, and this change affects
even our preaching of the very Gospel which frees men from the Law. Aukrust's
conclusion in his *Forkynnelse og historie*, pp. 344-6, is thus a matter of debate.

[42] In his *Urkristendom och reformation*, Lund 1932, pp. 171-5, and *Filosofi och
motivforskning*, Stockholm 1940, pp. 224-6, Nygren takes up for discussion the
practical problem of whether our present situation calls for a synthesis or a demar-
cation of limits. When he imagines, however, that there is a possibility of some
kind of "cultural synthesis" in this regard, he is not discussing the concept of *the
Law* in other than a negative and deprecatory way. This in fact is characteristic
of modern Protestantism.

separation from the world, and this in effect means against the world. This turns the Church into an idol—it "secularises" the Church—and makes it easier for the other collective groups in the world to become idols.[43]

There is a risk involved in having the demands of the Law set in an ideological framework, i.e. of having a religious view of life clothed in the conventional morality of a total view of life which does not admit the Gospel. It is a risk which is inherent in *all law*. It would be difficult to find in the twentieth century, either in the East or in the West, a "power" or "earthly government" which is not based on at least a semi-religious view of life. The compromise made in the Lutheran concept of the Law during the 1930's took place by and large in such a way that the Church failed to see the significance of the view of life which lay behind the political systems, and in consequence failed to maintain a critical distance from them. The transition from the simple demands which are made upon us each day to the total view of a particular attitude to life is charac-teristic not only of the amalgam which we have referred to as "idealism," but also of the demands which are made by the State upon its citizens. In particular we must stress that the Law which is derived from the Bible is as liable to be misapplied as any other Law. If what we find in the Bible really is *the Law*, i.e. demands, commandments, and requirements, then obedience to the Law requires that we turn its demands into an ideology. The result of this, however, is a self-righteousness which bears all the marks of a self-centred religion, and which excludes the Gospel. When the Gospel is first heard in the world of the Law it has always to destroy much that the Law has created during the period of its reign, whatever the source of that Law may have been.[44]

If Swedish theology has tended to avoid interpreting "idealism" as a part of the first use of the Law, this is because of the preoccupation of Lundensian theology with the basic motifs of *eros*, *nomos*, and *agape*. If we were to inquire into the historic origins of the universally accepted, but at times quite

[43] The term "secularising" is used here as synonymous with "Säkularismus" in Gogarten's *Verhängnis*, p. 138.
[44] Cf. Ivarsson, *Predikans uppgift*, pp. 74 ff.

vague, values which lead men to adopt particular attitudes, we would often find that these had their roots in ideas and concepts of Greek philosophy. To be true, these have been popularised and considerably changed in the meantime, but nonetheless they originated first in a milieu which was characterised, religiously speaking, by *eros*. At times we should also find that these values had their roots in the Bible, and especially the New Testament, though less frequently in that integral Old Testament or Jewish element which Nygren understands by *nomos*.[45] The meaning of *nomos* in Nygren's motif research is far narrower than "Law" in Paul, the early Church fathers, or Luther. It ought to be possible in motif research to use the term "Law" freely of sociological factors which do not stem organically from the heritage of Israel or Judaism, but which still have the function of Law in society, i.e. which are regulative or determinative of human conduct. It becomes less possible for us to do this, however, because there already exists a term to describe this corporate attitude to life, viz. "*eros*." It is particularly significant that immediately after the publication in 1930 of Part I of Nygren's work *Agape and Eros* there arose a lively debate on the subject of Christianity and idealism. The discussion arose because a practical attitude to life was involved. In Nygren's description of *eros* men recognised an attitude to life which characterised themselves, and which had moral significance for them.[46] The discussion was not about the relation between *nomos* and *agape*, or between the Law and *agape*. But this confrontation of *agape* and *eros*, i.e. of Christianity and idealism, makes it unusually difficult from several points of view to establish a true doctrine of the Law.

In particular this difficulty has increased by Nygren's approach since the emergence of the problem of "Christianity and idealism." Instead of reducing "idealism" into its constituent parts, Nygren reduces the problem, in so far as it remains a theological problem, to a discussion of *eros* and *agape*.[47]

[45] Cf. Anders Nygren, *Den kristna kärlekstanken*, VOL. II, 2nd edn., Stockholm 1947, Eng. trans. *Agape and Eros*, revised edn. London 1953, pp. x, xiii, 201, etc.
[46] Cf. Nygren, *Filosofi och motivforskning*, pp. 208-10, the introduction to the chapter on Christianity and idealism.
[47] Cf. *op. cit.*, pp. 208-26, where Nygren discusses this synthesis.

If, however, we put the problem in such a way, we can never discuss the first use of the Law, nor deal with it in its proper context, even when we are discussing the possibility of a "cultural synthesis" between Christianity and idealism.[48] When the Law disappears as an independent factor alongside the Gospel, and when the problem is reduced to one of "*eros* and *agape*," this means that we are regarding idealism exclusively as being at variance with the Gospel. It is this same Gospel which comes into contact with the values which govern human action in the environment in which it is preached; and the question of what function these values have in forcing men into, or alternatively in restraining them from, particular conduct is not asked. If we discuss the possibility of a cultural synthesis between Christianity and idealism in which in some form we can affirm the positive value of idealism,[49] but if at the same time we still do not deal even remotely with the concept of the Law—the terms "*nomos*" and "law" are both used here in their Jewish sense—then this will mean in practice that attitudes and positions which have been derived from outside Christianity will be accepted as beneficial for human society, *without being given a place in "the Law" or "the works of the Law."*[50]

[48] Cf. *op. cit.*, pp. 224-6. The whole problem calls for an analysis of the concept of "Law" and an interpretation of "idealism" (including that idealism which is involved in all that we mean by "eros") as an expression of the work of the Law. This has been the point at issue from the beginning. There arose widespread interest in the problem of Christianity and idealism for the simple reason that "eros" appeared to describe men's ethical valuations (there was, of course, no general interest in the purely historical problem). But to solve the question raised by reducing the problem to one of "eros and agape" is acceptable only if it is impossible to provide any answer to the general question, and if there is no existing theological method by which to reach a solution. If in this situation there is no suggestion made that the proper concept with which we have to deal is the Law, this omission proves that there is some defect in our theological system.

[49] See Nygren, *Filosofi och motivforskning*, p. 225.

[50] Cf. Nygren, *Urkristendom och reformation*, p. 173: "To insist that men today must first be converted to a belief in some kind of idealistic world view before going on to Christianity is no better than it was to demand in the synthesis of Judaism and Christianity that circumcision and observance of the Law should be the conditions of entrance to Christianity. When such a synthesis has outlived its usefulness, the connexion between the two exists only to be broken." This is the only passage in his analysis of our modern situation and its task (*Urkristendom och reformation*, pp. 169-75; *Filosofi och motivforskning*, pp. 224-6) in which Nygren uses the term "Law." For him "Law" is a Jewish concept which in our present situation has no meaning.

At this point Lundensian motif research and Barthian theology are very similar.[51]

The old doctrine of Creation and the Law assumed as self-evident that there is no good thing anywhere in the world which was not made by God and bestowed upon us by Him. I cannot regard with pleasure any part of the world, and I cannot accept it for my use without thanking God for it, i.e. without receiving it from His hands, and acknowledging Him as Giver and Creator. The question at once raised in modern theology is, How do I know this God who bestows and fashions men anew throughout the world? How do I get knowledge of His existence? Earlier theology looked in a different direction, and emphasised that even without knowing God men received life from Him, and were used by Him to perform His will and to do His work in the world. The first article of the Creed and the first use of the Law still point in this direction, i.e. to God and His works. Both, however, give rise to problems when the main question becomes that of knowledge. Then the second article becomes the first, and the Law is derived from the Gospel.

[51] Both for Lundensian theology and for Barth, the second article takes the place of the first. This explains why the idea of the Law has disappeared from each. Cf. Barth, *Christengemeinde und Bürgergemeinde*, pp. 7-35. Though Barth's use of the doctrine of *analogia relationis*, which he puts in place of the Law, distinguishes him from the motif theology of Lund, it does not destroy the basic similarity beween the two. For both, the second article is the point of departure.

CHAPTER III

THE SECOND USE OF THE LAW

Man and Guilt

THE second use of the Law is its essential use,[1] but it has no direct effect in the world. While the Law compels men to a certain course of action and brings about visible results in the world or in "the body," it has also another hidden effect. It burdens men's consciences with guilt and speaks of men's condition. The Law thus sets man before God, and puts him there as a captive and sinner, "without excuse." But the guilt which man sees in his own heart *coram Deo* has been committed in the world and has found concrete expression in his relation to his neighbour and the things of Creation which man has turned into his idols. He has put these in God's place rather than subjected them to himself.

We shall return later in the present section to the characteristic interplay which marks the relationship between the first and second uses of the Law. The guilt which is revealed by the second use of the Law in the conscience or *coram Deo* has not only been committed in the world. It is also revealed when the Law compels men to do certain actions. When the Law presses upon man and compels him to do certain things, it exposes the opposition which lies in his heart. This opposition is expressed in the word of denial addressed to his neighbour by which man reveals his egocentricity, in his word of assent to his idols, and in the pain which he suffers when he is deprived of money, honour, or pleasure. By this he reveals that his heart is godless. We might say that man's conscience has a continual foretaste of the Last Judgment. The Last Judgment accuses

---

[1] Cf. Arvid Runestam, *Den kristliga friheten hos Luther och Melanchthon*, Stockholm 1917, pp. 160 ff.

man before God and Christ, but it does so by pointing to simple everyday occurrences in the world in which "the least of these my brethren" have been given or have not been given bread, water, and clothing (Mt. xxv.31-46).[2] This final Judgment will prove to be a surprise even to those who in their earthly life heard Christ's word and belonged to His Church. The true meaning of the final Judgment will not be revealed until the event itself takes place. Man's insight into the nature of God and His will will increase, since God continues to have dealings with him. Consequently the proclamation of the Gospel or the preaching of Christ means that the man who hears the word of the Gospel becomes aware of his guilt and recognises in retrospect his terrible impurity in a way which, in comparison with any insight into guilt and Law previously held, is something quite new. Only when the Gospel is preached does man become aware of his guilt.[3] This is not the point at which to criticise this statement, but what the Gospel reveals are the experiences which a man has already had as a human being in his dealings with Creation, the place of God's works, though these were expressed in different and less intelligible forms. It may be appropriate at the beginning of this section to say first a few words about guilt as a human phenomenon independent of the preached Word.

Guilt is always individual in its nature. When theology or preaching strips guilt of its individual character in order to provide a more radical description of a sin against God which consists merely in unbelief and not in outward acts, the result is not a clearer insight into the nature of guilt, but rather the reverse. It means that guilt has been dispersed. The root of guilt is always to be found in the disruption of fellowship with God. This disruption, however, is expressed in man's actual relationships with his neighbour and his attitude to the rest of Creation. These are perverted when his fellowship with God has been destroyed. Guilt and the apprehension of guilt, therefore, are an expression of health and are a normal human

[2] In the New Testament the Last Judgment is consistently thought of as a judgment of men's works (cf. II Cor. v.10). See Wilfried Joest, *Gesetz und Freiheit*, 2nd edn., Göttingen 1956, pp. 165-9, 176-85. Joest submits a good number of New Testament passages, particularly from the exhortatory sections of the Epistles, to a penetrating analysis.

[3] Cf. Brunner, *Man in Revolt*, p. 116 f.

phenomenon. Guilt is an indication of health. The fact that guilt makes itself felt even where the word of the Gospel has not been preached is a witness to the truth that God continues to create and give life even outside the Church, and that men are and remain His, surrounded by His works and kept in His mercy. We have no reason to think of a guilty conscience as something for which a man ought to blush. We should rather think of guilt as being a normal and healthy phenomenon which there is no need for men to confess. In particular, however, we are not to regard it as a weakness, but as a sign that the world is God's.[4] This normal, healthy phenomenon, however, has an individual expression in every man, just as there is an individual expression for every other part of his normal state of health. Guilt is a part of human life, and is bound up with the activities and relationships of this life. Guilt, of course, means life and health in the same way as the Law and judgment mean life and health. It is part of an abnormal situation in which factors that are hostile to human life prevail and in which life is thus threatened. When a physician destroys the false feelings of guilt which exist in his patient, and in so doing removes his guilt, this act of healing is the means by which one group of demands is separated from the multitude which men experience. This separation is always being made when the first use of the Law is properly fulfilling its function. As the disappearance of the Law from theological thinking in general has created a gulf between Christian faith and culture, so it has also lessened the possibility of interpreting the work of psychiatry in the light of faith. Often enough the only distinction which remains is between the sick person, who is the responsibility of the physician, and the "purely religious" person who is a suitable subject for the care of the pastor, and whose guilt is regarded simply as guilt before God. It may well be that the physician is at the present day one of the powers that perform the first use of the Law, generally, however, and this has been the case for a century now, without using the name of "God." As one of these modern powers the

[4] In recent times it is the actual *confession* of sins which has become of primary importance in the act of confession, whereas in the Reformation it was *absolution* which occupied this place. In the Articles of Faith of the Swedish Church, for instance, it is stated, "The ministers of the Word of God are commissioned to forgive sins, but not to uncover hidden offences."

physician fulfils his function well when he destroys unreasonable feelings of guilt and makes his patient change his habits. But psychiatry also knows of cases in which healing cannot take place as long as the patient refuses to assume part of the responsibility for his illness and thus give himself the opportunity of self-correction and of abandoning his old habits.[5] In a situation such as this the physician is discharging the Law's function of constraint in regard to the patient. Guilt is the characteristic negative form in which the health of the patient is to be seen. The only question is whether he is capable of attaining to this state of health, i.e. of dying to his old life, which is the meaning of health. In such a situation, in which a man's whole existence is at stake, the second use of the Law continues to function in the world apart from the preaching of the Gospel.

If we look at the matter apart from the Gospel, which is Christ, we may put it in this way: the terrible thing is that a man's tribulations continue apart from the preaching of the Gospel. But a theology which deals with a bare and unrelated Gospel and has no place for the double concept of "Law and Gospel," and indeed can see no justification for such a concept, says in effect that the man who suffers tribulation knows nothing of guilt before God until the Gospel is preached to him. If we have tied ourselves to the formula "Gospel and Law," and made the question of knowledge central, we no longer regard the Law as a restraint and tribulation exercised by God in the world, but rather as a knowledge which is found in those who have received the Gospel. In this case the recognition of guilt comes only after the preaching of the Gospel.[6] The classical documents of Christianity show hardly any trace of this anxiety in modern theology. In these the Gospel is interpreted without further explanation as going out into the world to confront an already existing situation of distress, just as Jesus went out to those who were oppressed and burdened with guilt in order to heal and forgive. When men are healed, it is clear that they gain an insight into the nature of their affliction. The important thing, however, in this case is not the

[5] Cf. Heinz Häfner, *Schulderleben und Gewissen*, Stuttgart 1956, pp. 7, 179.
[6] See Søe, *Kristelig etik*, p. 21 f.

insight which men receive, but the healing itself, i.e. the Gospel as a *work* of God. In contrast to the regenerating and life-giving work of the Gospel there is a corresponding work of death and affliction in the world wherever compulsion meets and restrains unhealthy or sinful attitudes.

When theology loses the concept of the work of the Law and is compelled to work with an unrelated Gospel in the midst of a profane world in which God is inactive and where the natural laws alone are regulative, guilt before God becomes a correlative of this same Gospel, and only very few of those who suffer could be described as having "purely religious" sufferings. When such distinctions are made between those who are "physically sick" and those who are suffering from a "purely religious" affliction, we must at some time ask what was the group to which those whom Jesus helped and to whom He preached the Gospel belonged.[7] Sometimes we have the impression that it is the "physically sick" who represent the deepest suffering, and even the deepest guilt *coram Deo*, and that they bear this burden representatively in a merciless society in which the interest of the collective thrives and real fellowship is non-existent, and in which these victims have waited in vain for years for someone to "prove neighbour to the man who fell among the robbers" (Lk. x.36). A man who is aware that he is going in the wrong direction, and that he can attain health only if the pattern of his life is broken into by certain forces, may believe that he is in the presence of death when he is confronted by these forces. In a certain sense he is, but it is a death which is accompanied by life that meets him. It requires a superhuman effort to face such a death alone without support of a fellowship or a Gospel which assures a man that he is God's, even though he may die if he is not cured. We must ask if, when the Church waits for a "purely religious" crisis to occur in men, it is not passing by the victims of assault who come under the second use of the Law, i.e. who apply all the demands of the Law to their own hearts, and see

---

[7] The first to recognise Jesus as the Messiah was not Peter at Caesarea Philippi but the unclean spirit in the man in the synagogue at Capernaum (Mk. 1.24, cf. v.7). Cf. Julius Schneiwind, *Das Evangelium nach Markus*, Das Neue Testament Deutsch, VOL. I, 5th edn., Göttingen 1949, pp. 52, 87.

their impotence and also judge themselves.[8] Their guilt is worldly guilt and is related to an individual situation in which only their fellow men are involved—or their fellow men and the things of Creation, and "life" but not "God." Their need is not expressed as a religious need.

If God has no place in their picture of suffering, this may be because they have accepted a traditional metaphysical concept of God which is un-Biblical. What we vaguely call "life" may have more in common with the God of the Bible than the reality which we think we define by the term "God." When the Bible speaks about God, it does not speak about a reality which man encounters in a specifically religious act and of which he has some knowledge, as he has knowledge of other objects in other acts. God is Creator, and His relation to man is given in the simple fact that man lives. All of man's reactions to his own life are reactions within his relationship to God and this cannot be established by him through his acceptance of God, nor can it be broken by his denial of God. Rather it is established in birth, i.e. Creation, and although it may vary thereafter in content (it may display wrath or love, judgment or grace), it does not cease.[9] Even when man in unbelief rises up against God, he must still, because he is a creature, seek his life from God. He therefore seeks for something around himself in which to trust. The idols which he makes become his lords, and in consequence prevent him from ruling in freedom over Creation and subduing it to himself. He falls instead into bondage to the things that he uses and owns. If this idolatry is already in conflict with his humanity, his insight into his own unnatural condition increases when his idols are rejected in the course of his life and are revealed as being incapable of affording him help at the onset of death. Even here he does not cease to be in a relationship to God, nor is his only loss that which relates to money, prestige, or sex, and his only relationship that which he has with his idols. All

---

[8] It is interesting to compare the views of a psychiatrist and a New Testament scholar in regard to the meaning of conscience. The similarities are striking. The conscience adresses itself to particular actions and condemns them. Cf. Pierce, *Conscience in the New Testament*, pp. 66-74, 85 f., 111 f., with Häfner, *Schulderleben und Gewissen*, p. 133.

[9] Cf. the section above, "The Creator and Life," in Part I, chapter I.

this negative experience is an experience of the Creator, and
an experience of guilt in His presence. It is a constant reminder
of what man owes to God—trust, obedience, and faith (Rom.
I.18-32).[10]

A man's daily confrontation with the needs and demands
of his neighbour is a part of this experience of judgment and
revelation of guilt. His attitude of selfishness and disparagement
in regard to his neighbour is not a different reality from that
of a lack of belief in God and bondage to the creature. Lovelessness in regard to one's neighbour is exactly the same reality
as unbelief, but seen from the point of view of the neighbour,
i.e. from the point of view of one who requires but does not
receive a particular act of service. When a man defies God he
turns to the creature, which then becomes his treasured God.
In so doing, however, he closes the door on his neighbour's
need. In the purely human need of the excluded neighbour
we again have a reminder of what the Creator demands, and
this word of demand renders the one to whom it is addressed
guilty. We cannot separate guilt *coram Deo* from a feeling of
guilt in regard to our fellow men. Guilt *coram Deo* is expressed
in our relationship to our neighbour.[11] In the Last Judgment
guilt in the presence of God will be defined in terms of our
failures to help our neighbour. Guilt is not an unknown
quantity which suddenly appears when the Gospel is preached
any more than the Law is unknown until the Gospel is preached.
The Law is operative in the whole world, and is continually
engaged in asserting its demands. Objective guilt *coram Deo* is
perceived in man's concrete experiences of guilt, i.e. in his
refusal to give what was asked of him, viz. trust in God and
love toward his neighbour. Those who are acquisitive and
refuse to give to others increase in guilt. They are well aware

---

[10] Cf. G. Bornkamm, *Das Ende des Gesetzes*, pp. 23-6; Vajta, *Theologie*, pp. 8-10;
Gärtner, *The Areopagus Speech*, pp. 235 f.

[11] Cf. Prenter, *Skabelse og genløsning*, pp. 104-10. Prenter admits that it is "the
prophetic word of judgment" alone that has power to reveal sin, but he also
clearly defines the meaning of man's guilt in regard to his neighbour (e.g. p. 108).
See also Ivarsson, *Predikans uppgift*, pp. 74-6, n. 22, where Ivarsson takes up the
discussion with Prenter on this point. We should also compare this with Prenter's
Skabelse og genløsning, pp. 151-64, where the relationship between philosophy and
dogmatics is brought back to the relationship between Law and Gospel.

of this, for they are continually striving to oppose God's work of Creation. This work is not something that is distant from them, but is going on around them all the time, so that at every point they encounter it.[12]

When guilt is defined in terms of the first use of the Law, it is to be seen as the force which compels men to act for the advantage of others. God continues to create and to be involved in the world and not only with the individual who is now seen to be guilty before Him. Man is caught in the tension between God and the world, and is forced to turn out towards his neighbour and Creation. But while the Law exercises its positive function of compelling men to act, it also speaks of the man who *does* the Law. Here it speaks negatively, and its function is one of accusation. The first work of the Law, that of compulsion, is continually passing into the second work of the Law, that of accusation. It exercises both of these functions at the same time. It differs only in the mode of its reception. At one time I am forced to look outwards to the world which is purer than I am, and which has a right to my services. At another time I am forced to look inwards to myself, but I am less pure than the world, and remain so whatever I may do. The first and the second uses of the Law coincide.

If, however, we define guilt in terms of the second use of the Law, it will be seen not as a force which compels men to act in the interests of others, but as *health* in its negative aspect, i.e. health in the only form which it can have under the conditions of human perversity.[13] In its second use the Law does not speak of the world or its need of my services, but it speaks directly of myself. When it passes judgment upon me, it reveals throughout what I ought to have been. It bears in itself the image in which I have been created, and even as it accuses contains the original purity of Creation.[14] The image of the Law points forward to Christ, who is the image of God,

---

[12] The idea of the world as the result of God's work of Creation and as pointing to the divine Artificer is something quite different from this, and should not be confused with the matters discussed in Rom. 1.18 ff. See Gärtner, *The Areopagus Speech*, p. 138.

[13] Cf. Brunner, *Man in Revolt*, p. 202, and the quotation from Luther on pp. 522 f., and also Løgstrup, *Den etiske fordring*, pp. 189 f.

[14] Cf. Luther's interpretation of Exodus in W. A., 16, p. 447.26-34.

and who can therefore make me human again (Col. 1.15; Gen.
1.26). But while the Law points thus to Christ, and speaks of
the original and uncorrupted life of man, it still retains its
negative function of accusation, i.e. it demands man's death.
It is in precisely this way that it contains my health in its
negative aspect. Death does not detract from the purity of the
first Creation, but points us back to it. It brings us to the
resurrection from the dead and to likeness to Christ. These
are all parts of the same reality.[15] The second use of the Law
is therefore fulfilled when the image of Christ is proclaimed
in the Gospel. Nowhere do we see our guilt more clearly than
when the Gospel speaks to us. But what is the Gospel? It is
simply the story of Christ, the continued repetition of the
account of what happened to Him, and what He did and said.
The divinity and humanity of Christ cannot here be separated
from one another. To think of guilt as being revealed only
through the Gospel, and as having been unknown to men
before this time, is to intellectualise the Gospel and also to
separate Christ's divinity from His humanity. The guilt which
is revealed when a man hears Christ preached to him is the
same as he has encountered previously in his conscience,
except that it is extended and widened to include the whole
of his existence. This guilt is revealed and extended when
Christ's humanity is preached, for Christ "emptied Himself,
taking the form of a servant, being born in the likeness of men.
And being found in human form He humbled Himself and
became obedient unto death, even death on a cross" (Phil. II.
7 f.). It is here that we see the contrast between Christ's work
and Adam's. Adam erred from the true and living way—and
the man who hears the word of the Gospel is Adam. At the
same time the Gospel proclaims the "image of God," i.e. the
One in whose image Adam was created. Christ's divinity shines
forth without the slightest diminution of His humanity. It is

---

[15] The extent and significance of Baptism lies in the fact that it embraces all
this in a single act, the consequences of which continue to affect the one who has
been baptised. Baptism proves that God will not leave in the power of evil those
whom He has created in His image. At the same time, however, it points forward
to a daily death and resurrection for as long as the baptised Christian lives on
earth, and even beyond that. The significance of the Church is seen most clearly
if it is regarded from the point of Baptism as the act of recapitulation.

a part of the uniqueness of the Gospel that the Crucified represents vicariously all the dead who have ever suffered and all the living who still suffer, and that the man who hears the word of the Gospel sees his own share of guilt in the burden of suffering which others have had to bear. His guilt is that while his egocentricity remains unaltered and he himself is unharmed, he is still compelled, like Adam, to avoid the way of the Cross, faith, and selflessness. Man can see his total guilt only when he stands, as it were, outside himself. He sees no more than part of his guilt as long as he remains inside himself. This is why the second use of the Law can be fulfilled only when the Gospel is preached.[16] The realisation of his total guilt comes only when a man has glimpsed his total forgiveness. The vast extent of his old corrupted nature can be comprehended only when his new nature comes into being.

In the present theological situation, however, where the second article is put before the first, and where in consequence the first use of the Law is repudiated in many quarters, we must concentrate on the point which is disputed. It is quite true that the second use of the Law is fulfilled when the Gospel is preached, and that only faith reveals the depth of guilt. But what faith and the Gospel bring to accomplishment is something that is basic to every human activity. We should not, therefore, be afraid in our theology of starting with the common human experience of guilt.[17] It is easy to see how the theological quest of an earlier period, which was undertaken in the interests of apologetics to discover different human "points of contact," should have produced the anti-liberal reaction within present-day theology. We must also, however, be aware of the dangers

[16] Cf. Bring, *Dualismen hos Luther*, p. 225 f., and Ivarsson's reference to Bring in *Predikans uppgift*, p. 74, n. 22. Ivarsson attacks Prenter on the grounds that he gives too high a place to the preaching of the Law, "the prophetic word of judgment" (e.g. *Skabelse og genløsning*, p. 110). There is good reason to believe, however, that Prenter includes a preaching of the Gospel in this prophetic word of judgment: "The Law cannot reveal sin if it is separated from the Gospel" (*op. cit.*, p. 110). On this point Ivarsson and Prenter are agreed.

[17] When Häfner, *Schulderleben und Gewissen*, p. 179 f., states that the process of "*Personwerdung*" continues until death, and that in this process feelings of guilt have not simply a destructive but also a constructive part to play, he is speaking as a psychoanalyst about something which has particular theological significance. Cf. von Gebsattel, *Prolegomena einer medizinischen Anthropologie*, p. 390.

N

which accompany this anti-liberal reaction. These may ultimately be summarised as constituting a false Christology in which the humanity of Christ has been lost and His divinity treated docetically. It is obvious that a docetic Christology such as this regards the guilt which man experiences after the Gospel has been preached to him, i.e. which he experiences before Christ, as different from any guilt which he experiences in his relationship with his neighbour. It is a guilt which is derived from the Gospel, and is unknown outside the sphere in which the Gospel is preached. This specifically religious guilt tends to minimise ordinary human guilt and consciousness of guilt, and to destroy the connexion between guilt in the presence of God and this other type of guilt in regard to one's neighbour.[18] To minimise this guilt means ultimately that we become incapable of fulfilling the demands of the first use of the Law, or having any positive view of the works which men are compelled to do for their neighbour.[19] All this is a vicious circle in which one debatable attitude confirms another. It is a peculiar Christocentric circle which lacks any human aspects, and in particular lacks any of Christ's human aspects. In the meanwhile, however, the Gospel works with its own inward power; and since it deals with men who continue to be bound by the first use of the Law, it brings all human guilt to life and prevents it from being hidden from the presence of God. We may accentuate the problem if we express it in the following

[18] Soe, for instance, does this. See his *Kristelig etik*, pp. 21 f., 58, 206, n. 5.

[19] *Op. cit.*, pp. 203-6. It is a problem for Søe how from the standpoint of the Christian faith we can approve measures for the moral betterment of society if these do not bring or are not associated with faith in the Gospel. "Humanly speaking such a course is often a mere extra, or a safeguard against moral disintegration or sheer inhumanity. It is difficult to determine whether in this regard the Christian contribution has a positive or negative value" (p. 209). Søe, however, suggests that while the Christian can rejoice when any such inhumanity is eradicated, its removal cannot be justified on the grounds of the civil use of the Law. This raises for Soe the problem of the concept of sin which he has now separated from the first use of the Law. He therefore refers to Jn. xvi.9 as the central word concerning the "confession of sin": "(He will convince the world) of sin, because they do not believe in me" (p. 206, n. 5). If, however, our argument is consistent, we shall see that the denial of the first use of the Law puts a wedge between sin before God and sin against our neighbour. We should perhaps add that if we affirm the first use of the Law, we shall not find any difficulty in Jn. xvi.9. The passage makes good sense as it stands—the meaning of sin is made clear in the preaching of the Gospel.

way—theology is surrounded by human experiences of Christ which it cannot explain. It is often said that liberal theology has led our present generation to interpret Jesus as "the ideal man," and to formulate its conception of guilt accordingly. There is in fact some truth in this statement, but the real reason why men have the kind of burden of guilt which they have is simply that they are *men*. In their feelings of guilt they resemble the condemned in Jesus's picture of the Last Judgment. These passages concerning the future Judgment are from one point of view quite lacking in modern "theocentricity," and are particularly concerned with human relationships. It is men's outward physical acts which are almost exclusively the basis of the Judgment.[20]

The gulf between these New Testament passages concerning the Judgment on men's works on the one hand and the clear statements about the righteousness which is given in faith apart from works, and indeed in spite of any evil works which men may have done, on the other hand, corresponds in early Christian writings to the tension between Law and Gospel which we find in the Lutheran Reformation of the sixteenth century. In both these cases it is a question of a gulf and a tension which cannot be reconciled logically any more than the gulf and contrast between death and life can be. Death does not prove on closer analysis to be life any more than the Biblical texts concerning the Judgment prove on closer analysis to contain the Gospel. But death is conquered by life, because at Calvary there is One who undergoes death and yet destroys it, and after the victory of His Resurrection comes to preach the Gospel to the prisoners of death. In the same way the judgment which is contained in the word of judgment is transformed into the Gospel not because judgment in itself is grace, but because the Judge is *Christ* who, according to the scripture, has appeared on earth before the final Judgment and spoken

[20] Cf. Joest, *Gesetz und Freiheit*, p. 155 f. See, e.g., Mt. xxv.31-46 and also xvi. 27; Jn. v.29; Rom. ii.6; ii Cor. v.10. Works and the Last Judgment are mentioned together more frequently in the New Testament than faith and the Last Judgment. See also Eidem, *Det kristna livet enligt Paulus*, vol. i, pp. 78-85, where several Pauline passages are quoted. We cannot begin here to deal with the problem of the relationship between works and justification by faith, but I propose to take it up in my projected work on Gospel and Church.

His "piercing" word which discerns "the thoughts and inten-
tions of the heart" (Heb. iv.12).[21] Christ in His mercy is
always seeking the lost.[22] Judgment merges into the Gospel
simply because Christ is what He is, and not because man is
what he is. The words of the Bible are addressed to man, and
the words about judgment are no exception. They are addressed
to the old man who is condemned to die in order that the new
man may arise.

This means that the Law in its second use precedes and
prepares the way for preaching, though the substance of
preaching cannot be derived from it. It precedes the preaching
of the Gospel in the same way as death precedes and prepares
the way for Resurrection. Unless Resurrection is seen as a
mighty act, it cannot under any circumstances be derived from
death, for death is the opposite of Resurrection. If Resurrection
follows death it does so by destroying that which precedes
and thus opens the door to Resurrection. And if preaching
comes to the world of the Law, it abolishes the work of the
Law which still continues in the world. And yet this work of
the Law is God's. The unity of the divine works of judgment
and regeneration is hidden in God. It can be made a logical
unity only at the cost of losing all conception of sin and eliminating the certainty that even the man of faith bears about
in himself that which is condemned to death.[23] Since, however,
the second use of the Law is based on the first use of the Law,
i.e. on human society in its relationship to the rest of Creation,
theology is forced to begin in one way or another to begin at
two starting-points.[24] If we simply take the Bible and interpret
the Biblical words without dealing with men's actual condition,
the existing rule of Law as the direct opposite of preaching will
disappear, and so also will the first article of the Creed. The
first article will then have to be interpreted as a derivative of
the second article, and therefore of the Gospel, just as the Law

[21] Cf. Paul Feine, *Theologie des Neuen Testaments*, 6th edn., Leipzig 1934, p. 391.
[22] Cf. Joest, *Gesetz und Freiheit*, pp. 179 f., 194; Ivarsson, *Predikans uppgift*, pp.
73, 99 ff.
[23] Barth's use of the formula, "Gospel and Law," is connected with his peculiar
treatment of the concept of sin. See Barth, *Die kirchliche Dogmatik*, VOL. III, PT. II,
p. 244 f., and VOL. III, PT. III, p. 424.
[24] Cf. Wingren, *Theology in Conflict*, pp. 161 ff.

is derived from the Gospel. All these difficulties of theological interpretation are closely connected, and cannot be removed as long as we fail to adopt the method of two starting-points.

Preaching and the Law

The publication of my book *Theology in Conflict* in 1954 produced an article by the Danish theologian Hejne Simonsen in the *Dansk teologisk tidsskrift* in 1957. In this article Simonsen clearly defines the problem of preaching and the Law and examines its difficulties.[25] He maintains that theology must rest on two principles which he defines in the following way: "*First*, in the proclamation of the Gospel the Christian message is essentially based on and subordinate to the apostolic preaching of Christ; and *second*, the demands of the Law are binding on men in society before they encounter the Gospel."[26] Simonsen, however, denies that either preaching or the Law can be made an object of scientific observation or research. Thus the error in *Theology in Conflict* does not consist in the assertion that theology has two points of departure, but in the suggestion that these two points of departure, preaching and the Law, are phenomenological and can be made the object of scientific observation and analysis. Simonsen maintains quite consistently that theology must deal with this double point of departure and abandon its scientific character.[27] Only when theology sacrifices its scientific character can it come to grips with its object, and as long as it maintains this character, it lacks this contact.

We are not, however, to be quite so hasty and forthright in dismissing simple, everyday observation from theology. The kind of observations which can be made in essentials by anyone are an inseparable part of a historical phenomenon such as Christian preaching. In contrast with most other language which has been used to describe God in the course of history, Christian preaching is based on a given text which is to be

[25] Hejne Simonsen, "Teologiens metode hos Gustaf Wingren," in *Dansk teologisk tidsskrift*, 1957, pp. 81-92.

[26] *Op. cit.*, p. 91.

[27] *Op. cit.*, pp. 87, 89, 92.

interpreted in all preaching. In contrast with many other writings which have dealt with God in the course of history, this particular writing does not deal with the secrets of another world which have been acquired in moments of solitary contemplation, but describes the events which have happened in a history that is common to all men. These events are a part of everyday life, and cannot be separated from this connexion with the world without losing their meaning. If we subordinate preaching of the present day to the apostolic *kerygma*, we are assuming that it is possible to compare the two. In this case philology, like every other study, can contribute to our total understanding. If we dissolve every contact between systematic theology and scientific argument, we are not only sacrificing the scientific character of theology, but are also destroying the important distinction maintained by theology against all "Enthusiastic" piety, viz. the connexion between the Spirit and the external word. In the conflict of the anti-Gnostic Fathers with the Gnostics and of the Reformers with the Enthusiasts it was the interpretation of scripture which became the most important instrument in their task of explaining the meaning of faith. This took place long before the emergence of modern science, and indeed we might say that modern science has one of its strongest roots in the need of the Christian Church for an objective interpretation of scripture.[28]

Having said this, however, I must also add that the basic factor which underlies the two starting-points which we have referred to as "actual human need" and "preaching" is not, of course, accessible to scientific examination and argument in the sense that each of the two points "exists" by itself and can be observed and described without amplification from the other. When we say that we must have a double point of departure, what we mean is that each starting-point is to be explained by and interpreted in the light of the other. The word of the Gospel is addressed to particular men. Any exegesis which fails to explain the function of a text in relation to those whom it addresses limits its purpose quite arbitrarily. The actual demands made upon men serve to remind us of this purpose when we are analysing what we mean by the

[28] Cf. also Prenter, *Skabelse og genløsning*, pp. 188-91.

"Word." Thus, these actual demands which are revealed to us by the word of the Gospel embody the rule of the Law, sin, and Creation, i.e. human birth. Anthropology cannot be dealt with independently of the Gospel, but rather man's actual situation is revealed when the Gospel is preached to him. It is then that the demands which are made upon men cease to be unrecognised, that guilt is revealed, and men reinterpret the demands made upon them and come to know that they themselves have been created by the God of whom the Gospel now speaks. The "Word" or "Gospel" addresses man as a creature who stands accused before God, and if it fails to do so it lacks an essential part. Correspondingly, what we have referred to as the "actual demands" or the "Law" must be illuminated by the light which comes from the preaching of the Gospel.[29] If the Gospel has no discriminatory function in regard to the multitude of demands made upon men, we are left with the rigid and inflexible "order" of an earlier theology of order. Preaching and the Law illuminate one another. Neither can be analysed independently of the other. This is the meaning of our double phenomenological starting-point. The two points are open to observation only as *interpreted*. Any interpretation must proceed from given facts, and when these are interpreted, they are interpreted in the light of each other.[30]

From one point of view Simonsen is right in maintaining that neither the Law nor preaching can be made the object of scientific examination or research. When we examine the whole content of "the Law," we shall see that it contains more than

[29] Both Gogarten and Løgstrup speak of a radical demand without connecting this with a continuing preaching of the Gospel. Neither shows how this radical demand comes into being through the preaching of the Gospel, and neither uses Biblical theology to show how conventions are destroyed by the working of the preached word. Cf. Gogarten, *Politische Ethik*, pp. 1ff., 62, 115, 197, 214-20; Løgstrup, *Den etiske fordring*, pp. 125-32. Though neither Gogarten nor Løgstrup plead for a theology of order, their arguments support this, since they each dismiss the problem which could provide the basis of a criticism of order. There is no radical demand which is separate from the preaching of Christ's death.

[30] The only purely theoretical point in all this is our proposal that the content of the preached word shall be interpreted by theology. In any given situation in which the Gospel comes into conflict with a particular cultural ethos our task may change, and the central Gospel message reinterpreted in the light of the prevailing cultural situation. Cf. Wingren, *Theology in Conflict*, p. 165 f.

merely "actual demands," for it also contains the second use
of the Law, i.e. guilt in the presence of God as well as Creation,
i.e. birth. The content of the Law does not consist arbitrarily
of "actual demands," for the human situation, which is
phenomenologically bound to these demands, does in fact have
this deeper significance as soon as it is illuminated by the
preaching of Christ. So also when we examine the whole
content of preaching, we shall see that it contains more than
merely "actual proclamation," for it contains the whole of
God's work in Christ which is now addressed to man. The
content of preaching does not consist arbitrarily of "actual
proclamation," for the word of scripture which is read in
preaching does in fact have this deeper significance. Both
preaching and the Law are to be interpreted by each other,
in order that this greater content in each of them may become
clear. Our argument has been that phenomenologically there
are two starting-points, preaching and the Law. Both preaching
and the Law illuminate and explain one another, and this
process of reciprocal illumination is constant and unavoidable.
On the one hand we cannot work with a conception of the
Bible that interprets the Biblical content as impersonal and
unrelated rather than personal and particular, and as something
that addresses man as its object. On the other hand, however,
we cannot work with a static conception of the Law which
has no critical or sovereign principle to speak in regard to the
multitude of demands which are made upon man in society.
Both these points of departure are accessible to observation
and objective argument. So also is the deeper significance of
each, as long as we continue to remember that each illuminates
the other.[31]

In maintaining, however, that preaching and the Law can
illuminate each other, we must make a reservation. If we mean
that it is impossible for a scientific theology to allow the Old

---

[31] It will still be necessary for us to define what we mean by the "Word" or
"the Christian message" in relation to this position for which we have argued, and
to do so in terms of the traditional discipline of systematic theology. If we do so,
the necessity of having this double starting-point will follow logically, and each
will illuminate the other directly from the content of scripture. All this presupposes
an existing rule of Law which is in force before we encounter the Gospel in human
life. Cf. Simonsen's article in *Dansk teologisk tidsskrift*, p. 91.

and New Testaments to illuminate each other, then it is also impossible to allow preaching and the Law as our double point of departure to do so. It is precisely this that forms the basis of the whole of the present discussion. The dominant school of Protestant theology has reduced the Bible to the New Testament. It deals with the Old Testament in a secondary way from the point of view of a purely New Testament Gospel, i.e. it operates with a conception which is based on the New Testament alone, and which does not accept mankind's prehistory and the story of Creation and the Fall as its starting-point. This isolation of the New Testament from its Old Testament roots has its origin on the one hand in pietism and on the other hand in the modern preoccupation with the idea that every science requires some "given factor" with which to work. Christianity as a specific religion and the Christian Church as a particular phenomenon appear to be such a given factor. When, however, the writings of the New Testament are interpreted without reference to the fact that the whole of their message concerns the restoration of Creation, and where the early Christian *kerygma* is interpreted without being related to mankind's prehistory in Genesis, this New Testament *kerygma* changes its meaning and loses part of its substance. In the same way the second article of the Creed loses its meaning when it is not preceded by the first article, but is put first itself, and when the doctrine of Creation and the Law is derived from the second article and the Gospel. We can find a further illustration of the neglect of the Old Testament and the first article in the disappearance of a theological anthropology, in the loss of the idea of man as the one who is addressed in the *kerygma*, and in the denial of an existing rule of Law and the problem of guilt.[32] The primal man of the Old Testament is

[32] When we become aware of this lack of an anthropology and of man as the one who is addressed in the word of the Gospel, the easy solution is to fill this gap with an existentialist interpretation of man. This is what Bultmann does and what Barth did in his earliest dogmatic work, *Die christliche Dogmatik*, Munich 1927, though since 1932 and the first volume of the *Church Dogmatics* he has since modified his position. In regard to his early view see Barth, *Die christliche Dogmatik*, VOL. I, pp. 1 ff., 49, 111. When the New Testament is cut off from the Old, it puts a philosophy in its place. We find another example of the same thing in Nygren's methodology, in which he makes *agape* the basic motif of the New Testament, and separates if from the Jewish *nomos* motif of the Old Testament.

not an Israelite. He is the one who hears the missionary gospel of the New Testament, whatever may be his race—he is modern man, created by God, in bondage to the Law, and guilty.[33]

My work *Theology in Conflict* was directed at three present-day European theologians, each of whom has attempted to define the content of theology. My own interest, however, lay primarily in content rather than in method. My interest in method was aroused only when it became clear that their errors in content were due to presuppositions which lay behind their method of working. It is a fact that the belief in Creation has no place in dogmatic systems, that the Old Testament has no part in the basis on which the systematic theologian works, and that the universal Law creates a problem for any theological ethic that seeks a specifically Christian ethos. If it is difficult for us to put these various parts where they belong, it is not because we have failed to notice them. It is impossible not to see them. But even when we have seen them, we cannot deal with them systematically. To deal with them positively means that we must abandon a once valid method of working and seek a completely new starting-point. It is now clear, I believe, that our double phenomenological starting-point of Law and Gospel opens up to us new opportunities of dealing with these very points which hitherto we have been unable to relate properly. It is quite possible that some other starting-point may open up to us even better opportunities. If there is any one point which we have strongly emphasised in *Theology in Conflict* it is that method in theology is a question of convenience which is to be settled solely by reference to the subject-matter with which theology has to deal.[34] From whatever point we begin to systematise our theology there will be opportunities or difficulties which will simplify or render difficult our task. It is important that systematic theology should define as it were

[33] All that we have said above concerning Creation and the Law is intended to support our theory that the prehistory of the Old Testament occupies a place of central significance for theology. Cf. the summary at the end of the section "Bondage and Constraint" with which we conclude the first part of the present work. The transition from Christian orthodoxy to pietism can be seen in several ways, but it would be an interesting task to examine the connexion between the disappearance of the Old Testament in favour of an unrelated New Testament and the disappearance of the civil use of the Law in favour of a sectarian ethic.

[34] See Wingren, *Theology in Conflict*, pp. 167 f.

from within the unexpressed presuppositions in the methods which at present determine its content, and also that it should seek new and unrestricted starting-points. The problem of method in theology has too often been solved in the past by allowing other branches of study, in complete disregard of the subject-matter of theology, to determine the procedure which it is to follow if it is to be a science. Theology has then been allowed to continue as far as it can from this given starting-point, with no particular regard to its content.[35]

In the previous section, "Man and Guilt," we had occasion to discuss the preaching of Christ in the Gospel. The second use of the Law comes to its fulfilment only when Christ is proclaimed, and guilt is fully revealed to man only when he hears the Gospel. At the same time, however, we must remember that in discussing the preaching of Christ and the message of His work in an exposition which deals with Creation and the Law, we are introducing something which does not strictly belong at this point, and which relates to a completely different subject, viz. the Gospel and the Church. The very fact of Creation and the Fall has brought the work of the Law into being, but the Gospel is a new beginning which will finally destroy the reign of the Law. However it may come to men, the Law is always basically a summons to works. From the point of view of the kingdom of this world the Law does not stop at random, but is directed to a particular end. Even when the Decalogue is preached, we are still in a human situation which would still exist even apart from the Bible and the Christian congregation.[36] However the Law is sharpened, it cannot *as Law* give new Creation or resurrection from the

---

[35] Cf. also Prenter, *Skabelse og genløsning*, pp. 29-36.

[36] Even the civil use of the Law is the object of preaching. Dietrich Bonhoeffer, *Ethik*, 2nd edn., Munich 1953, Eng. trans. *Ethics*, New York 1955, pp. 271-85, stresses this preaching of the civil use of the Law. See also Ivarsson, *Predikans uppgift*, pp. 158-63. This means, as Ivarsson correctly states, that the ministry of preaching is brought into the service of the earthly government (p. 161). The task of preaching, however, is not fully performed when it serves the earthly government. It is only when the Gospel is preached that the Church is brought into being. It is only when the Gospel is preached and Christ is proclaimed that guilt is revealed. This is why it is important that the primary claim on those who hear the Gospel is not that of the death of Christ, for this was a quite unique event.

dead. As Law it continues to play its part in warding off sin. From the point of view of the Law, however, the preaching of the Gospel does not end at a particular point, but points beyond all that we call "Law" to the "kingdom that is not of this world."

Nevertheless, the Gospel of Christ must be preached in order that the function of the Law *coram Deo* in human society may be depicted. The Law as Law is essentially incomplete as long as the preaching of the image of Christ has failed to come to men. However precise a form a commandment may take, it can never make its accusation as particular as this human life can. It is a part of the Incarnation that in His humanity Christ can be all things to all men. All men can see their own humanity realised in Him, but also see the gulf between this true "image of God" and the image which they themselves have created in rebellion against the decree of the Creator. This is one of the reasons why the task of preaching can never be finished. It is continually coming to new generations of men. The Gospel proclamation of Christ is always new, for it exercises a different function in every man. It reveals to each man something that is unique, and builds him up in a way that is also unique.[37] The accusation against man consists in the fact that there is no accusation in the Gospel which is preached to him, but only a description of something that has taken place. The man who hears the Gospel is not allowed to find refuge in works, for there is no longer any need of works; but in hearing the Gospel he is brought into contact with a life which ends only in the kingdom that is not of this world.

We see the incapacity of the Law to produce works in the second use of the Law as a whole, even when this has not been intensified by the Gospel proclamation of Christ. As soon as the Law turns inwards and passes a verdict on the person of the doer of the Law, it burdens the conscience with guilt and "puts to death." It may do this while it is speaking of the external works which we do for our fellow men. It may do this even though Christ has not been preached. The second use of the Law in all its expressions points beyond the Law itself, and even within the reign of the Law states that the Law cannot

[37] Cf. Bring, *Dualismen hos Luther*, pp. 247 ff.

be an end, but must serve some other purpose. In the purely negative function of stopping every mouth and holding the world accountable to God (Rom. iii.19) we see that the Law can never be more than a means to an end. Even though the total depravity of human life can be recognised only where Christ is preached, all men realise simply from their own experience and the lives of others that as long as the Law forces them into doing something, its deepest function remains concealed.[38] The Law reveals its deepest function only when it turns inwards to man and "puts him to death," but it is when it does so that it shows how he has failed to conform to God's will. It is this grim revelation of man's failure that is the "principal use of the Law."[39] The Law now holds up to him God's decree in Creation—man made in the image of God (Gen. i. 26)—and says to the one whom it accuses, "You are not the man you were created to be; your life is far from you." The whole of the second use of the Law, in distinction from the first use, points away from works to "another kingdom."[40] The image of God is not altogether lacking in human expression. His image has taken human form, only it has not done so in the power of the Law. It is this human form of the image of God that is proclaimed in the preaching of Christ.[41]

It may be appropriate here to say a few words in preparation for my projected work *Gospel and Church*. Baptism will clearly be of particular importance. Any discussion of the Gospel

[38] Cf. G. Bornkamm, *Das Ende des Gesetzes*, pp. 29 ff. Bornkamm stresses the other aspect. Even though every man is aware of the Judgment, this can be expressed only when the Gospel is preached.

[39] Cf. Luther, *Commentary on Galatians*, W. A. 40-1, pp. 482.12, 512.18, 520.21, 534.14.

[40] See also Ivarsson, *Predikans uppgift*, pp. 96 ff. Ivarsson shows in an unusually penetrating way how during the period of the Reformation preaching was an event or act involving the hearer, and also how this type of preaching was lost in subsequent periods.

[41] Cf. Rom. iii.21 f. and the closely related verses in Rom. i.15 ff. The power evidenced in the preaching of the Gospel consists in the communication to the hearer of God's work in Christ through the preached word. But the divine part of this act cannot be separated from the human. Christ Himself is human, and the preaching of Christ retains all this humanity in its narrative form. Modern preaching is often impoverished because the preacher often explains and analyses without having regard to the naïve and anthropomorphic character of the Biblical narrative.

must start from a continuing event rather than from a past
event. Christ does not belong to the past, but encounters man
who stands under the Law in the present period. Both Baptism
and the Eucharist are events which continue in the present
among men. Neither Baptism nor the Eucharist has any
meaning in the present apart from men's participation in them
by undergoing Baptism or by eating bread or drinking wine.
Those who share in the Sacraments have all been created in
the image of God and are all far from realising His image.
Their real life lies in what they taste and experience, and not
in what they themselves are.

For them the Sacraments are the means of participating in
Christ. The work of Christ is the opposite of the work of Adam,
and the course of events described in the Gospel is the opposite
of that described in man's prehistory. The new Creation has
already begun, and therefore the Church is filled with the song
of praise. Since the work of Christ in His ministry on earth
reverses Adam's fall, it has the effect of restoring and recapitulating human life. The centre of this saving work is His death
and resurrection, and we are ingrafted into Christ in His death
and resurrection through Baptism. The Adam who is snatched
from the dominion of darkness and given in Baptism the life
for which he was created is no more a creature of the past
than Christ is, but is man, this man who is being baptised.
Recapitulation takes place in the Church, and is still going on.
The epic and narrative aspect of the Sacraments and the Gospel
is essentially the same as the epic character of man's prehistory
and the narrative of Adam and his descendants.[42] But the
Gospel is the account of abundant life, while man's prehistory
was the account of the onset of death.

The Gospel narrative describes events which constitute a
beginning. The Christian who has been baptised renews his
baptism daily; his death and resurrection are the objects of
hope, and this hope outstretches to include not only his own
future but also everything that can happen to humanity. The
Church is a people whose hope, prayers, and praises cannot be
separated from the responsibility which they have to the world.
In any description of the Gospel or the Church the relationship

[42] Cf. Dodd, *The Bible Today*, pp. 160-3.

of the Church to the Creation around it must have a central place. Here too mankind is affected retroactively by man's own prehistory and the destiny for which he was created, viz. free "dominion" over the things of the earth. As long as enmity and opposition continue, something of the primal decree of God in Creation remains unaccomplished. The world mission and ministry of the Church are characterised at the one time by the restoration of Creation and continuing opposition, the "not yet" of man's Creation.[43] All who are baptised experience this same dualism of fulfilment and expectancy. Their lives are led in the tension between freedom and Law, which belongs to the transitional period. While man lives in the world he continues to be affected by the Gospel and his Baptism, but in this he is one with the rest of the world in awaiting an event which will happen not only to him and to the Church, but to all men—the return of Christ, the Last Judgment, and the resurrection of the dead.

This last event has already begun with the work of the Spirit in the Church. Everything, therefore, that takes place in the Church takes place with the whole of Creation and for the whole of Creation. What happens in the Church is simply the continuation of what happened when Christ became man. And He became man in order to restore what God had created

[43] Cf. Billing, *Försoningen*, pp. 100 f., 120-4.

LIST OF ABBREVIATIONS
AND OF WORKS FREQUENTLY CITED

This list contains only those works frequently cited. Full details
of all other works cited are given in the appropriate footnotes.

AUKRUST, TOR. *Forkynnelse og historie.* Oslo 1956.
AULÉN, GUSTAF. *The Faith of the Christian Church.* Philadelphia 1948.
Original *Den allmänneliga kristna tron.* 5th edn. Stockholm 1957.
BARTH, KARL. *Christengemeinde und Bürgergemeinde.* Theologische Studien
VOL. XX. Zollikon-Zürich 1946.
—— *Die kirchliche Dogmatik.* VOL. III, PTS. II, III, IV. Zollikon-Zürich
1948, 1950, 1951.
—— *Dogmatics in Outline.* London 1949. Trans. of *Dogmatik im Grundriss.*
Zollikon-Zürich 1947.
—— *Evangelium und Gesetz.* Theologische Existenz heute VOL. XXXII.
Munich 1935.
—— *Rechtfertigung und Recht.* Theologische Studien VOL. I. Zollikon 1938.
BENKTSON, BENKT-ERIK. *Den naturliga teologiens problem hos Karl Barth.*
Lund 1948.
BILLING, EINAR. *De etiska tankarna=De etiska tankarna i urkristendomen.*
2nd. edn. Stockholm 1936.
—— *Försoningen.* 2nd edn. Stockholm 1921.
—— *Herdabref.* Stockholm 1920.
—— *Vår Kallelse.* Uppsala 1909.
BOHLIN, TORGNY. *Den korsfäste Skaparen.* Uppsala 1952.
BONHOEFFER, DIETRICH. *Creation and Fall.* London 1959. Trans. of
Schöpfung und Fall. 3rd. edn. Munich 1955.
BORNKAMM, GÜNTHER. *Das Ende des Gesetzes.* Beiträge zur evangelische
Theologie VOL. XVI. Munich 1952.
BORNKAMM, HEINRICH. *Luther und das Alte Testament.* Tübingen 1948.
BRING, RAGNAR. *Dualismen hos Luther.* Lund 1929.
BRUNNER, E. *Man in Revolt.* London 1939. Original *Der Mensch im
Widerspruch.* 3rd edn. Berlin 1941.
—— *The Divine Imperative.* London 1937. Trans. of *Das Gebot und die
Ordnungen.* 2nd edn. Tübingen 1933.
BULTMANN, RUDOLF. *Kerygma und Mythos.* VOL. I. Hamburg 1948.
CAIRD, G. B. *Principalities and Powers.* Oxford 1956.
CULLMANN, O. *Christ and Time.* London 1951. Trans. of *Christus und
die Zeit.* Zollikon-Zürich 1946.

CULLMANN, O. *Königsherrschaft Christi – Königsherrschaft Christi und Kirche im Neuen Testament.* Theologische Studien VOL. X. 2nd edn. Zürich 1946.
—— *The Earliest Christian Confessions.* London 1943. Trans. of *Die ersten christlichen Glaubensbekenntnisse.* Theologische Studien VOL. XV. Zollikon-Zürich 1943.
DAHL, N. A. *Background = The Background of the New Testament and its Eschatology.* Cambridge 1956.
DEWAR, LINDSAY. *An Outline of New Testament Ethics.* Philadelphia 1949.
DODD, C. H. *Fourth Gospel = The Interpretation of the Fourth Gospel.* Cambridge 1953.
—— *New Testament Studies.* Manchester 1953.
—— *The Bible Today.* Cambridge 1948.
DÜRR, LORENZ. *Die Wertung = Die Wertung des göttlichen Wortes im Alten Testament.* Mitteilungen der vorderasiatisch—aegyptischen Gesellschaft VOL. XLII, PT. I. Leipzig 1938.
EICHRODT, WALTER. *Theologie des Alten Testaments.* VOLS. II-III. Leipzig 1935, 1939.
EIDEM, ERLING. *Det kristna livet enligt Paulus.* VOL. I. Stockholm 1927.
ELERT, WERNER. *Das christliche Ethos.* Tübingen 1949.
GÄRTNER, B. *The Areopagus Speech = The Areopagus Speech and Natural Revelation.* Acta semin. neotest. upsal. VOL. XXI. Uppsala 1955.
GEBSATTEL. V. E. von. *Prolegomena einer medizinischen Anthropologie.* Berlin 1954.
GOGARTEN, FRIEDRICH. *Politische Ethik.* Jena 1932.
—— *Verhängnis = Verhängnis und Hoffnung der Neuzeit.* Stuttgart 1953.
HÄFNER, HEINZ. *Schulderleben und Gewissen.* Stuttgart 1956.
HILLERDAL, GUNNAR. *Gehorsam gegen Gott und Menschen.* Stockholm and Göttingen 1954.
IRENAEUS. *A. h. = Adversus haereses. Sancti Irenaei episcopi Lugdunensis libros quinque adversus haereses,* ed. W. W. Harvey. Cambridge 1857. *Sancti Irenaei episcopi Lugdunensis quae supersunt omnia,* ed. A. Stieren. Leipzig 1848-53.
IVARSSON, HENRIK. *Predikans uppgift.* Lund 1956.
JOEST, WILFRIED. *Gesetz und Freiheit.* 2nd edn. Göttingen 1956.
JOHNSON, AUBREY R. *The Vitality of the Individual in the Thought of Ancient Israel.* Cardiff 1949.
LAU, FRANZ. *Luthers Lehre = Luthers Lehre von den beiden Reichen.* Berlin 1952.
Luthers Theologie – "Äusserliche Ordnung" und "Weltlich Ding" in Luthers Theologie. Studien zur systematischen Theologie VOL. XII. Göttingen 1933.
LINDESKOG, GÖSTA. *Studien – Studien zum neutestamentlichen Schöpfungsgedanken.* PT. I. Uppsala universitets årsskriften VOL. XI. Uppsala and Wiesbaden 1952.
LØGSTRUP, K. E. *Den etiske fordring.* Copenhagen 1956.
LUTHER, MARTIN. W. A. – *Kritische Gesammtausgabe,* ed. J. C. F. Knaake. Weimar 1883—.

O

MICHEL, OTTO. *Der Brief an die Hebräer.* Meyers Kommentar VOL. XIII.
    9th edn. Göttingen 1955.
NYGREN, A. *Filosofi och motivforskning.* Stockholm 1940.
—— *Urkristendom och reformation.* Lund 1932.
ODEBERG, H. *Skriftens studium, inspiration och auktoritet.* Stockholm 1954.
OLSSON, HERBERT. *Luthers socialetik = Grundproblemet i Luthers socialetik.*
    VOL. I. Lund 1934.
ØSTERGAARD-NIELSEN, H. *Scriptura sacra et viva vox.* Forschungen zur
    Geschichte und Lehre des Protestantismus VOL. X, PT. X.
    Munich 1957.
PEDERSEN, JOHANNES. *Israel.* VOLS. I-II. London and Copenhagen 1926.
    Trans of *Israel*, VOLS. I-II. Copenhagen 1920.
PIERCE, C. A. *Conscience in the New Testament.* Studies in Biblical Theology.
    London 1955.
PRENTER, REGIN. *Skabelse og genløsning.* 2nd edn. Copenhagen 1955.
RAD, GERHARD VON. *Das erste Buch Mose.* Das Alte Testament Deutsch
    VOL. I. Göttingen 1949.
RAMSEY, PAUL. *Basic Christian Ethics.* New York 1951.
ROBINSON, JOHN A. T. *The Body.* Studies in Biblical Theology No. 5.
    London 1952.
SIMONSEN, HEJNE. "Teologiens metode hos Gustaf Wingren," in *Dansk
    teologisk tidsskrift*, 1957.
SØE, N. H. *Kristelig etik.* 4th edn. Copenhagen 1957.
—— *Religionsfilosofi.* Copenhagen 1955.
S.T.K. = *Svensk teologisk kvartalskrift.*
TÖRNVALL, GUSTAF. *Andligt regemente = Andligt och världsligt regemente hos
    Luther.* Lund 1940.
VAJTA, VILMOS. *Theologie = Die Theologie des Gottesdienstes bei Luther.*
    Stockholm 1952.
WINGREN, GUSTAF. *Man and the Incarnation = Man and the Incarnation: A
    Study in the Biblical Theology of Irenaeus.* Edinburgh 1959. Trans. of
    Människan och inkarnationen enligt Irenaeus. Lund 1947.
—— *Theology in Conflict.* Philadelphia and Edinburgh 1958. Trans. of
    Teologiens metodfråga. Lund 1954.
ZIMMERLI, WALTHER. *I Mose I-XI.* VOL. II. Zürich 1943.

INDEX OF NAMES

Althaus, P. : 109.
Aukrust, T. : 20, 38, 75, 159, 169.
Aulén, G. : 33, 37, 137, 152.

Barth, K. : 12, 13, 14, 17, 27, 39, 46, 72, 79, 93, 104, 126, 128, 156, 173.
Bauer, K. : 7.
Benktson, E.-K. : 12, 60.
Billing, E. : 20, 23, 27, 91-2, 123, 125, 130, 134, 135, 146, 197.
Björkman, U. : 37.
Bohlin, T. : 12, 14.
Bonhoeffer, D. : 23, 52, 97, 100, 108, 112, 193.
Bornkamm, G. : 50, 53, 62, 134, 180, 195.
Bornkamm, H. : 41, 90.
Bring, R. : 63, 95, 149, 183, 194.
Brun, L. : 93.
Brunner, E. : 30, 43, 48, 52, 175, 181.
Bultmann, R. : 15, 68-9, 70-1, 78, 83-4, 86-7, 88, 146, 159, 191.

Caird, G. B. : 55, 168.
Cairns, D. : 35.
Calvin, J. : 157.
Caspari, W. : 106.
Causse, A. : 131.
Cullmann, O. : 3, 5, 9-10, 12, 15-16, 32, 45,[1] 69-72, 78-80, 83-4, 86-8, 125, 146-7.

Dahl, N. A. : 35, 40, 42, 86, 165.
Dewar, L. : 93, 144.
Dillistone, F. W. : 38.

Dodd, C. H. : 11, 41, 68, 118, 126, 165, 196.
Dürr, L. : 31, 66.

Eichrodt, W. : 26, 49, 85, 131.
Eidem, E. : 42, 185.
Eklund, H. : 67, 68.
Elert, W. : 137, 142.

Feine, P. : 186.
Fromm, E. : 51.

Gärtner, B. : 5, 16, 26, 47, 53, 59, 85, 119, 133, 180-1.
Gebsattel, V. E. : 65, 183.
Gloege, G. : 87.
Gogarten, F. : 25, 28, 117, 170, 189.
Goppelt, L. : 88.
Grundtvig, N. F. : 27.

Häfner, H. : 177, 179.
Hägglund, B. : 6.
Haikola, L. : 46.
Hanson, S. : 5.
Hauge, R. : 34.
Heidegger, M. : 15.
Herner, S. : 95.
Hillerdal, G. : 13, 55, 93.
Hoh, J. : 6.
Hygen, J. B. : 73.

Irenaeus : 17, 128, 166.
Ivarsson, H. : 8, 24, 49, 53, 63-4, 68, 74, 118, 125, 133, 138, 155, 161, 170, 180, 183, 186, 193, 195.

Joest, W. : 175, 185.
Johansson, N. : 34.
Johnson, A. R. : 21, 85.
Josefson, R. : 74.
Justin Martyr : 60, 166.

Köberle, A. : 20.

Lau, F. : 137, 152-3.
Lindeskog, G. : 5, 59, 85, 95, 101, 133.
Lindström, H. : 88.
Løgstrup, K. E. : 23, 28, 29-31, 43, 47, 50, 53, 63, 94, 102, 141, 159, 163, 165, 181, 189.
Luther, M. : 7, 26, 38-9, 41, 44, 55, 62, 64, 68, 73-5, 81, 85, 98-9, 106, 118, 132-3, 135, 137-8, 143, 146, 149, 151, 153-5.

Melanchthon, P. : 88.
Michel, O. : 65, 115.

Nygren, A.: 7, 15, 53, 58, 169, 171-2, 191.

Odeberg, H. : 7, 127.
Olsson, H. : 62, 95, 124, 159.
Østergaard-Nielsen, H. : 23, 159.

Pedersen, J. : 19-20.
Pierce, C. A. : 54-5, 66, 139, 161, 179.
Prenter, R. : 8, 11, 34, 37, 43, 53-4, 87, 89, 125, 142, 155, 157, 180, 183, 188, 193.

Rad, G. von : 50, 88, 90, 96, 105, 107-8, 111, 116.
Ramsey, P. : 138, 143, 152, 158, 166.
Robinson, J. A. T. : 77, 92, 158.
Rückert, H. : 68.
Runestam, A. : 174.

Schartau, H. : 74, 133.
Schlink, E. : 126.
Schmidt, H. : 26.
Schmökel, H. : 131.
Schniewind, J. : 178.
Schumann, F. K. : 41-2.
Schweizer, E. : 145.
Simonsen, H. : 187, 190.
Skydsgaard, K. E. : 193.
Søe, N. H. : 17, 29, 39-40, 44, 52, 58, 60, 66, 94, 126, 144, 157, 161, 177, 184.
Strathmann, H. : 68.

Thielicke, H. : 42.
Thornton, L. S. : 18.
Thurneysen, E. : 13.
Tillich, P. : 74.
Törnvall, G. : 75, 138, 143, 154.
Traub, H. : 78.

Vajta, V. : 51, 64, 114, 180.

Wingren, G. : 16-17, 25, 48, 60, 84, 135, 140, 153, 156, 162, 186, 189, 192.

Zimmerli, W. : 95-7, 107, 110, 113, 116, 127, 136, 148.

INDEX OF SUBJECTS

Abuse of Creation : 43-4, 92-3, 116-7, 143-4, 153-4, 156, 163 ; *see also* USE OF CREATION.

acquisitiveness : 43, 48-51, 61-2, 68-9, 114-5, 150-1, 180.

Adam : 10, 25, 35-7, 40-1, 50, 61, 77, 85-91, 100-1, 115, 132, 182, 196.

" all nations " : 16-17, 118-20, 124-7, 133-4, 191-2.

anthropocentric emphasis in theology : 12-13, 28, 39-40, 60 n., 67, 157, 167-8.

anthropology : 16-17, 45-7, 102-5, 119-20, 189-92.

anthropomorphism : 11, 23, 195 n.

anti-liberal reaction in theology : 12, 34, 67 n., 183-4.

authorities, civil : 55 n., 56, 80, 81 n., 113-4, 148 n., 163-70 ; *see also* EARTHLY GOVERNMENT.

Baptism: 37-8, 73, 77 n., 116 n., 129, 131-2, 146, 161, 182 n., 195-6 ; *see also* EUCHARIST.

Bible, unity of : 6-11, 16-18, 123-35, 145-6, 191-2 ; *see also* NEW TESTAMENT.

birth and Creation : 19, 20-1, 25-7, 83-92, 94, 98-9, 103-4, 119-20, 167-8 ; *see also* LIFE.

body, the : 18-20, 26, 71-2, 78-81, 85.

bondage of man : 49-54, 65-6, 108-20, 128 n., 179-80.

Church : 32, 34, 37-8, 69-70, 92-3, 146-8, 158-9, 169-70, 196-7.

collectivism : 91-2, 116-8, 144, 170.

commandments : given by Christ, 42-3, 48-9, 140-3, 167 ; given to Israel, 92, 123-35.

confession of an article, and its denial : 4-6.

conversion : 5, 59 n., 119 n., 133 n.

covetousness : 51, 99-100, 151 n.

creation: as static order, 30, 43, 46-8, *see also* BIRTH AND CREATION, CREED, FIRST ARTICLE OF, LIFE, NEW CREATION, ETC. ; purer than man, 41, 43-4, 101-2, 115, 117.

creed : Trinitarian, 3-17, 23, 25, 29, 88, 120 ; *see also* SPIRIT, HOLY ; first article of, 7, 11-12, 25-9, 41, 53, 81 n. 89, 98, 119-20, 131, 156-7, 160-1, 168, 173, 186, 191 ; second article of, 11-14, 33-41, 67, 80 n., 81 n., 92-3, 155-6, 173 n., 191.

Cross, of Christ : 52, 56, 76, 79-80, 131, 139-40, 145, 182-3, 193 n.

Death : 20, 38, 49, 65, 69-82, 90-1, 97-8, 108, 111-20, 127, 132-3, 141-2, 144-6, 182, 194-5 ; and Resurrection, 37, 78-81, 128, 145-6, 182, 185-6, 196, *see also* RESURRECTION.

demands made upon men, evaluation of : 93-4, 117 n., 123-5, 130, 143-4, 155, 157-9, 165, 176, 189-90.

demythologising : 86-7 ; *see also* SCRIPTURE, EXISTENTIAL INTERPRETATION OF.

denial : *see* CONFESSION AND DENIAL.

Docetism : 36 n., 182-4, 195 n.

dominion, man's : 51-2, 65, 88-9, 91-3, 95-108, 197.

Early Church : 6-7, 18-20, 74, 81, 113-4, 124, 166-8 ; see also MARTYRDOM.
earthly government : 41-2, 54-5, 63, 80-1, 112-8, 135-48, 166-8, 193 n.
Ebed Jahveh : 37, 145.
Eucharist : 37-8, 196 ; see also BAPTISM.
experience, human : 67-9, 179-80, 183-4.

Faith : 51-2, 60-8, 72-8, 87-8, 91-2, 119-20, 129-31, 142.
fear : 65, 112-3, 163-7.
Folk Church : 135, 146-7.
forgiveness : 59, 74, 134-5, 176 n., 183 ; see also JUSTIFICATION.
freedom, man's in Creation : 97-108.

Gnostics : 4-7, 18, 168, 188.
God : worship of, 10-11, 11 n., 129 ; relation to, even when unacknowledged, 20-4, 26-8, 54-5, 56, 62, 65-8, 90-1, 119-20, 127-8, 179-80, see also UNRECOGNISED DEMAND ; existence of, 21-3, 53 ; sovereignty of, 29, 48 n., 53-5, 66-7, 103-8, 127, 129-30, 156-7.
good gifts given through evil men : 47-9, 54, 95-6, 103-4, 143.
Gospel : 5, 16, 32, 59-61, 70, 115, 119-20, 125, 127, 132, 141, 165, 169, 172, 177, 182-3, 185-6, 188-97 ; " Gospel and Law," 13, 68, 117 n., 125-6, 156, 166, 177, 186 n., 190-1 ; see also " LAW AND GOSPEL."
Government : see EARTHLY GOVERNMENT.
guilt : 53, 56, 61, 74-5, 134, 149, 174-85, 189-95.

Healing of the sick : 64, 177-8.

" Ideal man," Jesus as : 33, 38, 169, 185.

Idealism : 162-73.
idolatry : 50-1, 57, 62, 64-5, 68, 75, 91-3, 99-100, 102, 114, 117, 129, 154, 179.
image of God : 35-41, 79-80, 106 n., 128, 181-2, 194-7.
Israel : history of, 91 n., 118, 124-35, 146 ; laws of, 91-2, 123-35, see also COMMANDMENTS.

Judgment : Last, 16, 34, 39, 55-7, 69-78, 84 n., 113, 139, 174-5, 180, 185, 197 ; God's, 53-7, 61-3, 67-8, 72-9, 84, 87, 91, 119, 128, 139, 185-6.
justification : 13, 73-6, 185 ; see also FORGIVENESS.

Knowledge, problem of : 11-14, 28-9, 40-3, 51-5, 60 n., 66 n., 81 n., 151, 155-7, 173, 177.

Last Judgment : see JUDGMENT.
" Law and Gospel " : 72 n., 84, 117 n., 125, 177, 185 ; see also " GOSPEL AND LAW."
Law : natural, 42-3, 48 n., 60-3, 124-5 ; first use of, 56-7, 59, 84 n., 110-1, 149-73, 176, 181, 183-4, 186-9, 192 n., 193 n., ; second use of, 56, 84, 116 n., 149, 174-87, 193-5, see also COMMANDMENT, GIVEN TO ISRAEL.
life : as a gift of God, 18-24, 25-6, 29, 46-7, 65-6, 85-6, 98-9, 152-3, 164, 168, see also BIRTH AND CREATION ; offered by Christ, 35-6, 42, 61, 86 n., 100-1.

Mammon ; 51 n., ; see also IDOLATRY.
man: as object of God's dealings, 10, 14-7, 56, 69-70, 84 n., 87-8, 127-8, 186, 189-92, see also NEW MAN ; and woman, 27 n., 104-5, 108.
marriage : 143-4 ; see also MAN AND WOMAN.

martyrdom, period of : 51 n., 76 n., 79-80, 145 ; *see also* EARLY CHURCH.
methodology : 22-4, 192-3.
motif research : 171-3, 191 n.

Neighbour : 30-1, 50-1, 55-6, 69, 91-4, 98, 116-7, 130, 138, 150-66, 169, 180, 184; love for, 94, 116-7, 137-8, 150-1.
new creation : 29-30, 35, 76-7, 93-4, 111, 125, 142-5, 159-60.
new man : 35, 77, 183, 186 ; *see also* OLD TESTAMENT.
New Testament, separation of from Old Testament : 7-9, 14-17, 25, 28, 84 n., 116 n., 124, 132, 190-1 ; *see also* BIBLE, UNITY OF.

Old man : 49, 77, 91, 115 n., 182-3, 186 ; *see also* NEW MAN.
order, theology of : 30, 43, 91-2, 117, 125, 189.

Phenomenology : 10, 24-5, 186-93.
politics : 13, 92, 125-6, 170.
preaching : 10-11, 21 n., 38, 53-4, 60-1, 68, 70-1, 85, 119, 125-7, 129, 159 n., 175-95 ; *see also* DEMANDS, EVALUATION OF.
prehistory : 96-120, 126, 134, 192 n., 197 ; *see also* BIBLE, UNITY OF.

Recapitulation : 15-16, 24, 27 n., 37 n., 41, 63, 77, 166-7, 181-2, 190-1, 195-7.
Reformation : 42-3, 73-6, 80-1, 124, 156, 162-8.
restoration : *see* RECAPITULATION.
resurrection : man's, 18-19, 48-9, 78, 186 ; Christ's, 73, 77-9, 115-6, 185.
ruler, earthly : 156, 163-6.

Sacraments, epic character of : 37-8, 196 ; *see also* BAPTISM ; EUCHARIST.

Scripture, existential interpretation of : 15, 70, 73 n., 78, 84, 88 n., 191 n.
sequence of God's mighty acts : 11-17, 30, 41-2, 86, 119-20, 156-7, 160-1.
sin : 41-53, 69, 73-5, 79, 81, 90, 97, 101-2, 108-20, 130-4, 138-9, 141-6, 186.
Sovereignty : *see* GOD, SOVEREIGNTY OF.
Spirit, Holy : 9-10, 16, 31, 79, 85, 127, 145, 188.
sword, power of the : 54, 112 n.

Temptation : Christ's, 35-6, 40-1, 50-1, 52, 100-1, 131 ; Adam's, 36-7, 40-1, 49, 100-1.

Unrecognised demand, the : 22, 57-69, 124-5, 189.
use of Creation : 43-4, 88-9, 95-6, 105-7 ; *see also* ABUSE OF CREATION.

Vocation : 47, 97-9, 103-7, 135, 146, 152-3, 160.

Woman : *see* MAN AND WOMAN.
works : 98-118, 151-6, 162-73 ; *see also* SEQUENCE OF GOD'S MIGHTY ACTS.
world, man's place in : 42-3, 83-4, 88-95, 106-7, 114-5, 131-2, 149, 151-2, 159-60, 176-7, 196-7 ; *see also* EARTHLY GOVERNMENT.
world mission of the Church : 5, 10 n., 16, 59, 68 n., 70, 109 n., 127, 133, 191 ; *see also* PREACHING ; GOSPEL.
worship of the creature : *see* IDOLATRY.
wrath of God : 53-7, 61-2, 66, 68-70, 72-3, 77, 79-80, 90, 115-6, 161.

INDEX OF BIBLICAL PASSAGES

Gen. I-XI   98, 126, 134.
I-IX   148 n.
I-II   45.
I   89.
I.1-26   88.
I.26   29, 35, 95, 129 n., 182, 195.
I.26-7   35.
I.26-8   106 n.
I.27   27 n.
I.28   51, 95, 98, 103, 108.
I.28-9   32, 50, 88.
II   115.
II.5   96.
II.5ff.   89.
II.7   19 n., 86 n.
II.15   96, 98.
II.17   35-6, 49.
II.18-20   95.
III   9, 29, 35, 37, 40, 45, 49-50, 104 n., 109 n., 115, 133.
III.1   49.
III.1-15   36 n., 49.
III.5   37, 49.
III.8   50, 65.
III.16   108.
III.16-19   98, 104 n., 108 n.
III.17   90, 111.
III.17-18   41, 108.
III.17-19   36, 68, 96 n., 116.
III.18   90.
III.19   49, 90, 108, 111, 115.
III.23   96.
IV   50, 104 n.
IV.1-16   111.
IV.2   98.
IV.7   69.
IV.12   104 n., 108 n., 111.
IV.20-2   98.
V.29   96, 104 n., 111 n.

Gen. VI.5ff.   104 n.
VI.22   107.
VII.7   107.
VII.22-3   107.
VIII.21   90 n., 96 n., 111 n., 112, 136.
VIII.22   105.
IX   113 n., 133, 136.
IX.1   95, 112.
IX.1-7   96.
IX.1-17   112.
IX.2   95, 112.
IX.2-3   95, 97.
IX.5   97.
IX.5-6   133, 136.
IX.6   97, 112, 116, 143.
IX.7   112.
IX.8-17   105 n., 136.
IX.13   113 n.
IX.17   113 n.
IX.20   90 n., 98.
XI   127 n.
XI.1-9   94.
XI.4   107.
XI.7-9   127.
XII.3   125, 133.
XLV.5-8   5, 96 n.
L.20   5, 96.

Ex. XX.1ff.   129.
XX.16   158.
XXIII.9   92 n., 130.

Deut. V.6-8   129.
V.20   158.
XXXII.39   21 n.

1 Sam. II.6-7   21 n.

Job X.8-9   85 n.
XII.10   26 n., 85 n.

Job XXXI.13-15	130.	Is. XLIV.9-24	52 n.
XXXI.15	26, 85.	XLIV.19	100.
XXXIII.4	85-6, 86 n., 94.	XLIV.24	85 n.
XXXIII.6	85-6, 86 n., 94.	XLIV.15ff.	4 n.
XXXIV.14	26 n., 85 n.	XLV.20	100 n.
		XLV.23	4, 5 n.
Ps. II	44 n.	XLVI.6-7	52 n.
VIII.7-8	95.	XLVI.6-11	100 n.
X.4	22 n.	LXIV.12	66 n.
XIV.1	22 n.		
XXVIII.1	66 n.	Jer. I.5	26, 85 n.
XXXIII.6	31.	XXXI.31	6 n.
LIII.2	22 n.		
LVI.5	20 n.	Lam. III.22-3	141.
LXXXIII.2	66 n.		
XCVI.5	130 n.	Mt. IV	35.
CIV.27-30	26 n., 85 n.	IV.1-11	40.
CIV.29	85.	IV.9-11	51.
CIV.30	31 n., 85.	V.21ff.	42.
CXIX.73	85 n.	V.44-5	41 n., 59 n.
CXXVII	99 n.	V.45	18, 89.
CXXXIX.5	26.	V.47	71 n.
CXXXIX.7ff.	26 n.	VI.24	51 n.
CXXXIX.13	26.	VI.24ff.	100 n.
CXXXIX.13-16	85.	VI.25-32	18.
CXLIII.7	66 n.	VII.11	41, 48.
		VII.12	62 n., 93 n., 150.
Prov. XX.12	85.	VIII.5-13	64.
		VIII.10-12	57 n.
Is. X.5-12	129.	IX.28-9	64.
X.5-15	95 n.	X.15	57 n.
X.5-27	5.	X.32-3	4.
XI.6-9	88 n.	XI.22-4	57 n.
XXV.8	20, 49 n.	XII.41-2	57 n.
XXXI.3	20.	XIII.24-30	57 n.
XXXIV.16	31 n.	XIII.25	81.
XL-XLVI	62 n., 130.	XIII.28	81.
XL.18ff.	5 n.	XIII.37-43	57 n.
XL.19ff.	52 n.	XIII.47-50	57 n.
XL.19-24	100 n.	XV.21-8	64.
XLI.1ff.	5 n.	XVI.27	185 n.
XLI.2-4	129.	XIX.4-6	5 n.
XLI.4	130.	XXIV.14	17, 127.
XLI.5ff.	52 n.	XXIV.40-1	57 n.
XLI.6-7	100 n.	XXV.31-46	56 n., 175, 185 n.
XLIII.7	26, 85 n.	XXV.32	17, 58 n., 127.
XLIV.9-20	100 n.	XXV.40	69 n.

Mt. xxv.42   69.
xxv.45   69 n.
xxvi.39   36 n., 37.
xxvi.42   36 n., 37.
xxvi.52   112 n.
xxviii.19   17, 127.

Mk. i.13   40, 88 n.
i.24   178 n.
ii.23-8   143 n.
v.7   178 n.
v.36   64.
vii.14-23   44 n., 101.
ix.24   63.
x.37-40   37.
x.46-52   64.
xi.22-4   64.
xii.28ff.   150.
xii.29ff.   93 n.
xiii.3-29   147.
xiv.36   131.
xvi.15   101.

Lk. iv.1-13   40.
iv.18   31 n.
v.17-20   64.
viii.22-5   64.
x.25-37   57 n.
x.29   155 n.
x.36   155 n., 178.
xii.50   131.
xiv.26   93 n., 144 n.
xxiv.47   5, 17.

Jn. i.1-14   31.
i.14   31, 101.
iii.17   140.
iii.36   56 n.
v.29   185 n.
ix.22   4 n.
xvi.9   184 n.
xviii.11   37 n.
xix.11   5.
xx.17-28   11 n.
xx.29   68 n.
xx.31   8.

Acts ii   127 n.
ii.5-12   127.
ii.36   3.
iii.13-14   4.
iv.24-8   95 n.
iv.24-30   5 n.
iv.27-8   5, 96, 129.
v.30-2   3.
xiv.15-17   5.
xiv.16   17, 127.
xiv.17   17 n., 18.
xvii   17 n., 54 n., 66 n.
xvii.23   119 n.
xvii.24ff.   17 n.
xvii.24-31   5.
xvii.25   18, 40, 85.
xvii.26   17, 55 n., 127.
xvii.27-8   26 n.
xvii.28   40, 55 n.

Rom. i-iii   133.
i-ii   17 n., 54 n., 66 n.
i   50, 60.
i.15-17   195 n.
i.16-17   54.
i.16-32   133.
i.18   56 n., 66.
i.18ff.   181 n.
i.18-32   49, 53, 130, 180.
i.18-ii.16   5.
i.19ff.   17 n., 60, 133.
i.19-25   91 n.
i.23   60.
i.24   54.
i.25   60.
i.25-32   114.
i.28   54.
i.28-32   50.
i.29-32   49.
i.30-2   60.
ii.2-3   54.
ii.5   54.
ii.6   56 n., 185 n.
ii.14-15   17 n., 42, 48, 57 n., 67 n., 133 n.
iii.1   134.
iii.9   133 n.

Rom. III.19	133 n.		I Cor. X	36.
III.19-20	134, 195.		XI.25	6 n., 37.
III.19ff.	125.		XI.31	49.
III.21-2	54, 195 n.		XI.32	54, 139 n.
III.22-3	134.		XV.24-8	115 n.
IV.17-18	78.		XV.26	49 n., 115, 142.
V.12	49, 115.		XV.29ff.	77 n.
V.12-19	35.		XV.30	77 n.
V.15	35.		XV.31	77 n.
V.17	35.		XV.44	79.
VI.1-22	142 n.		XV.45ff.	86 n.
VI.3-5	129 n.		XV.45-9	35 n.
VI.3-8	38.		XV.50-7	101.
VI.5	79.			
VI.9	100 n.		II Cor. III.6	6 n.
VI.9-10	36.		III.14	4 n., 6 n.
VII.8ff.	54 n.		IV.4-6	35 n.
VII.22-5	79.		IV.8-14	129 n.
VIII.11	31 n., 71 n., 79.		V.10	56 n., 175 n., 185 n.
VIII.19	90 n.		V. 21	131.
VIII.19ff.	101, 115 n.		XII.7-10	76 n., 95 n., 129
VIII.19-22	88 n.			and n.
VIII.20	41, 90, 111 n.		XII.9	19 n.
VIII.21-2	41.		XII.9-10	142.
VIII.23	79.		XIII.5	63.
VIII.29	38.			
IX.4-5	129 n.		Gal. III.1	38.
X.6-8	26 n.		III.8	133.
X.9	3.		III.8-18	124.
XII.19	80 n.		III.22ff.	125.
XIII	66 n., 80, 114.		III.27	35.
XIII.1ff.	80 n.		V.1-2	143 n.
XIII.1-6	5, 54 n., 167 n.		V.14	93 n., 150.
XIII.3	56 n.		V.17	49, 63, 79.
XIII.3-4	56, 164 n.			
XIII.4	55, 80, 112 n., 161.		Eph. IV.24	35.
XIII.9	93 n., 150.		IV.25	158.
XIII.14	35.		V.5	51 n., 151 n.
XIV.14	44 n., 101 n.		V.6	56 n.
XVI.18	51 n.			
XVI.26	17, 127.		Phil. II.7-8	182.
			II.10-11	5 and n., 10.
I Cor. II.7-9	36 n.		II.11	3.
V	139.		III.10-11	38, 79.
V.4-5	129.		III.19	51 n.
V.5	129 n., 139 and n.		III.20-1	38.
VIII.6	40.			

Col. I.15   35, 129 n., 182.   I Pet. II.13-14   5.
     I.16-17   31.   II.13ff.   80 n.
     III.5   51 n., 151 n.   II.14   56 and n.
     III.6   51 n., 56 n.   II.18   80.
     III.10   35.   II.18-23   140.
                                               II.20   80.
I Thess. II.16   55 n.   II.21-3   80.
                                               II.23   80 n.
I Tim. IV.3-4   5 n.
       IV.4-5   44 n.   II Pet. III.16   4 n.
       VI.13   85.

Tit. I.15   44 n., 101 n.   I Jn. III.8   39.

Heb. I-v   100.
     I.2   31, 40 n.   Jas. II.19   5.
     II.10   40.
     II.10-18   40.   Rev. IV.11   5 n., 88 n.
     II.14   40.   VII.9-10   127.
     II.14-15   29, 39.   XII.9   49.
     II.15   65 n., 115.   XIV.7   5 n., 88 n.
     II.18   40.   XX.2   36 n., 49.
     IV.12   186.   XX.10   36 n., 49.
     V.7-9   36 n.   XX.10ff.   49.
     X.12   101.   XXI.4   41 n., 101.
     X.13   101 n.   XXII.5   101.